Hidden Prophecies in the Song of Moses

By J. R. Church

About the Cover

The cover design of the "Tabernacle At Night" was inspired by Nobert McNulty's painting "Moses' Tabernacle in the Wilderness." With permission, artist Tim Deibler recreated the concept of the night scene for our book with astounding beauty. We wish to thank both artists for their creative insight.

Lithograph Reproductions of McNulty's painting, suitable for framing are offered in the back of this book.

All scripture references are from the King James Version unless otherwise stated.

Hidden Prophecies in the Song of Moses

First Edition, 1991

Copyright © 1991 by **J. R. Church**

Printed in the United States of America

Published by:

Prophecy Publications

P. O. Box 7000

Oklahoma City, OK 73153

Library of Congress Catalog Card Number 90-92076

ISBN 0-941241-05-X

Introduction

Some early theologians predicted that the world would last for 6,000 years, at the end of which, Christ would return and establish a heavenly kingdom. Such predictions can be found in the writings of Irenaeus, the Epistle of Barnabas, the Testament of Adam and the Secrets of Enoch as well as in other rabbinic literature. Were these early Jewish and Christian theologians correct? We shall soon know. We live in the final decade of, not only the twentieth century, but the sixth millennium of human history as well.

Those early theologians were commenting on a theme set by Moses in Psalm 90:4 which says, *"For a thousand years in thy sight are but as yesterday when it is past, and as a watch in the night."*

Was Moses right or wrong? In this book, we shall examine the concept and explore the Song of Moses for its underlying prophetic theme.

This book is a sequel to our earlier work, HIDDEN PROPHECIES IN THE PSALMS, in which we demonstrated how the Psalms appear to contain a prophetic scenario for the rebirth of Israel and the return of Jesus Christ. We presented historical evidence to show how those events are actually coming to pass in this century.

During this time we had the opportunity for further research. Though our concept for the Psalms remains unchanged, we thought it necessary to add certain new insights to this sequel. This book is not a revision of our previous work, but an addition to it.

So much more has been learned over the past few years. We became convinced that the Song of Moses found in Deuteronomy 32 would be incomplete without the group of eleven Mosaic psalms recorded in Psalms 90-100. The Deuteronomy chapter, coupled with these eleven psalms, make a dynamic dozen, corresponding to the twelve tribes of Israel.

The glory of this completed song can be compared to the beauty of a grand chandelier hanging above a prophetic dining table. This Mosaic masterpiece became the central theme upon which the prophets built their prophetic scenarios.

It is incredible to think that the Song of Moses should be divided as it is, with the first stanza left in the book of Deuteronomy, and the other eleven stanzas removed to the Psalms. Also, it is amazing that this division in the Song of Moses should be overlooked by both Christian theologians and rabbinical scholars over the centuries.

Concerning the concept set forth in this volume, we ask only for a fair hearing. Read carefully, for you may overlook some prophetic golden nugget, simply because this author was unable to utilize the vocabulary necessary to place that gem in its proper setting for adequate impact.

I, therefore, beg for your indulgence as we unfold glory upon glory. Let the Holy Spirit orchestrate this Song of Moses upon heavenly harps and make its music move you toward rapture!

Table of Contents

The Decade of Destiny 7
An Exciting Discovery! 13
Moses and the Rock 35
Themes of the Prophets 52
Psalm 90 76
Psalm 91 97
Psalm 92 110
Psalm 93 117
Psalm 94 124
Psalm 95 132
Psalm 96 138
Psalm 97 145
Psalm 98 153
Psalm 99 158
Psalm 100 165
The Great Sabbath 170
Moses and the Messiah 196
Grace in the Wilderness 224
The Mosaic Tabernacle 260
The Passover 280
The Day of Pentecost 287
The Feast of Trumpets 317
The Days of Awe 329
The Day of Atonement 338
The Feast of Tabernacles 349

Chapter One

The Decade of Destiny

Human history is approaching the conclusion of its sixth millennium. Even allowing for calendar corrections, mankind is within only a few years of the beginning of the seventh millennium. This twentieth century has witnessed two world wars, widespread famine and disease, along with an increase in earthquake activity. It seems more than a coincidence that these events are occurring as we approach the conclusion of the sixth millennium and the beginning of the seventh.

Some early theologians believed that Christ would return at the end of 6,000 years. What a thought! What a possibility! Even if we considered this proposed time schedule to be only approximate, we can still see prophetic scriptures being fulfilled around us today.

Irenaeus, born in A.D. 140, worked intensely against powerful Gnostic heresies and wrote a treatise on the virtues of the Christian faith. Among his writings was found this statement:

"For in so many days as this world was made, in so many thousand years shall it be concluded ... and God brought to a conclusion upon the sixth day the works He made ... This is an account of the things formerly created, as also it is a prophecy of what is to come ... in six days created things were completed: it is evident, therefore, that they will come to an end after six thousand years." [1]

According to Irenaeus the history of the human race from creation to the consummation will span a 7,000 year period of time. The seventh millennium is to be the reign of Christ.

Irenaeus was not alone in his belief. There are other ancient writings which concur. Among them are THE SECRETS OF ENOCH, THE EPISTLE OF BARNABAS, THE TESTAMENT OF ADAM and other writings of early theologians.

THE SECRETS OF ENOCH, dating from at least the first century (also called II Enoch), is translated from Slavonic. In it, God is said to show Enoch the age of the world and its existence of 7,000 years:

"And I appointed the eighth day also, that the eighth day should be the first-created after my work, and that the first seven revolve in the form of the seventh thousand, and that at the beginning of the eighth thousand there should be a time of not-counting—endless..." [2]

THE EPISTLE OF BARNABAS was among a collection of New Testament books, bound in a single volume (later called the SINAITICUS), discovered in 1844 at the monastery of Saint Catherine located at the foot of Mount Sinai. It dates back to at least

---

[1] *The Writings Of Irenaeus*, volume 1, p. 577.

[2] Rutherford H. Platt, Jr. Ed. *The Forgotten Books of Eden*, "The Secrets of Enoch," (Alpha House, Inc., 1927, World Bible Publishers, Inc.), p. 92.

the fourth century A.D. and reflects the theology of some early Christian theologians:

"And God made in six days the works of his hands; and he finished them on the seventh day, and he rested the seventh day, and sanctified it. Consider, my children, what that signifies, he finished them in six days. The meaning of it is this; that in six thousand years the Lord God will bring all things to an end. For with him one day is a thousand years; as himself testifieth, saying, Behold this day shall be as a thousand years. Therefore, children, in six days, that is, in six thousand years, shall all things be accomplished. And what is that he saith, And he rested the seventh day: he meaneth this; that when his Son shall come, and abolish the season of the Wicked One, and judge the ungodly; and shall change the sun and the moon, and the stars; then shall gloriously rest in that seventh day." [3]

In the TESTAMENT OF ADAM (middle or late third century) the career of the world is said to last for 6,000 years after the Flood, or for 7,000 years in all. Seth, the supposed author, writes about the deathbed account of his father Adam:

"You have heard, my son Seth, that a Flood is coming and will wash the whole earth because of the daughters of Cain, ... who killed your brother Abel out of passion for your sister Lebuda, since sins had been created through your mother, Eve. And after the Flood there will be six thousand years (left) to the form of the world, and then its end will come." [4]

---

[3] *The Lost Books of the Bible,* "The Epistle of Barnabas," (Alpha House, Inc., 1926, World Bible Publishers, Inc.), p. 161.

[4] James H. Charlesworth, Ed., *The Old Testament Pseudepigrapha*, Vol. 1, "Testament of Adam," (Garden City, NY: Doubleday & Company, Inc. 1983), p. 994.

In an article entitled "Chronomessianism," published in 1976 in the HEBREW UNION COLLEGE ANNUAL YEARBOOK, Rabbi Ben Zion Wacholder quoted a statement from the ancient Talmud:

"Just as the seventh offers a release to the Jew, so the world will be released during the seventh millennium."[5]

Rashi commented upon a statement made in the Talmud (Sanhedrin 97d) wherein it says that the world is to exist 6,000 years:

"In the first 2,000 there was desolation, for 2,000 years the Torah or Law flourished, and the next 2,000 was to be the messianic era. But through our many iniquities, all these years have been lost." [6]

That was written about 200 years after Christ, and the writer states that the Messianic era did not come to pass because of their sins. The seventh millennium was predicted to see the exhaltation of Messiah.

Please note: According to the Jewish calendar, the Temple was destroyed in the year 3830—which would place the writing of that Talmudic commentary right at the 4,000-year mark.

Rashi commented on the 2nd century Talmudic statement that the first 2,000 years of human history was desolation, the second 2,000 years saw the flourishing of the Torah, and that the third 2,000

---

[5] RabbI Ben Zion Wacholder, "Chronomessianism," 1976, *Hebrew Union College Annual Yearbook.*

[6] *Talmud* (Sanhedrin 97d).

year period, the Messianic age, did not come to pass. He said, "This is supposed to be the age of the Messiah and where is He? He didn't come, because of our sins." [7]

About the time of this writing, Bar Kochba led the Jews in a revolt against the Romans (A.D. 135), having been declared to be the Messiah by Israel's high priest. He was killed by the Romans. The revolt was crushed and the Jews were scattered from their land and sold on the slave markets of the world.

According to these early theologians, seven millenniums of world history are somehow related to the seven days of creation. Those seven days were thought to prophetically represent seven one thousand year periods of human history.

The apostle Peter was evidently drawing upon this concept when he wrote in the third chapter of his second epistle that the day of the Lord was represented by 1,000 years duration:

"But, beloved, be not ignorant of this one thing, that one day is with the Lord as a thousand years, and a thousand years as one day.

"But the day of the Lord will come as a thief in the night; in the which the heavens shall pass away with a great noise, and the elements shall melt with fervent heat, the earth also and the works that are therein shall be burned up" (II Peter 3:8,10).

The *"day of the Lord"* implies a final sabbath, the seventh millennium of human history. According

---

[7] Ibid.

to Peter, it should begin with our Lord's coming as *"a thief in the night"* and conclude 1,000 years later as *"the heavens pass away and the elements melt with fervent heat."* This is consistent with other prophecies in the Bible and the book of Revelation in particular. After the millennial reign of Christ, God will renovate the earth and the heavens with fire. He will create new heavens and a new earth *"wherein dwelleth righteousness."*

All of those early theologians who wrote about the six days of creation and their prophetic implications that the world should last for six thousand years were actually following the theme set by Moses in Psalm 90:4.

"For a thousand years in thy sight are but as yesterday when it is past, and as a watch in the night" (Psalm 90:4).

It is for this reason that we became involved in a careful and detailed study of the Song of Moses. Psalm 90, as we shall see, is an intregal part of that prophetic song written by Moses on the day of his death. The Song of Moses recorded in Deuteronomy 32 is only the first of twelve prophetic stanzas which lay out for us both the "fall" of Israel and its "rising again" in these last days.

Chapter Two

An Exciting Discovery!

"And I saw another sign in heaven, great and marvelous, seven angels having the seven last plagues; for in them is filled up the wrath of God.

"And I saw as it were a sea of glass mingled with fire: and them that had gotten the victory over the beast, and over his image, and over his mark, and over the number of his name, stand on the sea of glass, having the harps of God.

"And they sing the song of Moses the servant of God, and the song of the Lamb ..." (Revelation 15:1-3a).

An air of overwhelming expectation fills the celestial hall. Attention is drawn to seven mighty angels holding vials filled with God's wrath. Suddenly, the saints begin to sing, as though prompted by some unseen choir director. It is not a mighty anthem. It is a song filled with pathos, sorrow and judgment. It is the Song of Moses.

Question: Why should they sing this particular song during the Tribulation Period? Just what does the Song of Moses have to say that is so important? Until now, it has been a little known and often overlooked part of Scripture. Is there a fascinating discovery waiting to be made?

I think so. And it is fitting that the Song of Moses should be mentioned in the book of Revelation. Chapters 4-19 of Revelation are Jewish in character and are concerned with the judgments of God in the time of Jacob's trouble. Events of the Tribulation Period will bring the nation of Israel to a state of siege which can only be broken by the visible return of Christ.

During this time, just prior to the seven vial judgments, the saints in heaven will sing the Song of Moses. They await the victory. Soon, satan will be bound and the Messianic kingdom will be established. It is natural enough then that the saints in heaven should sing the Song of Moses. Please note, it is a Jewish song, written for Jewish people. Moses composed this song as a prophecy. It is a tightly condensed prophetic scenario for Israel's dispersion and return, the archetype of God's revelation to the Old Testament prophets. And in Revelation 15, the final fulfillment of that prophecy is ready to be completed.

Who Hath Ears to Hear?

Let us look back at the Song of Moses in Deuteronomy 32. Its prophetic nature is incredibly important and deserves our close consideration:

> *"Give **ear**, O ye heavens, and I will speak; and **hear**, O earth, the words of my mouth ..."* (Deuteronomy 32:1).

Moses expressed God's plan for Israel in a poetic discourse unique in the Pentateuch. Echoes of this song are heard throughout the Old Testament.

It is no ordinary song. It is not a "tehillim," the Hebrew word for "psalm." Instead, it is a "sherah," a parable or riddle set to rhythm. A parable is an obscure story, usually calling for great thought or special enlightenment to unravel its meaning.

You may recall that Jesus spoke in parables. In Matthew 13, the disciples became concerned about these obscure teachings. After telling one of these parables or riddles, Jesus said,

> *"Who hath **ears to hear**, let him **hear**"* (Matthew 13:9).

Jesus followed a theme set in the Song of Moses—that Israel should be spiritually deaf. Therefore, His parables about the kingdom are couched in symbolic language, not easily understood. Jesus used parables, not to make theology easier, but rather, more difficult to understand! His veiled language frustrated the disciples:

> *"And the disciples came and said unto him, Why speakest thou unto them in parables?*
>
> *"He answered and said unto them, Because it is given to you to know the **mysteries** of the kingdom of heaven, but to them it is not given.*
>
> *"For whosoever hath, to him shall be given, and he shall have more abundance: but whosoever hath not, from him shall be taken away even that he hath.*
>
> *"Therefore I speak to them in parables: because they seeing see not; and **hearing they hear not**, neither do they understand"* (Matthew 13:10-13).

As a child, I was told that a parable is an earthly story with a heavenly meaning. That is correct.

But, I was also told that parables should make theology easier to understand. Not so! Jesus used parables to hide the true meaning of the mysteries of the kingdom of heaven. He even used the term *"mysteries"* in His explanation to the disciples.

A modern term for parable would be what we call a riddle. In our day, a riddle is a type of verbal puzzle. It may take the form of a question, statement or story, but the listener is required to discern its secret meaning by applying all of the information at his command.

Let us approach the Song of Moses, then, as a parable. Its opening words, *"Give ear ... and hear"* imply a mystery in its message. A special gift of spiritual hearing must be given by the Holy Spirit, otherwise we would be unable to understand.

We suggest that Deuteronomy 32 gives only the first of twelve stanzas in the Song of Moses. The other eleven are recorded in Psalms 90-100. According to Jewish theologians, Moses dedicated each of eleven Psalms (90-100) to a tribe. Rabbi Avrohom Chaim Feuer wrote,

"The fourth book of the Psalms begins with eleven consecutive works composed by Moses (Psalms 90-100). Rashi explains that these correspond to the eleven blessings which Moses bestowed upon eleven of the tribes as enumerated in Deuteronomy 33. The tribe of Simeon was excluded from Moses' blessings because the Simeonites had led the orgy that resulted in the death of thousands of Jews (see Numbers 25:1-15)." [1]

---

[1] Rabbi Avrohom Chaim Feuer, *Tehillim,* Psalms—A New Translation with a Commentary Anthologized from Talmudic, Midrashic and Rabbinic Sources, (Brooklyn, NY: Mesorah Publications. Ltd., 1985) p. 1121.

Here are eleven psalms dedicated to the eleven tribes. Notably, one tribe was left out—the tribe of Simeon. Jewish theologians have suggested why they think Simeon was excluded from Moses' blessings, but he was not ignored at all. I suggest that the first stanza (Deuteronomy 32) was dedicated to Simeon and that the other eleven stanzas (Psalms 90-100) were dedicated to the other tribes.

In Deuteronomy 33, we find the other eleven tribes named. What Moses had to say about each of those tribes represents a synopsis or overview setting the theme for each part of the song (Psalms 90-100) dedicated to its particular tribe. The 32nd and 33rd chapters of Deuteronomy, then, become a set of parables, riddles or prophecies encompassing all twelve parts of the Song of Moses.

The Binding of Simeon

I believe the answer to the mystery lies in the story of Joseph. It is important to understand that Joseph imprisoned Simeon while his brothers returned home. Simeon languished in an Egyptian jail until his brothers returned with Benjamin. During that time, Simeon was out of earshot. The name Simeon means "hearing."

Joseph was a type of Christ. When his brothers first saw the exalted Joseph, they did not recognize him. They were spiritually deaf. However, when they returned with Benjamin, Simeon was restored and Joseph was revealed. In like manner, Israel has not recognized Jesus as Messiah. The Chosen People have been made spiritually deaf.

One day, however, their spiritual hearing will be restored. At that time, Christ will be received and Israel will be delivered. The story is a prophecy that Israel should be spiritually deaf during the time between their first and second encounters with Jesus.

Let us take a closer look at the story in Genesis 42. Following their first encounter with Joseph, the brothers were imprisoned for three days:

> *"And Joseph said unto them, That is it that I spake unto you, saying, Ye are spies:*
>
> *"Hereby ye shall be proved: by the life of Pharaoh ye shall not go forth hence, except your youngest brother come hither.*
>
> *"Send one of you, and let him fetch your brother, and ye shall be kept in prison, that your words may be proved, whether there be any truth in you: or else by the life of Pharaoh surely ye are spies.*
>
> *"And he put them all together into ward **three days**"* (Genesis 42:14-17).

It is important to note that their imprisonment lasted for three days; for Moses, the chronicler of this event, wrote in the Song of Moses:

> *"For a **thousand years** in thy sight are but as yesterday when it is past ..."* (Psalm 90:4).

These days of imprisonment may be a prophetic picture of 3,000 years of Israel's exile—from the days of the Old Testament until this generation.

Hosea added his commentary to this concept:

> *"Come and let us return unto the LORD: for he hath torn, and he will heal us; he hath smitten, and he will bind us up.*
>
> *"After **two days** will he revive us: in the **third day** he will raise us up, and we shall live in his sight"* (Hosea 6:1-2).

Israel's prolonged punishment may be a fulfillment of the prophetic scenario set in the story of the brothers being imprisoned for three days:

> *"And Joseph said unto them the third day, This do, and live; for I fear God:*
>
> *"If ye be true men, let one of your brethren be bound in the house of your prison: go ye, carry corn for the famine of your houses:*
>
> *"But bring your youngest brother unto me; so shall your words be verified, and ye shall not die. And they did so"* (Genesis 42:18-20).

Joseph proposes to keep Simeon in prison while the rest return to fetch Benjamin. Consider the conversation between the unsuspecting brothers:

> *"And they said one to another, We are verily guilty concerning our brother, in that we saw the anguish of his soul, when he besought us, and **we would not hear** ..."* (Genesis 42:21).

They refused to hear. The theme of Israel's spiritual deafness is thus introduced. Then Reuben, oldest of the twelve, continues the theme:

> *"And Reuben answered them, saying, Spake I not unto you, saying, Do not sin against the child; and **ye would not hear?**"* (Genesis 42:22).

For the second time they turned a deaf ear. Little did they know, as they talked among themselves, that Joseph could hear and understand their conversation. They could not understand him, however, because Joseph spoke with them in the language of the Egyptians using an interpreter:

"And they knew not that Joseph understood them; for he spake unto them by an interpreter" (Genesis 42:23).

For the third time the story emphasizes the theme of hearing while not being able to understand. This was the same situation which frustrated the disciples in Matthew 13. Remember, in verse 9 of the Matthew account, Jesus said, *"Who hath ears to hear, let him hear."* Just as Joseph deliberately covered his identity by using another language, Jesus couched his teachings in cryptic parables which could not be easily understood.

Joseph imprisoned Simeon and sent the others back to fetch Benjamin.

"And he turned himself about from them, and wept; and returned to them again, and communed with them, and took from them Simeon, and bound him before their eyes" (Genesis 42:24).

The fact that Simeon means "hearing" points up the prophetic impact of the story. Since the whole narrative refers to Christ and His relationship with Israel, it seems obvious that the binding of Simeon should refer to Israel's spiritual deafness.

The whole story is set within the time-frame of a seven-year famine, a prophetic scenario of Israel's future Tribulation Period. The Brothers were sent back home to fetch Benjamin, whose name means "son of my right hand." When Benjamin was born, the dying Rachel named him Benoni, meaning "son of sorrow." Jacob, however, changed his name to Benjamin. This is a prophetic statement about the character of Jesus Christ. When He came the first time, He was a *"man of sorrows,"* but today, He sits at the "right hand" of the Father.

When the brothers returned with Benjamin, Simeon was restored and Joseph was revealed. So it will be during Israel's future seven-years of tribulation. Israel's spiritual hearing (Simeon) will be restored and the greater Joseph (Christ) will be revealed. The prophetic reason for the restoration of Israel in this generation is to allow Israel to fetch "the son of my right hand" of whom Benjamin is a type.

The Parables of Christ

During the ministry of Christ, parables were used—not to explain the mysteries of heaven, but to hide their meaning from the Jews. Jesus spoke in dark sayings—in parables or riddles.

Furthermore, when pressed about the matter, Jesus invoked a prophecy found in Isaiah which explains the problem of Israel's deafness:

> *"And in them is fulfilled the prophecy of Isaiah, which saith, By hearing ye shall hear, and shall not understand; and seeing ye shall see, and shall not perceive"* (Matthew 13:14).

It was to the prophet Isaiah that God used the theme first given in the story of the binding of

Simeon. He told Isaiah:

> *"Go, and tell this people, **Hear** ye indeed, but **understand not;"** (Isaiah 6:9).

Isaiah was told that Israel would become spiritually deaf, and that they would be scattered among the nations for an extended period of time. In the last days, however, they would return to their Promised Land, after which, their spiritual hearing would be restored.

In Acts 28, the apostle Paul tried to convince the elders in Rome to receive Christ. Frustrated with Jewish unbelief, he finally said:

> *"Well spake the Holy Ghost by Isaiah the prophet unto our fathers,*
>
> *"Saying, Go unto this people, and say, **Hearing** ye **shall hear, and shall not understand;** and seeing ye shall see, and not perceive"* (Acts 28:26-27).

The theme of Israel's spiritual deafness continues throughout the Old and New Testaments. History attests to the fact that Israel has suffered exile among the nations for these millennia. Incidentally, if they should be without spiritual hearing during their exile, it is logical to conclude that when they are returned to their Promised Land their hearing should be restored.

With the turn of the 20th century, the Chosen People embarked upon a return to their Promised Land. Someday soon, their spiritual hearing should be restored. A possible reference to that is recorded in Psalm 92:11:

*"Mine eyes also shall see my desire on mine enemies, and mine **ears shall hear** my desire of the wicked that rise up against me"* (Psalm 92:11).

Sometime during the Tribulation Period, religious Jews will begin to understand the mysteries of the prophets. At what point this will occur is not certain. Some theologians think Israel will wake up from their forefather's rejection of Christ shortly after all saints have been taken in the rapture—leaving Israel behind.

The Mosaic Blessings

In the chapter immediately following the curse of Deuteronomy 32, Moses gives a blessing to each of the other eleven tribes. These blessings also appear to be written in cryptic terminology. They are riddles which cannot be understood until one reads the other stanzas to the Song of Moses in Psalms 90-100. Each blessing offers a prophetic theme set for its corresponding psalm. The name Simeon was excluded. This is consistent with God's prophetic policy—that the Chosen People should be without spiritual hearing throughout the years of their exile from the Promised Land.

Upon examining Deuteronomy 32, we found that Simeon was not left out of the Song of Moses after all. Moses directed the very first part of his song to Simeon. This first stanza in the Song of Moses was kept imprisoned under the Law while the other eleven parts of the song were placed under Grace in the nineteenth book of the Old Testament—namely the Psalms!

We can find a reference to Simeon's first stanza in Psalm 49:1-4. It follows the birth of Israel which appears in Psalm 48. Once the nation is born, an injunction to *"hear"* is given:

> *"**Hear** this, all ye people; **give ear**, all ye inhabitants of the world:*
>
> *"Both low and high, rich and poor, together.*
>
> *"My mouth shall speak of wisdom; and the meditation of my heart shall be of understanding.*
>
> *"I will incline mine ear to a parable: I will open my dark saying upon the harp"* (Psalm 49:1-4).

This command to *"hear"* and *"give ear"* in Psalm 49:1 is comparable to Deuteronomy 32:1:

> *"**Give ear**, O ye heavens, and I will speak; and **hear**, O earth, the words of my mouth"* (Deuteronomy 32:1).

The command to *"hear"* in Psalm 49:1 appears to be a direct reference to the first stanza of the Song of Moses (directed to Simeon) in Deuteronomy 32, and may be a clue that the meaning of the riddle is about to be unfolded.

Psalms 90-100 are virtually the climax of all the Psalms, describing events of the Tribulation Period. They include the restoration of Temple worship, the rise of the antichrist, the abomination of desolation, the gathering of all nations to Armageddon, and the glorious appearing of the Messiah to judge the world and establish His kingdom.

Once the nation of Israel is established in Psalm 48, God invites them and all the inhabitants of the world to *"hear."* God said He would *"incline His ear to a parable"*—perhaps the parable in the Song of Moses. God said He would *"open His dark saying upon the harp."* Again, it appears to be a reference to the *"dark saying"* in the Song of Moses. Psalm 49 sets the Mosaic theme for modern Israel—from its birth in Psalm 48 directly to the climactic events found in the rest of the Song of Moses as recorded in Psalms 90-100.

All twelve songs appear to form the Song of Moses; Deuteronomy 32 being the first stanza of the song and Psalms 90-100 being the other eleven. They tell the story of Israel's future and declare that Israel has not been forever forsaken; that one day God will return them to their Promised Land; and will send the Messiah to establish the kingdom of heaven. No wonder, then, Revelation 15:3 culminates the scenario by reminding us that the saints in heaven sing the Song of Moses.

The Last Words of Jacob

The dying Jacob gathered his sons around his bed (Genesis 49) and gave prophecies of that which would befall each tribe in the last days. He said:

> *"Gather yourselves together, and **hear**, ye sons of Jacob; and **hearken** unto Israel your father"* (Genesis 49:2).

He used the theme set forth in the binding of Simeon. His prophecy showed that in the last days, Israel would again be given the skill to *"hear"* and understand spiritual things.

He That Hath an Ear ...

This theme is also carried out in the book of the Revelation. I think the blessing given in chapter 1 addresses the spiritual deafness of Israel:

> *"Blessed is he that readeth, and they that hear the words of this prophecy ... for the time is at hand"* (Revelation 1:3)

Letters are addressed to seven churches in Revelation 2-3, and each message ends with:

> *"... he that hath an ear, let him hear what the Spirit saith unto the churches"* (Revelation 2:7, 11, 17, 29; 3:6, 13, 22).

In Revelation 13 the theme is repeated:

> *"If any man have an ear, let him hear"* (Revelation 13:9).

This verse is found in the chapter which describes the antichrist and his satanic system of world government. And the chapter concludes with a similar statement:

> *"Here is wisdom. Let him that hath understanding count the number of the beast: for it is the number of a man; and his number is Six hundred three score and six"* (Revelation 13:18).

This is the chapter that describes the beast out of the sea and the dragon who gave him his power. The term dragon is synonymous with serpent and may be yet another clue to the subject of spiritual deafness predicted in the Song of Moses.

It is a fact that serpents are deaf. They cannot hear sounds that travel through the air. They hear by sensing vibrations from the ground.

The symbolism of the serpent refers back to the Garden of Eden and the curse given to the serpent that beguiled Eve. The serpent is a type of satan. The *"seed of the serpent"* is a type of the antichrist—opposite to the *"seed of the woman:"*

> *"I will put enmity between thee and the woman, and between thy seed and her seed; it shall bruise thy head, and thou shalt bruise his heel"* (Genesis 3:15).

The concept that serpents are deaf is even found in the Psalms!

> *"Their poison is like the poison of a serpent: they are like the **deaf adder** that stoppeth her ear;*
>
> *"Which will not hearken to the voice of charmers, charming never so wisely"* (Psalm 58:4-5).

Psalm 58 tells us that serpents are deaf. This scripture, with all the others, provide an overwhelming amount of evidence to prove Israel's spiritual deafness.

That brings us to the rest of the Song of Moses, in Psalms 90-100. These Psalms drive home the theme of spiritual deafness. Here's how we came to that conclusion. The number nine is the ninth letter in the Hebrew alphabet. According to the Lexicon, the ninth letter, teth, means "serpent." Therefore, we consider Psalms 90-99 to be "serpent" psalms. Prophetically, they tell the story of the rise and fall of the antichrist and his system of world government. Psalm 99, incidentally, was dedicated to Dan, whose symbol was a many-headed serpent. The fact that the number 99 has two nines in it appropriately represents more than just one head on the serpent. It must be more than mere coincidence that the psalm dedicated to the "serpent" tribe should be numbered 99! Early Jewish theologians speculated that the tribe of Dan would produce the antichrist. The symbol of satan, the antichrist and the coming world government in the book of the Revelation is represented by a seven-headed, ten-horned serpent!

Asher Concludes the Song of Moses

As we studied Deuteronomy 32, 33 and Psalms 90-100, another pattern emerged. While reviewing the 12 stanzas, I noticed that the first and last were different from the middle 10. The first stanza (Deuteronomy 32) describes the "fall" of Israel. The last stanza (Psalm 100) describes the "rising again" of Israel. And the middle 10 (Psalms 90-99) describes Israel's confrontation with the serpent (satan) and the seed of the serpent (antichrist).

Psalm 100 was dedicated to the tribe of Asher. The name Asher means "blessing" and his corresponding psalm rejoices over the Messiah and His heavenly kingdom. There is not one negative statement in Psalm 100:

"Make a joyful noise unto the LORD, all ye lands.

"Serve the LORD with gladness: come before his presence with singing.

"Know ye that the LORD he is God: it is he that hath made us, and not we ourselves; we are his people, and

the sheep of his pasture.

"Enter into his gates with thanksgiving, and into his courts with praise: be thankful unto him, and bless his name.

"For the LORD is good; his mercy is everlasting; and his truth endureth to all generations" (Psalm 100:1-5).

The stanzas about judgment and wrath are concluded with Psalm 99. Psalm 100 records only joy and thanksgiving. Early Jewish theologians recognized the prophetic nature of Psalm 100.

"Rabbi Hirsch explains that this song ... deals with the gratitude that will be due to God in the **Messianic Age**, when the world has **reached perfection**. Psalm 100 serves as a **finale** to the previous psalms concerning the approach of the Messianic Era." [2]

These verses declare the Kingship of Christ and the blessings of the kingdom. Jesus Christ, the Messiah will come to establish a golden age for the human race. Is it possible that this concluding decade of the sixth millennium of human history will witness the fulfillment of Psalm 100?

It seems fitting to note that the number 100 just happens to be the 19th letter (koph) of the Hebrew alphabet. Furthermore, the entire collection of 150 psalms just happen to comprise the 19th book of our Old Testament. Therefore, this concluding psalm in the Song of Moses just may represent the conclusion of the 1900's!

---

[2] Ibid., p. 1215.

Simeon and Anna

As we have noted, the Song of Moses sets the theme for all biblical prophecy. A reference can even be found in the story of Simeon and Anna found in Luke's gospel:

> *"And, behold, there was a man in Jerusalem, whose name was **Simeon**; and the same man was just and devout, waiting for the consolation of Israel: and the Holy Ghost was upon him.*
>
> *"And it was revealed unto him by the Holy Ghost, that he should not see death, before he had seen the Lord's Christ"* (Luke 2:25-26).

Simeon was the name of the man to whom it was revealed that the baby brought by Joseph and Mary was Israel's anointed Messiah. Simeon's spiritual eyes were not dim nor his spiritual hearing impaired. Simeon knew that the nation as a whole would not accept their Messiah. The old prophet held the child and said to Mary:

> *"This child is set for the **fall** and **rising again** of many in Israel"* (v. 34).

He knew that Israel would be spiritually deaf, reject their Messiah, and fall. *"This child is set for the fall ... of Israel."* Even the name of the man who gave the prophecy of the future fall of Israel matched the one to whom the first stanza of the Song of Moses was directed. It was no mere coincidence that his name was Simeon. But, the prophetic scenario does not stop there. While Simeon was predicting the "fall" and "rising again" of Israel, an elderly prophetess approached. Note what tribe she was from:

> *"And there was one **Anna**, a prophetess, the daughter of Phanuel, of the tribe of **Asher**: she was of a great age, and had lived with a husband seven years from her virginity;*
>
> *"And she was a widow of about fourscore and four years, which departed not from the temple, but served God with fasting and prayers night and day.*
>
> *"And she coming in that instant gave thanks likewise unto the Lord, and spake of him to all them that looked for redemption in Jerusalem"* (Luke 2:36-38).

Anna, of the tribe of Asher, completed the prophetic scenario found in the Song of Moses. The concluding psalm (100) was directed to Asher. The psalm itself is filled with thanksgiving—just as Luke wrote that she *"... gave thanks ...and spake of him to all them that looked for redemption!"* Simeon and Anna followed the prophetic scenario in the Song of Moses perfectly—Simeon representing the *"fall"* of Israel and Anna representing the *"rising again!"* The first and last stanzas to the Song of Moses (Deuteronomy 32 and Psalm 100) reflect that same theme. The intervening Psalms (90-99) represent Israel's encounter with the symbolic serpent. They tell the story of the Tribulation Period.

Simon Peter Also Reflects the Song of Moses

There was another Simeon in the New Testament. He represented a new beginning as well. Through the first Simeon, we see the fall of Israel, and its spiritual hearing deafened. This other Simeon not only relates to the first stanza of the Song of Moses, but depicts the theme of the song.

At the council held in Jerusalem concerning the conversion of Gentiles, James referred to Peter as Simeon. It must be more than a coincidence that the term was used. It refers to the theme found in Simeon's stanza (Deuteronomy 32:21) that God should redeem *"those which are not a people"* (Gentiles) and make Israel jealous.

> *"And after they had held their peace, James answered, saying, Men and brethren, hearken unto me:*
>
> *"Simeon hath declared how God at the first did visit the Gentiles, to take out of them a people for his name"* (Acts 15:13-14).

Here is the other Simeon, better known as Simon Peter—Simeon, the "Rock." The name Peter means "rock." In the very name of Simon Peter, we have a commentary on the Song of Moses!

The first stanza of the Song of Moses was dedicated to Simeon. And the theme of it, (mentioned five times in Deuteronomy 32) is the *"Rock."* We have the very name of Simon Peter hidden within the terminology of the Song of Moses.

Our Savior also pointed up the significance of Peter the "Rock."

> *"When Jesus came into the coasts of Caesarea Philippi, he asked his disciples, saying, Whom do men say that I the Son of man am?*
>
> *"And they said, Some say that thou art John the Baptist: some, Elijah; and others, Jeremiah, or one of the*

prophets.

> *"He saith unto them, But whom say ye that I am?*
>
> *"And Simon Peter answered and said, Thou art the Christ, the Son of the living God.*
>
> *"And Jesus answered and said unto him, Blessed art thou, Simon Barjona: for flesh and blood hath not revealed it unto thee, but my Father which is in heaven.*
>
> *"And I say also unto thee, That thou art* **Peter**, *and upon this* **rock** *I will build my church; and the gates of hell shall not prevail against it"* (Matthew 16:13-18).

It was to Simon Peter that the Lord gave the privilege of preaching the Gospel on the Day of Pentecost to the Jews. And it was to Simon Peter that God gave the privilege of preaching the Gospel to the Gentiles at the house of the Roman centurion, Cornelius. So Simon Peter could also be called "Simeon, the Rock." Both the "hearing" and the "rock" were imbedded in his name. I think it is most significant and not by any stretch of the imagination a coincidence.

When Jesus said *"Thou art Peter and upon this rock will I build my church,"* He may have been refering to a prophetic message hidden in the Song of Moses. Peter was acting out what had been prophesied by Moses, 1,500 years before.

We feel this points up the importance of the Song of Moses. We see in Simon Peter a commentary on the Song of Moses. We see in Simeon and Anna a commentary on the Song of Moses. Perhaps most stones and rocks used in Scripture are symbolic of a theme established in the Song of Moses.

In Psalm 118:22, we have a reference to Christ as the great cornerstone, *"The stone which the builders refused is become the headstone of the corner"* (Psalm 118:22).

A story about the cornerstone of the Temple is told in Jewish folklore. It seems that plans for fashioning the cornerstone were sent to Solomon's quarry. The stonemasons followed the design and sent the finished stone to the Temple site. Instructions did not reach the Temple builders, however, and they couldn't figure out how to make the seemingly odd shaped stone fit into the building. They promptly sent it back to the quarry with demands that the problem be corrected. An argument ensued between the stonemasons in the quarry and the builders at the Temple site—an argument so heated that the builders finally brought the cornerstone to the brow of the hill (that later became Golgotha) and pushed it over the cliff. According to Simon Peter, that cornerstone was Christ!

> *"Wherefore also it is contained in the scripture, Behold, I lay in Zion a **chief corner stone**, elect, precious: and he that believeth on him shall not be confounded.*
>
> *"Unto you therefore which believe he is precious: but unto them which be disobedient, the stone which the builders disallowed, the same is made the head of the corner,*
>
> *"And a stone of stumbling, and a **rock** of offence, even to them which stumble at the word, being disobedient: whereunto also they were appointed"* (I Peter 2:6-8).

Peter, the very person Christ called a "rock," commented on that same theme established in the Song of Moses. Let's take a closer look at the "Rock."

Chapter Three

Moses and the Rock

The five books of Moses represent a foundation for the entire Bible, providing models, types and symbols, from which are developed the great prophetic scenarios. One such symbolism is the *"rock,"* which students of the Bible now recognize as symbolic of Christ, the *"Rock"* of our salvation.

The writings of Moses clearly expound upon the *"rock"* as the image of God's grace and the redemption offered to humanity through the sacrifice of Christ. Let's take a detailed look at Deuteronomy 32 and see just what the Song of Moses has to say about the *"rock."*

Remember that Moses wrote his song on the last day of his life. He must present the song, then make the ascent up Mt. Nebo, where he will die. Why must he die? Because, as we shall see, he smote a *"rock"* when God had told him merely to speak to the *"rock."*

In his song he wants Israel to understand the *"rock"* as a symbol. It is obviously the main thought on his mind as he prepares for death.

Five Rocks in Deuteronomy 32

In Deuteronomy 32, Moses mentions the *"rock"* five times. He begins by saying:

> *"He is the rock, his work is perfect: for all his ways are judgment: a God of truth and without iniquity, just and right is He"* (Deuteronomy 32:4).

According to Moses, God is the *"Rock."* In verse 15, Moses returns to the theme of the *"rock"* as he writes that Israel:

> *"... forsook God which made him, and lightly esteemed the rock of his salvation"* (v. 15).

In verse 18 he repeats the theme:

> *"Of the rock that begat thee thou art unmindful, and hast forgotten God that formed thee"* (v. 18).

And in verse 30 he predicts that Israel will be scattered among the nations having been evicted from their land by God, their *"rock:"*

> *"How should one chase a thousand, and two put ten thousand to flight, except their rock had sold them and their LORD had shut them up?"* (v. 30).

Verse 31 concludes by declaring that idols are not to be compared with the reality of God:

> *"... for their rock is not as our rock"* (v. 31).

The rock of idolatry worshiped by the heathen cannot be compared with the true *"Rock"*—the God of Israel. Nevertheless, one Gentile shall chase a thousand Jews, and two shall put ten thousand to flight. Why? Because God, the *"Rock"* of Israel, has sold His Chosen People into slavery.

Moses Smites the First Rock

Now let us review the story of the *"rock."* It begins in Exodus 17 while the children of Israel are encamped at Rephidim near the mountains of Horeb. When the people complain to Moses that they have no water, the Lord instructs him:

> *"Go on before the people, and take thee of the elders of Israel; and thy rod, wherewith thou smotest the river, take in thine hand and go.*
>
> *"Behold, I will stand before thee there upon a **rock** in Horeb; and thou shalt smite the **rock**, and there shall come water out of it, that the people may drink. And Moses did so in the sight of the elders of Israel"* (Exodus 17:5-6).

The smiting of this *"rock"* was a prophecy. The *"rock"* represented the Messiah, who was to be smitten. This prophecy was fulfilled at Calvary. Out of His being smitten, however, came the water of salvation to all who believe. In I Corinthians 10, the Apostle Paul warns the people in Corinth how they should deal with the *"Rock:"*

> *"... they drank of that spiritual **rock** that followed them: and that **rock** was Christ"* (I Corinthians 10:4).

The *"rock"* smitten by Moses in Exodus 17 represented the crucifixion of Jesus Christ. However, Christ should be smitten only one time. And that brings us to the great sin of Moses.

Moses Smites the Second Rock

Several years later, there came a time when the people thirsted again. By this time, Moses and Aaron had wandered through a lot of desert wasteland with the people, and had withstood their endless complaints.

> *"There was no water for the congregation: and they gathered themselves together against Moses and against Aaron"* (Numbers 20:2).

When Moses brought their petition before the Lord, he was directed once again to provide water out of a *"rock,"* but this time he was not to smite the *"rock;"* he should only speak to the *"rock:"*

> *"Take the rod, and gather thou the assembly together, thou, and Aaron thy brother, and speak ye unto the **rock** before their eyes; and it shall give forth his water, and thou shalt bring forth to them water out of the **rock**: so thou shall give the congregation and the beasts drink.*
>
> *"And Moses took the rod from before the LORD, as he commanded him.*
>
> *"And Moses and Aaron gathered the congregation together before the rock, and he said unto them, hear now, ye rebels; must we fetch you water out of the rock?*
>
> *"And Moses lifted up his hands, and with his rod he **smote the rock twice**: and the water came out abundantly, and the congregation drank, and their beasts also. And the LORD spake unto Moses and Aaron, Because ye believed me not, to sanctify me in the eyes of the children of Israel, therefore ye shall not bring this congregation into the promised land which I have given them"* (Numbers 20:8-12).

On this occasion, Moses disobeyed the Lord. Instead of speaking to the *"rock,"* he struck it twice. For his transgression Moses was told that both he and Aaron must die. They would not be allowed to accompany the Chosen People into the Promised Land. Why? Because the *"rock"* represented Christ, and Christ should not be smitten twice.

Moses must now pay the ultimate price for smiting the *"rock."* He writes this song with references about the *"rock"* because he wants Israel to know that the future Messiah is the *"Rock"* rejected and smitten by Israel.

Five—The Number of Grace

Please note, in Deuteronomy 32, Moses referred to the *"rock"* of Israel's God five times. In the first three references he says that the people have *"forsaken,"* *"lightly esteemed"* and *"forgotten"* their *"rock."* In the fourth reference, he writes that because of this, their *"rock"* had *"sold them,"* that is, abandoned them to their enemies. The fifth time that Moses mentions the *"rock,"* it is to say that the God of Israel is the true *"rock,"* not like those imitators worshiped by the enemy. Yes, there are five references to the *"rock"* in Deuteronomy 32. And five is the number of God's grace.

For example, after the passing of four world kingdoms given in the book of Daniel, the fifth kingdom is brought to power by the *"stone ... cut out without hands"* (Daniel 2:34).

Deuteronomy, the fifth book of the Bible, is devoted to extolling the grace of God. This is particularly true in the Song of Moses.

In I Samuel 17, the Philistines and their champion, Goliath, stand against Israel. The giant struck fear in the warriors of Israel, but David offers to go up against him while declining to use Saul's armor and sword. With only a shepherd's staff in his hand and a sling, he goes out to meet the giant. David's actions become a commentary on the five-fold *"rock"* in Deuteronomy 32, as he selects *"five smooth stones"* for his slingshot.

The Rock in the Psalms

The *"rock"* also becomes one of the themes found in the Psalms. We find the *"rock"* used 24 times throughout the Psalms. Five writers of the Psalms used the term. When David wrote in Psalm 18:2, *"The LORD is my rock ..."* he was commenting on the Song of Moses.

When the Sons of Korah sang in Psalm 42:9, *"I will say unto God my rock, Why hast thou forgotten me?"* they were commenting on the Song of Moses. When Asaph wrote in Psalm 78:35, *"And they remembered that God was their rock ..."* he was commenting on the Song of Moses.

When Ethan wrote in Psalm 89:26, *"Thou art my father, my God, and the rock of my salvation ..."* he was commenting on the Song of Moses.

Three Rocks in the Mosaic Psalms

Finally, though Moses listed the *"rock"* five times in Deuteronomy 32, he mentioned it three more times in the other portions of his song. They are:

*"To show that the LORD is upright: he is my **rock**, and there is no unrighteousness in him"* (Psalm 92:15).

*"But the LORD is my defense; and my God is the **rock** of my refuge"* (Psalm 94:22).

*"O Come, let us sing unto the LORD: let us make a joyful noise to the **rock** of our salvation"* (Psalm 95:1).

Psalm 95:1 marks Moses' final use of the term, *"rock,"* in the Song of Moses. And it is a fitting declaration. Please note: Moses concludes with the term *"rock of salvation,"* just as David concluded his Song of Deliverance (II Samuel 22:47) with the same term—*"rock of salvation."* Also, Ethan used the same term in Psalm 89 in reference to the Covenant of David. All three uses of the term *"rock of salvation"* connects Moses and David together in a special relationship.

This makes a total of eight times the *"rock"* is used in the Song of Moses. According to many theologians, the biblical number "eight" is the number of "new beginning." We are assured once again that God is not finished with Israel. He has not forever forsaken them. One day, He will restore them and establish a new beginning, the Millennial Kingdom of Christ.

Why is the *"rock"* mentioned five times in Deuteronomy 32 and three times in Psalms 90-100? I might mention that since 1948 Israel has fought five wars (1948, 1956, 1967, 1973 and 1982). During the future Tribulation Period Israel could face three more battles—Gog and Magog, the abomination of desolation, and Armageddon. Could there be a connection? In the case of David's *"rock"*s, each represented a battle with a giant. Perhaps the *"rock"*s in the Song of Moses also bear a similar prophetic design.

The Lion, the Bear and Goliath

Before David fought Goliath, he told King Saul that he had killed a lion and a bear:

> *"Thy servant slew both the lion and the bear: and this uncircumcised Philistine shall be as one of them ..."* (I Samuel 17:36).

Just as David killed the lion and the bear, we should note that Israel took care of Great Britain's control of Jerusalem in 1948. The symbol of Great Britain is a lion. The next army coming against Israel should be that of a "Russian bear." Israel must yet face the bear. However, once Israel is finished with the lion and the bear, the young nation must face the giant—the Goliath of history—Armageddon. Then the Messiah will come to judge the wicked, and save the righteous. Christ will establish a world kingdom and will rule as King of kings and Lord of lords. This is the ultimate message of the Song of Moses—the coming of the Messiah to establish His Kingdom while bringing the wrath of God upon the wicked.

The Last Words of Moses

Furthermore, this theme of war and victory is also given in the last words of Moses:

"There is none like unto the God of Jeshurun [another term used for Israel], *who rideth upon the heaven in thy help, and in his excellency on the sky.*

"The eternal God is thy refuge, and underneath are the everlasting arms: and **he shall thrust out the enemy** *from before thee; and shall say, Destroy them.*

"Israel then shall dwell in safety alone: the fountain of Jacob shall be upon a land of corn and wine; also his heavens shall drop down dew.

"Happy art thou, O Israel: *who is like unto thee, O people saved by the LORD, the shield of thy help, and who is the sword of thy excellency! And* **thine enemies shall be found liars unto thee; and thou shalt tread upon their high places"** (Deuteronomy 33:26-29).

The theme of these verses is that God is going to destroy the enemy, and set up a kingdom for Israel. God promised that Israel will tread upon the high places of their enemies.

The ZONDERVAN PICTORIAL ENCYCLOPEDIA OF THE BIBLE, says that Moses' last words, in Deuteronomy 33:26-29, find their echo in the prayer recorded in Psalm 90. So the theme of Psalm 90 actually follows the same theme found in the last words of Moses. I am convinced that Psalms 90-100 are the concluding stanzas to the Song of Moses that began in Deuteronomy 32.

David's Song of Deliverance

What is so fascinating about this prophetic theme is its connection with the final Song of Deliverance written by David. Just as the Song of Moses precedes his last words, David's song precedes the last words of David in II Samuel 22. Moses' song, preceding his last words, has FIVE *"rock"*s in it. And David's song, preceding his last words, has FIVE *"rock"*s in it! That could not possibly be a coincidence! Catch the theme in David's last words. It is the same as the theme in Moses' last words:

"Now these be the last words of David. David the son of Jesse said, and the man who was raised up on high, the anointed of the God of Jacob, and the sweet psalmist of Israel, said,

"The spirit of the Lord spake by me, and his word was in my tongue.

*"The God of Israel said, the **rock** of Israel spake to me"* (II Samuel 23:1-3a).

David's last words record the last words God spoke to him just before he died. You're about to read a message given to David by the *"rock"* of Israel. And who is the *"rock?"* Christ is the *"Rock!"* Now get this. The *"Rock"* of Israel says:

"He that ruleth over men must be just, ruling in the fear of God.

"And he shall be as the light of the morning, when the sun riseth, even a morning without clouds; as the tender grass springing out of the earth by clear shining after rain" (II Samuel 23:3b-4).

God is saying that the one who is to rule Israel, that is, the Messiah, will be like the sun coming up on a morning without clouds. What a beautiful way to describe the coming of Christ to reign on the earth! The prophet Malachi added:

> *"... unto you that fear my name shall the Sun of righteousness arise with healing in his wings ..."* (Malachi 4:2).

Everything will be so clean and wonderful when Jesus comes! That's what God, the *"rock"* of Israel said to the dying David. After quoting the *"rock,"* David goes on with his prophetic last words:

> *"Although my house be not so with God; yet he hath made with me an everlasting covenant, ordered in all things, and sure: for this is all my salvation, and all my desire, although he make it not to grow.*
>
> *"But the sons of Belial shall be all of them as thorns thrust away, because they cannot be taken with hands:*
>
> *"but the man that shall touch them must be fenced with iron and the staff of a spear; and they shall be utterly burned with fire **in the same place"*** (II Samuel 23:5-7).

Moses concluded his last words by saying, *"they shall tread upon their high places."* And David finished his last words by saying, *"they shall be utterly burned in the same place."* Obviously, the last words of David offer a reference to the last words of Moses. They express the same theme.

Moses and David Compared

Moses wrote five books of the Law, and corresponding to these David compiled five books of the Psalms. David's writings are intertwined with those of Moses. For example, David opened the Psalms with a phrase from the last words of Moses, who said, *"Happy art thou, O Israel, who is like unto thee?"* David opened the Psalms with, *"Blessed is the man."* Rabbis have written that David used the last words of Moses to introduce the Psalms. So one can see how David's writings closely follow the theme established in the Song of Moses.

David's Five Rocks

Just before David's last words, the Bible records his song—just as Moses' song is recorded in the chapter prior to Moses' last words. And David's song also talks about the *"rock!"* David also mentions the *"rock"* five times:

*"And he said, The LORD is my **rock**, and my fortress, and my deliverer;*

*"the God of my **rock**; in him will I trust;*

*"For who is God, save the LORD? and who is a **rock**, save our God?*

*"The LORD liveth; and blessed be my **rock**; and exalted be the God of the **rock** of my salvation"* (II Samuel 22:2-3,32,47).

Please note: David's last use of the *"rock"* connects it to the all-important word *"salvation."* David used the same term, *"rock of my salvation,"* that Moses penned in his concluding use of the *"rock"* in Psalm 95:1. Also, Ethan used the term *"rock of my salvation"* in Psalm 89:26—the psalm that deals with the Covenant of David and the introduction of the remaining stanzas to the Song of Moses (Psalms 90-100). Such a term, used by all three scriptures, points us to a special prophetic relationship between David and Moses.

David mentioned the *"rock"* five times in I Samuel 22. What do these *"rock"*s have to do with David? Just as Moses wrote about the *"rock"* he smote, now David writes about the *"five smooth stones"* he used when he faced Goliath. In the previous chapter (II Samuel 21), David talks about killing five giants:

> *"These four were born to the giant in Gath, and fell by the ¹hand of David, and by the hand of his servants"* (II Samuel 21:22).

We have five giants in all—Goliath and four others who were felled by David and his men. That was the reason David emphasized the *"rock."* However, he also meant to compare his song with the Song of Moses, since both songs preceded the recording of their last words.

There is a prophecy connected with David's use of the *"rock."* Just as David went out to fight Goliath, someday Jesus, the scion of David, will come to fight the giant of all wars, Armageddon!

Psalm 89's Covenant of David

Psalm 89 discusses the Covenant of David—the same theme that David addressed in his last words. Note, the last words of David refer to Psalm 89 and the last words of Moses refer to Psalm 90!

"He shall cry unto me, Thou art my father, my God, and the rock of my salvation" (Psalm 89:26).

There's the *"rock"* again. Psalm 89 corresponds with the last words of David and with David's Song of Deliverance. Ethan concludes the third book of the Psalms and prepares the hearer for the coming of Messiah. Psalm 89 ends on a very upbeat, prophetic note. The stage is set for the Song of Moses (Psalms 90-100) and the events that lead up to the Second Coming of Christ:

"Wherewith thine enemies have reproached, O LORD; wherewith they have reproached the footsteps of thine anointed" (Psalm 89:51).

This is prophetic language relating to the coming of Jesus. It leads us right into the next book of the Psalms—the Song of Moses!

We know that I Corinthians 10:4 says that the *"Rock"* is Christ. We know that both Moses and David emphasized the *"rock."* Moses wrote the five books of the Law and David wrote the five books of the Psalms. David placed Moses' song in Psalms 90-100, which tells about the conclusion of what began in Deuteronomy 32-33.

And by the way, David did not take those other eleven stanzas out of Deuteronomy to put them here. God kept them out of the book of Deuteronomy. God had Deuteronomy published with only one of twelve stanzas in the Song of Moses. And it was David who was given the privilege of placing those other eleven stanzas of Moses' song in Psalms 90-100.

Nebuchadnezzar's Dream, A Rock Cut Out Without Hands!

The prophetic significance of the *"rock"* was revealed by one of the great prophets of Israel—Daniel, who interpreted a dream of Nebuchadnezzar. The Babylonian king saw all of the great world empires depicted as a "giant" of a man. This monster man had a head of gold, arms and chest of silver, a midsection of brass, legs of iron and feet with toes made of iron mixed with clay. Suddenly, a *"rock"* cut out without hands smote the image, and ground it to powder. Then this *"rock"* became a mighty mountain and filled the whole earth.

"And in the days of these kings shall the God of heaven set up a kingdom, which shall never be destroyed: and the kingdom shall not be left to other people, but it shall break in pieces and consume all these kingdoms, and it shall stand for ever.

*"Forasmuch as thou sawest that the **stone** was cut out of the mountain without hands, and that it brake in pieces the iron, the brass, the clay, the silver, and the gold"* (Daniel 2:44-45a).

Daniel gives the conclusion to the dream when he says that this *"rock"* represents the coming Messiah to establish His Kingdom and bear rule over all the earth! That's what David's Song of Deliverance and the Song of Moses is all about. The *"Rock"* cut out without hands is about to come! He is practically on His way!

Zechariah's Burdensome Stone

Another use of the *"rock"* can be seen in Zechariah 12:3. In this prophecy, Jerusalem and Christ are connected:

> *"And in that day will I make Jerusalem a burdensome* **stone** *for all people: all that burden themselves with it shall be cut in pieces, though all the people of the earth be gathered together against it"* (Zechariah 12:3).

God has made Jerusalem a burdensome stone. This prophecy may help us to understand why Moses smote the *"rock."* We know that the *"rock"* represented Christ but have been puzzled about the second *"rock."* If the second event of smiting also only represented Christ, then perhaps we should look for a second smiting of Christ. However, if the *"rock"* had a double meaning and also represented Jerusalem as Zechariah implies, then the scenario makes better sense.

I am comfortable with the *"rock"* representing Christ. However, prophetic passages often have double meanings. That may be the case here. Suppose the *"rock"* also represented Jerusalem. In which case the Roman destruction of Jerusalem in A.D. 70 could represent a fulfillment of the first blow. The final blow could come during the Tribulation Period—just as Zechariah implies. Remember, on that second occasion, Moses smote the *"rock"* twice!

And what happened to the *"rock"* when Moses smote it? It gave forth water—which takes us again to the prophet Zechariah:

> *"In that day there shall be a **fountain** opened to the house of David and to the inhabitants of Jerusalem for sin and for uncleanness"* (Zechariah 13:1).

Out of Jerusalem—the burdensome stone—a fountain is opened in the house of who? Of David! That ties David and Moses together. Zechariah was offering a prophetic commentary on the Song of Moses and David's Song of Deliverance. Water came out of the *"rock"*—the *"Rock"* of our salvation!

In Revelation 15:3, the saints in heaven sing both the *"song of Moses and the song of the Lamb."* Perhaps the *"song of the Lamb"* is none other than the "Song of Deliverance" written by David.

There are, indeed, hidden prophecies compiled by David in the Psalms. When we started this study in the Song of Moses, we had no idea that it would further solidify the prophetic nature of the Psalms. Let us rejoice in the fact that in our day, God seems to be telling us that the conclusion of His plan is near, indeed! Perhaps the Song of Moses in Psalms 90-100, which tells the story of the Tribulation Period, is about to be fulfilled!

Chapter Four

Themes of the Prophets

"Give ear, O ye heavens, and I will speak; and hear, O earth, the words of my mouth" (Deuteronomy 32:1).

We have noted two incredible concepts about the Song of Moses. First, it is comprised of more than just one chapter. Deuteronomy 32 opens the Song of Moses while Psalms 90-100 continue and conclude it. Second, Deuteronomy 32 begins with a prophetic reference to Simeon. As we have already suggested, this cryptic reference to Simeon, whose name means "hearing," sets a prophetic theme found throughout the Bible that Israel should be spiritually deaf throughout the years of their exile.

Now we shall discuss a third concept. The Song of Moses actually sets the theme for the entire prophetic nature of the Bible. Moses predicted the exile of Israel; the rise of Gentile Christianity; and the eventual return of the Jews to the land of their inheritance, where they will face the antichrist and suffer the awesome Armageddon. The Song of Moses concludes with beleaguered Israel saved by the Messiah who will come to judge the world and set up His dynamic kingdom.

Let's consider some of the terminology used by Moses and follow each theme through some of the other prophets of the Bible. As I studied the song, I recognized certain key phrases which I had come across in other parts of the Bible. I came to the conclusion that the other prophets were actually expounding on the Song of Moses as they wrote their predictions about the future.

The Early and Latter Rain

For example, Moses wrote:

"My doctrine shall drop as the rain, my speech shall distil as the dew, as the small rain upon the tender herb, and as the showers upon the grass" (Deuteronomy 32:2).

Here, Moses set the theme for the prophecies about the early and the latter rain. When Solomon wrote of the rain, he could have drawn his theme from the Song of Moses. When Isaiah wrote about the rain, he may have been commenting on the Song of Moses. When Jeremiah, Hosea, Joel and Zechariah wrote of the latter rain, they all appear to have alluded to the Song of Moses. Of these, Joel's prophecies are quite significant:

*"Be glad then, ye children of Zion, and rejoice in the LORD your God: for he hath given you the former rain moderately, and he will cause to come down for you the rain, the **former rain**, and the **latter rain** in the first month"* (Joel 2:23).

Many theologians believe Joel was referring to the pouring out of the Holy Spirit—the early rain came on the day of Pentecost (Acts 2) and the latter rain will occur in the future Tribulation Period. Only five verses later Joel writes his prophecy:

"... it shall come to pass afterward, that I will pour out my spirit upon all flesh; and your sons and your daughters shall prophesy, your old men shall dream dreams, your young men shall see visions;

"And also upon the servants and upon the handmaids in those days will I pour out my spirit" (Joel 2:28-29).

This prophecy may be only half completed. That which occurred 2,000 years ago on the day of Pentecost was just the beginning. We may be awaiting a latter rain—the pouring out of the Spirit upon Jerusalem in the latter days. Why do we think this? Because Joel continued:

"And I will show wonders in the heavens and in the earth, blood, and fire, and pillars of smoke.

"The sun shall be turned into darkness, and the moon into blood, before the great and terrible day of the LORD come" (Joel 2:30-31).

Obviously, these events did not occur on the day of Pentecost recorded in Acts 2. Therefore, they await a later fulfillment. The symbol of the early rain appears to refer to the days surrounding the first coming of Christ and the latter rain could refer to those future events near His second coming. James had this same concept in mind when he referred to the prophetic nature of the early and latter rain:

"Be patient therefore, brethren, unto the coming of the Lord. Behold, the husbandman waiteth for the precious fruit of the earth, and hath long patience for it, until he

*receive the **early and latter rain**.*

"Be ye also patient; stablish your hearts: for the coming of the Lord draweth nigh" (James 5:7-8).

His prophetic theme of the early and latter rain was an Old Testament concept presented in the Song of Moses.

Remember the Days of Old

Here's another theme. Moses wrote:

*"Remember the **days of old**, consider the years of many generations ..."* (Deuteronomy 32:7).

This same terminology is used in a psalm written by Asaph:

*"I have considered the **days of old**, the years of ancient times"* (Psalm 77:5).

This was also the theme expressed in Isaiah where the Lord said:

*"Remember the **former things of old**: for I am God, and there is none else; I am God, and there is none like me,*

"Declaring the end from the beginning, and from ancient times the things that are not yet done, saying, My counsel shall stand, and I will do all my pleasure" (Isaiah 46:9-10).

In this passage, God declares that His people should remember *"the former things of old,"* for in them is set the prophetic theme for the future of Israel. Here is a verse that not only uses the same terminology found in the Song of Moses, but also may give a clue as to where the people should look in order to find the prophecy—namely, the Song of Moses.

The Inheritance of Jacob

For another example, consider the following:

*"For the LORD'S portion is his people. Jacob is the lot of his **inheritance"** (Deuteronomy 32:9).*

These words form the terminology used in a psalm by the Sons of Korah:

*"He shall choose our **inheritance** for us, the excellency of Jacob whom he loved"* (Psalm 47:4).

The theme of this verse refers to the inheritance of the land promised to Jacob and the use of this terminology comes right from the Song of Moses.

The Apple of His Eye

For another example of the importance of the Song of Moses to all future prophets in the Bible, let us consider the following passage:

*"He found him in a desert land, and in the waste howling wilderness; he led him about, he instructed him, he kept him as the **apple of his eye"** (Deuteronomy 32:10).*

The phrase, *"the apple of his eye"* was used by Zechariah in describing the return of Israel:

"Ho, ho, come forth, and flee from the land of the north, saith the LORD: for I have spread you abroad as the

four winds of the heaven, saith the LORD.

"Deliver thyself, O Zion, that dwellest with the daughter of Babylon.

"For thus saith the LORD of hosts; After the glory hath he sent me unto the nations which spoiled you: for he that toucheth you toucheth the **apple of his eye"** (Zechariah 2:6-8).

In using this phrase, Zechariah was commenting on the Song of Moses. By the way, please note that the *"land of the north"* appears to be Russia. In 1882, the first group of Jews left Kharkov for their Promised Land. A second wave came in 1904-1914 and a third wave of Russian Jews came in the years 1919-1924. In 1990 over 150,000 Jews from the Soviet Union arrived in Israel to establish a new life.

The next part of the verse spoke of *"the four winds of the heaven."* This appears to represent Jews returning from Europe and the rest of the world—as the fourth wave fled Polish persecution during the 1930's; a fifth wave came because of the Nazi holocaust; and finally, they have come from all nations since the birth of Israel. But the prophecy further targets Mystery Babylon— *"Deliver thyself, O Zion, that dwellest with the daughter of Babylon."* Perhaps Mystery Babylon is not the Soviet Union, or Europe, or any other country which has thus far seen waves of Jews leave for their homeland. Mystery Babylon appears to be a country where many of the world's Jewry still lives—outside Israel!

The phrase, *"the apple of his eye"* was also a key factor in Psalm 17 where the Psalmist referred to the future restoration of Jerusalem:

> *"Keep me as the **apple of the eye**, hide me under the shadow of thy wings"* (Psalm 17:8).

The nation of Israel and its capital, Jerusalem, according to Moses, are the apple of God's eye.

As an Eagle ... Spreadeth Abroad Her Wings

> *"As an **eagle** stirreth up her nest, fluttereth over her young, **spreadeth abroad her wings**, taketh them, beareth them on her wings:*
>
> *"So did the LORD lead him ..."* (Deuteronomy 32:11-12).

Not only is *"apple of the eye"* used in Psalm 17:8, but the rest of the verse which talks about hiding *"under the shadow of God's wings"* is also indicative of the passage in the Song of Moses which promises to care for Israel as an eagle hen *"spreadeth abroad her wings"* to protect her young. When Jesus wept over Jerusalem, He was using a theme from the Song of Moses:

> *"O Jerusalem, Jerusalem, which killest the prophets, and stonest them that are sent unto thee; how often would I have gathered thy children together, as a hen doth gather her brood **under her wings**, and ye would not.*
>
> *"Behold, your house is left unto you desolate: and verily I say unto you, Ye shall not see me, until the time come when ye shall say, Blessed is he that cometh in the name of the Lord"* (Luke 13:34-35).

In this passage, Jesus was quoting from the

Song of Moses. He used the terminology of the eagle who spreads her wings for the protection of her young. This terminology is also tied to another stanza in the Song of Moses:

> *"Surely he shall deliver thee from the snare of the fowler ...*
>
> *"He shall cover thee with his feathers, and **under his wings** shalt thou trust"* (Psalm 91:3-4).

Here the Lord promises to protect his people *"from the snare of the fowler"* using the symbolism of the protective mother eagle.

Turning to the Gentiles

The Song of Moses further declares that God will disperse the Jews among the nations and turn to the Gentiles:

> *"And he said, I will hide my face from them, I will see what their end shall be: for they are a very froward generation, children in whom is no faith.*
>
> *"They have moved me to jealousy with that which is not God; they have provoked me to anger with their vanities: and I will move them to **jealousy with those which are not a people** ..."* (Deuteronomy 32:20-21).

Here is God's promise that he will turn from the Jews to a people *"which are not a people."* He will make eternal life available to the Gentiles, and by doing so, He will move Israel to jealousy. This is a prophecy of Gentile Christianity which followed the smiting of Israel's Messiah on the cross. God promises to make Israel jealous by turning to the Gentiles. A reference to this part of the Song of

Moses is found in Paul's epistle to the Romans:

*"But I say, Did not Israel know? First, Moses saith, I will provoke you to **jealousy by them that are no people**, and by a foolish nation will I anger you"* (Romans 10:19).

Paul quoted from the Song of Moses. All three chapters in Romans 9, 10 and 11 are a commentary on the Song of Moses. And this is the theme: Israel will be forsaken temporarily while God turns to the Gentiles, making Israel jealous. Israel must become spiritually deaf and blind to God's purpose, just as the brothers of Joseph were made to carry out the will of God by selling their brother into Egyptian slavery. They meant it for evil, but God meant it for good.

Eventually, the sons of Jacob discovered that the rejected Joseph had become their salvation. And, in like manner, someday Israel will receive spiritual hearing and sight—that they might recognize Jesus as their Messiah and be delivered. Also, the apostle Paul quoted Isaiah, who, in turn, gave his commentary on the Song of Moses:

*"But Isaiah is very bold, and saith, I was found of **them that sought me not**; I was made manifest unto them that ask not after me"* (Romans 10:20).

This is a statement from Isaiah 65:1 and is yet another commentary on the Song of Moses which predicted that God would turn to the Gentiles. The apostle Paul continues:

"Have they stumbled that they should fall? God forbid: but rather through their fall salvation is come unto the

Gentiles, *for to provoke them to* ***jealousy***" (Romans 11:11).

One of the main themes in the Song of Moses is this prediction that God will turn to the Gentiles and provoke the Chosen People to jealousy.

Jeshurun

Now let's consider another term used in the Song of Moses. A description of Israel as Jeshurun, meaning "upright" was used.

*"But **Jeshurun** waxed fat, and kicked: thou art waxen fat, thou art grown thick, thou art covered with fatness; then he forsook God which made him, and lightly esteemed the Rock of his salvation"*(Deuteronomy 32:15).

The term is used again in Deuteronomy 33:5:

*"And he was king in **Jeshurun**, when the heads of the people and the tribes of Israel were gathered together"* (Deuteronomy 33:5).

Also, in verse 26, the term is used:

*"There is none like unto the God of **Jeshurun**, who rideth upon the heaven in thy help, and his excellency on the sky"* (Deuteronomy 33:26).

This same term, used for the upright in Israel, is also found in Isaiah 44:2:

*"Thus saith the LORD that made thee, and formed thee from the womb, which will help thee; Fear not, O Jacob, my servant; and thou, **Jeshurun**, whom I have chosen"* (Isaiah 44:2).

When Isaiah penned these words, he was commenting on the Song of Moses. The whole passage in Isaiah 44 promises that one day, deaf Israel will be able to hear and understand prophetic mysteries again. One day Israel will understand that God will pour out His Spirit upon them, just as Moses referred to the rain. And one day Israel will understand that the Lord will send His redeemer, just as Moses predicted in Psalms 90-100.

It is amazing to me that the prophetic portions of the Bible are so consistent with the themes set and the terminology used in the Song of Moses!

The Day of Vengeance

According to the Song of Moses, God will scatter the Chosen People among the nations of the world where they will be forsaken for a period of time. But that is not the end of the story. There will come a day when the Lord will regather the Jews to their Promised Land and will pour out his vengeance upon the Gentiles:

"For their vine is the vine of Sodom, and the fields of Gomorrah: their grapes [that is, the grapes of the Gentile nations] *are grapes of gall, their clusters are bitter:*

"Their wine is the poison of dragons, and the cruel venom of asps.

"Is not this laid up in store for me and sealed up among my treasures?

*"To me belongeth **vengeance**, and recompence; their foot shall slide in due time; for the day of their calamity is at hand, and the things that shall come upon them make haste"* (Deuteronomy 32:32-35).

The word *"vengeance"* is another key to the understanding of this prophecy. It takes us forward into the future—to the day of God's vengeance. This appears to be a reference to Armageddon. In verse 41 the Lord declares:

"If I whet my glittering sword, and mine hand take hold on judgment; I will render vengeance to mine enemies, and will reward them that hate me" (Deuteronomy 32:41).

This prophecy will be fulfilled at the end of this age. Verse 43 declares the restoration of Israel and God's judgment of the nations:

"Rejoice, O ye nations, with his people: for he will avenge the blood of his servants, and will render vengeance to his adversaries, and will be merciful unto his land, and to his people" (Deuteronomy 32:43).

The use of the term *"vengeance"* sets the theme repeated by Solomon, Isaiah, Jeremiah, Ezekiel, Micah, Nahum, Luke, Paul and Jude. These all gave commentaries on the Song of Moses when they referred to the day of God's vengeance.

Among them, Isaiah will suffice as an example. In Isaiah 61:1-2, the prophet wrote:

"The Spirit of the Lord God is upon me; because the LORD hath anointed me to preach good tidings unto the meek; he hath sent me to bind up the brokenhearted, to proclaim liberty to the captives, and the opening of the prison to them that are bound;

"To proclaim the acceptable year of the LORD, and the day of vengeance of our God; to comfort all that mourn" (Isaiah 61:1-2).

Isaiah's use of the term *"vengeance"* was a commentary on the Song of Moses.

This passage was quoted by Christ in Luke 4, except for the last part of the prophecy. Jesus left out the part about the *"day of vengeance"* because that part of the prophecy was scheduled for the far future.

Isaiah also used the term *"vengeance"* two chapters later, when describing the glorious appearance of Christ at Armageddon:

> *"Who is this that cometh from Edom, with dyed garments from Bozrah? this that is glorious in his apparel, traveling in the greatness of his strength? I that speak in righteousness, mighty to save.*
>
> *"Wherefore art thou red in thine apparel, and thy garments like him that treadeth in the winefat?*
>
> *"I have trodden the winepress alone; and of the people there was none with me: for I will tread them in mine anger, and trample them in my fury; and their blood shall be sprinkled upon my garments, and I will stain all my raiment.*
>
> *"For the **day of vengeance** is in mine heart, and the year of my redeemed is come"* (Isaiah 63:1-4).

Over and over again, the word *"vengeance"* is used to describe the Second Coming of Christ. The term is also found in the opening verse of Psalm 94. It is in that part of the Song of Moses dedicated to the tribe of Gad, which means "troop," and is descriptive of those armies who will gather against Israel in the end time:

> *"O LORD God, to whom **vengeance** belongeth; O God, to whom **vengeance** belongeth, shew thyself.*

"Lift up thyself, thou judge of the earth: render a reward to the proud" (Psalms 94:1-2).

What a prophecy! Israel will not be forever forsaken. God has promised that one day He will be merciful unto His land, the land of Israel, and to His people, the people of Israel. He will render vengeance upon the wicked when He comes. The exciting part of this promise in the Song of Moses is that its fulfillment began in 1948 with the restoration of the nation.

The Restoration of Israel

The concluding verses in Deuteronomy 32 introduce the restoration of Israel while the other eleven stanzas in the Song of Moses (Psalms 90-100) expand upon the prophecy to give further details of how those events will come to pass.

In Deuteronomy 33, Moses pronounces a prophetic blessing to each of the other tribes, giving a synopsis of each psalm (90-100) to which they are ascribed.

Psalm 90

For example, Psalm 90 was dedicated to Reuben, and Moses said of Reuben in Deuteronomy 33:6:

*"Let Reuben **live and not die**"* (Deuteronomy 33:6).

Psalm 90, then, is a song of repentance, indicating that the Chosen People will repent as the Messianic era approaches. In keeping with God's plea for repentance, Psalm 90 says:

*"Thou turnest man to destruction; and sayest, **Return,** ye children of men"* (Psalm 90:3).

Psalm 91

Psalm 91 was dedicated to Levi as a prophetic reference to the future restoration of Temple worship. Moses said of Levi:

"Let thy Thummim and thy Urim be with thy holy one, whom thou didst prove at Massah, and with whom thou didst strive at the waters of Meribah;

"Who said unto his father and to his mother, I have not seen him; neither did he acknowledge his brethren, nor knew his own children: for they have observed thy word, and kept thy covenant.

"They shall teach Jacob thy judgments, and Israel thy law: they shall put incense before thee, and whole burnt sacrifice upon thine altar.

"Bless, LORD, his substance, and accept the work of his hands: smite through the loins of them that rise against him, and of them that hate him, that they rise not again" (Deuteronomy 33:8-11).

The Lord is asked to *"accept the work of His hands,"* namely a reconstructed Tabernacle—a sanctuary on the Temple Mount. In like manner, Psalm 90's *"secret place"* is a reference to the Holy of Holies in that restored sanctuary.

*"He that dwelleth in the **secret place** of the most High shall abide under the shadow of the Almighty"* (Psalm 90:1).

The passage also alludes to an enemy who rises against Israel. It describes a time of great war.

Psalm 92

Psalm 92 was dedicated to Judah and is a prophetic picture of Israel under siege. A synopsis of the psalm is found in Deuteronomy 33:7:

"And this is the blessing of Judah: and he said, Hear, LORD, the voice of Judah, and bring him unto his people: let his hands be sufficient for him; and be thou a help to him from his enemies" (Deuteronomy 33:7).

In keeping with that theme, Psalm 92:9 says:

"For, lo, thine enemies, O LORD, for, lo, thine enemies shall perish; all the workers of iniquity shall be scattered" (Psalm 92:9).

Psalm 93

Psalm 93, continues the theme of Psalm 92 and is dedicated to Benjamin. The two tribes shared Jerusalem. The boundary between them was the Tyropeon valley. Today's Western Wall marks their ancient boundary. The Jews who pray at the Western Wall are standing in the territory of Judah. The Temple site is located in the territory of Benjamin. Moses referred to this border in Deuteronomy 33:12:

"And of Benjamin, the beloved of the LORD shall dwell in safety by him" (Deuteronomy 33:12).

In the end time, the two tribes should be safe from the wrath of God, which wrath is apparently called for in Psalm 93:3:

"The floods have lifted up, O LORD, the floods have lifted up their voice; the floods lift up their waves" (Psalm 93:3).

Psalm 94

Psalm 94 is dedicated to Gad. It appears to be a reference to military prowess and takes us to a future invasion of the holy city. Moses referred to it in this manner:

*"And of Gad, blessed be he that enlargeth Gad: he dwelleth as a lion, he teareth the arm with the crown of the head. And he provideth the first part for himself, because there, in a portion of the lawgiver, was he seated; and he came with the heads of the people, **he executed the justice of the LORD**, and his judgments with Israel"* (Deuteronomy 33:20).

The term Gad, meaning "troop," draws upon a picture of armies surrounding Jerusalem while the reference to a lion implies the coming of Christ (the Lion of Judah) to execute judgment and establish His kingdom. In like manner, Psalm 94 pleads for divine relief from an invading army:

*"... O God, to whom **vengeance** belongeth, shew thyself.*

"They break in pieces thy people, O LORD, and afflict thine heritage" (Psalm 94:1,5).

In keeping with the theme set forth in Deuteronomy 33:20, Moses promised an answer to their cry for help:

*"But the LORD is my defence; and my God is the rock
of my refuge.*

*"And he shall bring upon them their own iniquity, and
shall cut them off in their own wickedness; yea, the
LORD our **God shall cut them off**"* (Psalm 94:22-23).

Psalms 95 and 96

The theme of Psalms 95 and 96 can be seen in the
rejoicing of Issachar and Zebulun recorded in the
Mosaic blessing:

*"And of Zebulun he said, **Rejoice**, Zebulun, in thy going out; and, Issachar, in thy tents"* (Deuteronomy 33:18).

In keeping with that theme of rejoicing, Psalm
95 opens with:

*"O COME, let us **sing** unto the LORD: let us make a
joyful noise to the rock of our salvation"* (Psalm 95:1).

Psalm 96, following the same happy theme, is
dedicated to Zebulun and opens with:

*"O SING unto the LORD a new song: sing unto the
LORD, all the earth.*

*"**Sing** unto the LORD, bless his name; shew forth his
salvation from day to day.*

"Declare his glory among the heathen [Gentiles]*"*
(Psalm 96:1-3).

Psalm 97

The theme of Psalm 97 can be seen in the Mosaic
blessing given to Joseph:

"And of Joseph he said, Blessed of the LORD be his land, for the precious things of heaven, for the dew, and for the deep that coucheth beneath,

"And for the precious fruits brought forth by the sun, and for the precious things put forth by the moon,

"And for the chief things of the ancient mountains, and for the precious things of the lasting hills,

"And for the precious things of the earth and fullness thereof, and for the good will of him that dwelt in the bush: let the blessing come upon the head of Joseph, and upon the top of the head of him that was separated from his brethren.

*"His **glory** is like the firstling of his bullock, and his horns are like the horns of unicorns: with them **he shall push the people together to the ends of the earth:** and they are the ten thousands of Ephraim, and they are the thousands of Manasseh"* (Deuteronomy 33:13-17).

This lengthy blessing appears to present God's plans to bless the whole earth. We are reminded that Joseph was separated from his brethren. That prophetic scenario points us to Christ, once rejected by Israel, only to return and be crowned King of kings. In keeping with this theme, Psalm 97 says:

*"**The LORD reigneth;** let the earth rejoice; let the multitude of the isles be glad thereof.*

"Clouds and darkness are round about him: righteousness and judgment are the habitation of his throne.

"A fire goeth before him, and burneth up his enemies round about.

"His lightnings enlightened the world: the earth saw, and trembled.

*"**The hills melted like wax at the presence of the LORD, at the presence of the Lord of the whole earth.***

"The heavens declare his righteousness, and all the people see his glory" (Psalm 97:1-6).

It is a magnificent description of the Second Coming of Christ, of whom Joseph was a type.

Psalm 98

Psalm 98 is dedicated to Naphtali. Its theme is found in the Mosaic blessing:

"And of Naphtali he said, O Naphtali, satisfied with favour, and full with the blessing of the LORD: possess thou the west and the south" (Deuteronomy 33:23).

The verse implies the setting up of a world kingdom by the Messiah, especially seen in the phrase, *"possess thou ..."* In keeping with this theme, Psalm 98 says:

"O SING unto the LORD a new song; for he hath done marvelous things; his right hand, and his holy arm, hath gotten him the victory.

"The LORD hath made known his salvation: his righteousness hath he openly shewed in the sight of the heathen [Gentiles].

"He hath remembered his mercy and his truth toward the house of Israel: all the ends of the earth have seen the salvation of our God" (Psalm 98:1-3).

Indeed, as the Mosaic blessing declares, Israel is *"satisfied with favour, and full with the blessing of the LORD!"* In Psalm 98, Christ has come to save Israel and rule the world!

Psalm 99

Psalm 99 is dedicated to Dan, whose name means "judge." To him was given the awesome task of bringing judgment upon the house of Israel. In fact, Jewish theologians have speculated that Dan would produce the antichrist. It is noted in a commentary on an apocryphal writing entitled, *The Testaments of the Twelve Patriarchs.* In this ancient manuscript, dating back to 150 B. C., the last words of each of the twelve sons of Jacob are recorded. In the portion on the last words of Dan, the dying patriarch is reported to have said:

> "For I know that in the last days you will defect from the Lord, you will be offended at Levi, and revolt against Judah; but you will not prevail over them ... To the extent that you abandon the Lord, you will live by every evil deed ... and you are motivated to all wickedness by the spirits of deceit among you. For I read in the Book of Enoch the Righteous that your prince is Satan ..." [1]

The Testaments of the Twelve Patriarchs is preserved in a volume entitled, PSEUDEPIGRAPHA. In a footnote, James H. Charlesworth wrote:

> "No known Enochic text supports this, although Jewish and patristic speculation linked Dan and the Antichrist, possibly on the basis of the idolatry attributed to Dan in Judges 18:11-31 and the prophecies of judgment linked to Dan in Jeremiah 8:16-17." [2]

---

[1] H. C. Key, "Testaments Of The Twelve Patriarchs," *The Old Testament Pseudepigrapha,* Vol. 1, ed. James H. Charlesworth (Garden City, NY: Doubleday, 1983), p. 809.

[2] Ibid.

Dan receives a Mosaic blessing which corresponds with Psalm 99:

> *"And of Dan he said, Dan is a lion's whelp: he shall leap from Bashan"* (Deuteronomy 33:22).

The tribe actually moved into the territory of Bashan above the Sea of Galilee and captured the city of Laish (which means "lion") changing the name of the village to Dan. By the time of the reign of David, however, most of the tribe had disappeared from the land. Around 1050 B.C. the book of I Chronicles listed the genealogies of the other eleven tribes, excluding Dan!

Furthermore, Dan is not recorded in Revelation 7. The tribe made a mysterious leap from Bashan, leaving no obvious trail. They are regarded as a "lost tribe." Will they produce the antichrist? Have they been the guiding force behind all of Israel's troubles down through history? The dying Jacob said of Dan:

> *"Dan shall **judge** his people, as one of the tribes of Israel.*
>
> *"Dan shall be a serpent by the way, an adder in the path, that biteth the horse heels, so that his rider shall fall backward"* (Genesis 49:16-17).

Dan shall judge his people! In keeping with this theme, Psalm 99 says:

> *"The LORD reigneth; let the people tremble ...*
>
> *"The king's strength also loveth **judgment**; thou dost establish equity, thou **executest judgment** and righteousness in Jacob ...*

"Thou ... wast a God that forgavest them, though thou **tookest vengeance** *of their inventions"* (Psalm 99:1,4,8).

Psalm 100

Psalm 100 is filled with praise, indicative of the name Asher, which means "blessing:"

*"Let Asher be **blessed** with children; let him be acceptable to his brethren, and let him dip his foot in oil.*

"Thy shoes shall be iron and brass; and as thy days, so shall thy strength be" (Deuteronomy 33:24-25).

The thrust of this blessing is that the Chosen People will be blessed with material blessings for a very long period of time—perhaps a thousand years— *"as thy days, so shall thy strength be."* The rejoicing of Psalm 100 follows the theme as the kingdom is established and God's judgment of mankind is concluded!

"Make a joyful noise unto the LORD, all ye lands.

"For the LORD is good; his mercy is everlasting; and his truth endureth to all generations" (Psalm 100:1,5).

There is nothing in this psalm about judgment or sin. Nothing negative is recorded. All is happiness and joy.

The Last Words of Moses

Finally, upon the conclusion of these twelve stanzas, Moses makes a final statement before he ascends Mt. Nebo to die. He says in Deuteronomy 33:29, *"Happy art thou, O Israel ..."* Here is a clue as to when the fulfillment might commence. For these words were picked up by David to introduce the Psalms, *"Blessed is the Man."*

Yes, Psalm 1:1 refers back to the riddle found in the Song of Moses. To those who understand the prophecy, Psalm 1:1 indicates that the time has come for its ultimate fulfillment. That must surely be the reason why at least the first 89 Psalms appear to contain a year-by-year account of the Jewish people for at least the first 89 years of this century. We cannot say that Psalms 90-100 offer a year-by-year scenario. They seem to repeat several themes. We can say that these themes, however, are prophetic, and will be carried out during the Tribulation Period. A few of those themes given in Psalms 90-100 are:

1. The restoration of Temple worship.

2. Devastating wars.

3. The wrath of God upon a sinful world.

4. The coming of Messiah.

5. The establishment of His kingdom.

Will Psalms 90-100 see its fulfillment in the decade of the 1990's? We can only wait and see.

Chapter Five

Psalm 90
Dedicated to Reuben

In Deuteronomy 33 Moses delivers a blessing to each of eleven tribes, giving a synopsis of each psalm to which they are ascribed (Psalms 90-100). For example, Psalm 90 was dedicated to Reuben, and Moses said of Reuben in Deuteronomy 33:6:

"Let Reuben live and not die" (Deuteronomy 33:6).

The theme of Psalm 90 is repentance, prophetically implying that the Chosen People will return to the Lord as the Messianic era approaches.

*"LORD, thou hast been our dwelling place in **all generations**.*

"Before the mountains were brought forth, or ever thou hadst formed the earth and the world, even from everlasting to everlasting, thou art God" (Psalm 90:1-2).

The 1990's could be the most important decade in history. They conclude not only the twentieth century, but the sixth millennium as well. According to ancient rabbinical theology, God has laid out human history into seven millenniums, corresponding to the days of creation. Just as God rested on the seventh day, the seventh 1,000 year period should bring a great Sabbath rest. This is also the teaching of Revelation 20:4:

> *"... They lived and reigned with Christ a thousand years."* (Revelation 20:4).

The big question now concerns Psalms 90-100. Do they have a specific message for the decade of the 90's? What about Psalm 90? Does it hold a special message for 1990? Let's take a look.

The Last Generation

Normally, one would interpret Psalm 90 as simply saying that the great Creator has always loved mankind and offered His forgiveness to a wayward human race. However, what if the seventh millennium really is designated to be God's great Sabbath rest? What if Psalm 90 really does represent the beginning of the 1990's—the concluding decade of the sixth millennium? The Psalms happen to be the 19th book of the Old Testament. Could Psalm 90, therefore, represent a prophecy directed to those who live in 1990?

Let us read again God's message as if it were given specifically to the generation that will see the conclusion of the sixth millennium and the beginning of the seventh! *"LORD, thou hast been our dwelling place in all generations."* Not most generations, but ALL!—that is, if this present generation really is the last one!

In Psalm 48:13, the Psalmist writes, *"Tell it to the generation following."* The Hebrew term trans-

lated *"following"* is "acharon." It means, "LAST"
generation. Did the "LAST" generation begin with
the birth of Israel in 1948? Psalm 48 gives a description of *"a woman in travail"* (Psalm 48:6).
Since the *"woman in travail"* obviously gives birth
to a baby (a new generation) the reference to that
generation must be the focus of verse Psalm 48:13.
And if verse 13 refers to the generation born when
the woman travails, then that must be the generation designated as the "LAST" generation! If so,
then the Mosaic reference to *"ALL GENERA-
TIONS"* in Psalm 90:1 is certainly appropriate.

Not only is the term "LAST" generation found in
Psalm 48, it is also found in Psalm 102—following
these Mosaic psalms (90-100)! Psalm 102 speaks of
a *"set time"* (v. 13) *"when the LORD shall build up
Zion"* (v. 16). Jerusalem has become the largest
city in Israel over the past decade. According to
the passage, those events shall precede the coming
of Christ. The psalmist declares, *"When the
LORD shall build up Zion, he shall appear in His
glory"* (Psalm 102:16). The psalmist writes in verse
18, *"This shall be written for the generation to
come."* The Hebrew term is the same mentioned
earlier—"acharon," the "LAST" generation!

If Psalm 48 introduces the "LAST" generation
and Psalm 102 describes its conclusion, then the
message in Psalm 90 appears to be most important! Notice how perfectly God has packaged the
Song of Moses (Psalms 90-100). The term *"ALL
GENERATIONS"* both opens and closes the song.
The same phrase is found in the last verse of the
concluding psalm of the Song of Moses:

*"For the LORD is good; his mercy is everlasting: and his truth endureth to **all generations**"* (Psalm 100:5).

We observe the term *"ALL GENERATIONS"* in both the first verse of Psalm 90 and the last verse of Psalm 100. This Mosaic composition is couched within the framework of *"ALL GENERATIONS"*— a very important consideration, ONLY, if these psalms refer to the LAST generation.

The number "100" happens to be the 19th letter of the Hebrew alphabet. Could that be a prophetic reference to the conclusion of the 1900's? If so, then the prophetic importance of the term *"ALL GENERATIONS"* becomes all the more apparent. This phrase both opens and closes these eleven psalms and is positioned within the framework of the "LAST GENERATION" introduced in Psalm 48 and concluded in Psalm 102.

The Tribulation Period

"Thou turnest man to destruction" (Psalm 90:3a).

This scripture also reads with apocalyptic overtones. Moses writes, *"Thou turnest man to destruction."* Well, if this really is that generation which will be thrown into great tribulation, then the scripture becomes most fitting.

Have we arrived at that dreadful time when the human race will be turned to destruction? The apostle, John, predicts a time when a third of the earth will be burned with fire (Revelation 8:7). Half of earth's population will die. The vials of God's wrath will be poured out in judgment.

The Last Call for Repentance

"Return, ye children of men" (Psalm 90:3b).

If this generation is the one designated to see the judgment of God—the one upon which the Tribulation Period will fall, then it is understandable that God should give men one last chance to repent. Psalm 90 was dedicated to Reuben and that its theme is repentance:

> "In his blessings, Moses blessed Reuben first, saying, 'Let Reuben live and not die' (Deuteronomy 33:6), referring to Reuben's sin and to his subsequent repentance (Genesis 35:22). With his sincere remorse and penitence, Reuben introduced the principle of complete repentance to the world (Bereishis Rabba 84:19). Thus, this psalm relates to Reuben, the symbol of repentance." [1]

Have we arrived at that point in history John wrote about—the age of Laodicea? It is there that John wrote of God's final plea for repentance just before the apocalyptic events of Revelation 4 occur:

> *"Behold, I stand at the door and knock: if any man hear my voice, and open the door, I will come in to him, and will sup with him, and he with me"* (Revelation 3:20).

It is appropriate, then, that God should offer one last opportunity to repent. That is exactly what God is saying, *"Return, ye children of men."*

---

[1] Feuer, *Tehillim*, p. 1121.

Six Yesterdays Are Past

"For a thousand years in thy sight are but as yester-day when it is past ..." (Psalm 90:4a).

Rabbi Avrohom Chaim Feuer cites ancient rab-binical thought on the concept that each day of creation prophetically represented a thousand years of human history and that the seventh day of rest represented the Messianic age—a thousand year reign of the Messiah:

"It is both unreasonable and unwise to pass judgment on a work of art before it has been completed; even a mas-terpiece may look like a grotesque mass of strokes and colors, prior to its completion. Human history is God's masterpiece. Physical creation was completed at the end of the sixth day, but the spiritual development of man-kind will continue until this world ends, at the close of the sixth millennium. Thus it is both unfair and impos-sible to judge God's equity before the denouement of hu-man history, despite the fact that history appears to be a long series of tragic injustices.

"On the seventh day of the first week of creation, on the Sabbath, Adam surveyed God's completed work and he was stirred to sing of the marvelous perfection which his eyes beheld.

"Similarly, when the panorama of human history is completed, the seventh millennium will be ushered in as the day of everlasting Sabbath. At that time all Adam's descendants will look back and admire God's completed masterpiece." [2]

Historically speaking, we have arrived at the last decade of the sixth millennium. The teaching of

---

[2] Ibid., p. 1145.

the rabbi will either come to pass, or we will soon know that he was wrong. However, we must understand that his commentary did not represent his thoughts alone. He was repeating the cardinal teachings of historic Judaism. Author Joseph Good made the following observation:

"The article entitled 'Millennium' from the Encyclopedia of the Jewish Religion, edited by J. R. Zwi Werblowsky and Geoffrey Wigoder, 1986 by Adama Books, page 263; states that the belief in each day of the week of creation representing a one thousand year day of G-d, with the seventh day being 'the day of the L-rd,' or millennium. This belief could first be found in the Slavic version of the pseudepigraphal Book of Enoch (33:1-2). It was further developed by the 'tannaim' (the Rabbis shortly before, during, and immediately following Jesus' lifetime), who based their interpretation on Psalm 90:4. They explained that as the days of creation were six in number, the world would last for six thousand years. The seventh 'world day,' the sabbath, was to be the one thousand years of the Messiah (Sanhedrin 97a; Avodah Zarah 9a)." [3]

This concept is also reflected in the teaching of another rabbi, Simon Peter, who, in his commentary on this Mosaic passage writes:

"One day is with the Lord as a thousand years, and a thousand years as one day" (II Peter 3:8).

Now, if Peter and other early rabbinical theologians are correct, then we should read Psalm 90

---

[3] Joseph Good, *Rosh Hashanah and the Messianic Kingdom To Come*, p. 52, reports on 'Millennium' from the *Encyclopedia of the Jewish Religion*, edited by J. R. Zwi Werblowsky and Geoffrey Wigoder, 1986 by Adama Books, page 263.

as a special message to the generation which has reached the end of 6,000 years. Moses writes, *"For a thousand years in thy sight are as YESTERDAY WHEN IT IS PAST!"* The millennial day is PAST! We have arrived at the conclusion of it. Moses did not simply say that a thousand years is as a day like Peter did, but that it is PAST! It is as yesterday!

A Thief in the Night

"... and as a watch in the night" (Psalm 90:4b).

Moses divided the millennium into two parts, most of which is taken up in the *"yesterday."* But the rest of it concludes with *"a watch in the night."*

"Rashi, [a twelfth century rabbi] maintains that one day of God consists of less than one thousand years, for God warned Adam not to eat of the tree of knowledge, saying, 'For in the day that thou eatest thereof thou shalt surely die' (Genesis 2:17), which implies that Adam's entire lifespan was considered a single day in God's eyes. When Adam's life ended after 930 years (Genesis 3:5), it was the end of God's day. Thus, one thousand years in God's eyes are like one yesterday plus a short watch in the night composed of seventy years." [4]

If this rabbinical concept reflects Moses' true meaning, then we are not only approaching the end of the sixth millennial day, but are presently in the final *"watch in the night!"* Is that *"watch"* 70 years long? In verse 10, Moses explained:

---

[4] Feuer, *Tehillim* p. 1124.

> *"The days of our years are threescore and ten; and if by reason of strength they be fourscore years, yet is their strength labor and sorrow"* (Psalm 90:10a).

If the taking of Jerusalem by the British on December 9, 1917 marked the beginning of the *"watch in the night"* then we have already passed the 70th year and may be presently progressing through the *"labor and sorrow"* years! On December 8, 1987, Palestinian protesters began throwing rocks at the Jews! Since then, the "intifada" has continued. Could we presently be in the remaining decade of the *"watch in the night?"* Under such circumstances, we should consider the possibility that Psalm 90 bears a special message for our generation. Peter further explains his "millennial day" concept by addressing the *"watch in the night:"*

> *"But the day of the Lord will come as a thief in the night ..."* (II Peter 3:10).

Paul also writes about the Second Coming in terms reminiscent of this *"watch in the night:"*

> *"But of the times and the seasons, brethren, ye have no need that I write unto you.*
>
> *"For yourselves know perfectly that the day of the Lord so cometh as a thief in the night"* (I Thessalonians 5:1-2).

John also added to this concept:

> *"Behold, I come as a thief. Blessed is he that watcheth"* (Revelation 16:15).

Our Savior was not merely using a colloquialism when he referred to this same concept:

> *"Watch therefore: for ye know not what hour your Lord doth come.*
>
> *"But know this, that if the goodman of the house had known in what watch the thief would come, he would have watched, and would not have suffered his house to be broken up.*
>
> *"Therefore be ye also ready: for in such an hour as ye think not the Son of man cometh"* (Matthew 24:42-44).

In respect to these passages, it is essential that we view Psalm 90 and its *"watch in the night"* as prophetic and that we be busy watching!

As the Days of Noah

> *"Thou carriest them away as with a flood"* (Psalm 90:5a).

The *"flood"* in this passage was considered by Radak (a twelfth century rabbi) as a "rushing stream." Mankind will be judged with the speed and fury of a mighty torrent. Such will be the case when God throws this unbelieving world into great tribulation. Daniel uses the symbol of a flood as he writes about the antichrist:

> *"And in his estate shall stand up a vile person, to whom they shall not give the honor of the kingdom: but he shall come in peaceably, and obtain the kingdom by flatteries.*
>
> *"And with the arms of a flood shall they be overflown from before him, and shall be broken; yea, also the prince of the covenant"* (Daniel 11:21-22).

John uses a similar application in Revelation:

> *"And the serpent cast out of his mouth water as a flood after the woman, that he might cause her to be carried away of the flood.*
>
> *"And the earth helped the woman, and the earth opened her mouth, and swallowed up the flood which the dragon cast out of his mouth"* (Revelation 12:15-16).

Our Savior also referred to the judgment of the Tribulation Period when he said:

> *"But as the days of Noah were, so shall also the coming of the Son of man be.*
>
> *"For as in the days that were before the flood they were eating and drinking, marrying and giving in marriage, until the day that Noah entered into the ark,*
>
> *"And knew not until the flood came, and took them all away; so shall also the coming of the Son of man be"* (Matthew 24:37-39).

Even though God promised that He would never again destroy the world by a flood, the Tribulation is predicted to come with the fury of a flood. Psalm 93 paints the picture all the more vividly:

> *"The floods have lifted up, O LORD, the floods have lifted up their voice; the floods lift up their waves"* (Psalm 93:3).

The term *"flood"* used in Psalm 90 is specifically symbolic. Moses writes that God will carry the wicked away *"AS with a flood."* The word *"AS"* informs us of the symbolic nature of this descriptive term. Isaiah also used the metaphor to describe what I believe to be the Battle of Gog and Magog:

"Woe to the multitude of many people, which make a noise like the noise of the seas; and to the rushing of nations, that make a rushing like the rushing of mighty waters!

"The nations shall rush like the rushing of many waters: but God shall rebuke them, and they shall flee far off, and shall be chased as the chaff of the mountains before the wind, and like a rolling thing before the whirlwind.

"And behold at eventide trouble; and before the morning he is not. This is the portion of them that spoil us, and the lot of them that rob us" (Isaiah 17:12-14).

Because of the juxtaposition of this passage following the predicted destruction of Damascus, I am led to believe that Isaiah was describing a Soviet invasion. That future battle of Gog and Magog will most likely introduce the Tribulation Period since Ezekiel 39:9 indicates that Israel will be burning the weapons of that war for seven years.

Isaiah emphasized the concept that a mighty army will come with the fury of a raging torrent. Psalm 91 also gives a view of war. Does that mean the 1991 war in the Middle East?

Watch and Pray!

"... they are as a sleep" (Psalm 90:5a).

The theme is broad enough to cover the entire human race. The whole world is spiritually asleep and will be taken by surprise when the day of the Lord comes *"as a thief in the night."*

More specifically, however, Israel is asleep. The Jewish calendar year 5750 (1990) is made up of a

set of numbers, which when viewed as a set of letters, translates into a sentence, "You shall sleep."
(Note: In Hebrew, numbers are represented by letters of the alphabet).

This *"sleep"* may have been the subject of a parable given by Christ. He told about a group of vir-
gins who fell asleep while waiting for the Bridegroom to come. In our study on the prophecies behind Pentecost we discovered that the Jews "stay
up all night ... to decorate the bride!"[5] Rabbis explain this by saying that on the morning of the
first Pentecost, when God descended on Mount
Sinai to give the Ten Commandments, everyone
overslept! Moses had to go around and wake ev-
erybody up![6]

The Jews believe that sometime during the night
of Pentecost, heaven opens up for a brief instant,
and they don't want to miss it![7] The apocalyptic
overtones of such a Jewish custom are intriguing.
Paul explains the rapture in similar terms:

> *"Behold I shew you a mystery; We shall not all sleep,*
> *but we shall all be changed,*
>
> *"In a moment, in the twinkling of an eye, at the last*
> *trump: for the trumpet shall sound, and the dead shall*
> *be raised incorruptible, and we shall be changed"*
> (I Corinthians 15:51-52).

---

[5] Michael Strassfeld, *The Jewish Holidays*, (New York: Harper and Row, 1985), p. 74.

[6] Ibid.

[7] Ibid.

Many Christian theologians have long believed
that when the rapture of the bride of Christ takes
place, Israel will be left behind to endure tribulation. Such a dilemma for Israel may be the subject
expressed in the following Mosaic passage:

"...in the morning they are like grass which groweth up.

*"In the morning it flourisheth, and groweth up; in the
evening it is cut down, and withereth.*

*"For we are consumed by thine anger, and by thy
wrath are we troubled.*

*"Thou hast set our iniquities before thee, our secret sins
in the light of thy countenance.*

*"For all our days are passed away in thy wrath: we
spend our years as a tale that is told"* (Psalm 90:5b-9).

History attests to the fact that God drove Israel
from their land to dwell among the nations. Generation after generation has come and gone. Indeed, Israel's days were passed under the wrath
of God. Their years have been like *"a tale that is
told."* Stories of Jewish suffering make a heart
rending and seemingly never-ending series!

Rabbi Feuer addresses Jewish suffering in his
commentary on this passage, *"we are consumed
by your fury"* and *"we are terrified by your wrath:"*

"Now the Psalmist turns his attention to the special
perils of the exile (Radak), for if mortal men are vulner-
able in times of tranquility, they are certainly in even
greater danger when they are exposed to the Divine fury
unleashed in exile (Eitz Yosef). Rashi explains that the
word 'fury' also means nose. Among the most prominent
physical manifestations of anger are flaring nostrils and

heavy nasal breathing. In contrast, 'wrath' is a hostile, violent feeling which is kept inside (Malbim)." [8]

Concerning the statement, *"Thou hast set our iniquities before thee, our secret sins in the light of thy countenance,"* the rabbinical commentary says that God remembers everything forever (Rabbi Yoseif Titzak). Since our past sins remain before You eternally, You never stop punishing us for them (Radak). The term, *"secret sins,"* refers to immaturity or youth. The psalmist refers to sins committed in the immaturity of youth.[9]

It is apparent that Israel is the subject of this passage, having suffered God's judgment over the centuries. Jewish scholars, however, attribute the sins of ancient Israel to a national adolescent immaturity. For this reason, God will not punish them forever, but will be reconciled to Israel when they reach maturity.

The Last Watch in the Night

"The days of our years are threescore years and ten; and if by reason of strength they be fourscore years, yet is their strength labour and sorrow; for it is soon cut off, and we fly away" (Psalm 90:10).

As we have already considered, a *"watch in the night"* is said to cover a period of 70 years. Rashi suggested they are the years we spend surrounded by the iniquities and immaturity mentioned in verse 8. Since Moses lived 120 years, why did he

---

[8] Feuer, *Tehillim*, p. 1125.

[9] Ibid., p. 1126.

write of a lifespan being 70 to 80 years? Perhaps he was referring to a future generation who would see Jerusalem restored and the throne of Messiah established. Again, if we really can depend on the six millennium concept taught by early theologians, then these 70 to 80 years since the taking of Jerusalem in 1917 become the years to watch!

What is meant by *"soon cut off, and we fly away?"* Does this only refer to death? If taken in the context of a Jewish return to the Promised Land to await the coming of Messiah one might speculate that the 80 years could be cut short with a *"flying away"* or rapture taking place. That is not to say that the catching away of believers will take place in any particular year, but that it draws near— perhaps sometime within the 80 year span.

A Call for Elijah

"Who knoweth the power of thine anger: even according to thy fear, so is thy wrath.

"So teach us to number our days, that we may apply our hearts unto wisdom" (Psalm 90:11-12).

Rabbi Meiri identifies the anger of God's wrath as "the fury which stirred God to cast the Jews into exile." He posed the question, "Who can predict how long God's fury will persist and how long the exile will endure?"[10]

A Jewish interpretation of verse 12 says, "According to the count of our days so make known, then we shall acquire a heart of wisdom." The

---

[10] Ibid., p. 1128.

word *"So ..."* is translated from a Hebrew term pronounced, "kane," which has a numerical value of 70 and compares to the previous teaching in verse 10, *"The days of our years are threescore years and ten ..."*[11] These rabbinical interpretations give a prophetic view to the passage. Since God cast Israel into exile, there should come a day when God will restore the nation. The count of *"our days"* are made to refer to national Israel, not just those of a single individual. The prayer for *"wisdom"* to *"number the days"* seems to be that of the generation upon whom the restoration will come. Since Israel has been revived in this century, after two thousand years of exile, we suggest that the prayer is about to be answered!

The statement, *"... that we may apply our hearts to wisdom,"* was interpreted by Rabbi Radak (twelfth century) to have a prophetic meaning. He said that the word *"apply"* translated from the Hebrew root word "bow" functions as a noun— "the prophet." Radak gives this interpretation:

> "When the days of this world are finally counted out, we will witness the advent of the prophet Elijah, who will herald the advent of Messiah. The enlightened teachings of the prophet will bring a heart of wisdom to mankind, as Scripture states, 'The earth shall be filled with the knowledge of HASHEM [the LORD] as water covers the sea.' (Isaiah 11:9)." [12]

This astounding interpretation by a twelfth century rabbi reflects the teaching of historic Ju-

---

[11] Ibid.

[12] Ibid., p. 1129.

daism about Psalm 90. The implication of this part of the Song of Moses is overwhelming—that its message should be applied to the concluding days of the sixth millennium!

How Long?

"Return, O LORD, how long? and let it repent thee concerning thy servants" (Psalm 90:13).

The prayer continues with a plea for the LORD to *"return."* Even though Jewish theologians cannot accept the fact that their Messiah came the first time 2,000 years ago, they nevertheless cry out for his *"return!"* Moses, on behalf of Israel asks *"how long"* will God wait before reconciliation. He pleads for God to repent of His judgment on Israel.

The question, *"How long?"* is especially significant during this final decade of the sixth millennium. This question appears 18 times in 12 passages in the Psalms. In our commentary, HIDDEN PROPHECIES IN THE PSALMS, we suggested that at this point in the prophecy, it seems, the Jewish people are digging into the Bible. They are desperately trying to number their days, and from all indications, their question is about to be answered.[13]

The question appears for the last time in Psalm 94:3-6. If the question is to be asked at all, it is at least the prerogative of the Jews. They are the Chosen People. Though they have suffered as no

---

[13] J. R. Church, *Hidden Prophecies In The Psalms,* (Oklahoma City: Prophecy Publications, 1986), p. 23.

other nation, they have not been forever forsaken.
The promise of deliverance will come. Messiah
will appear to establish a millennium of peace.
God will keep His promise.

The Dawn of the Messianic Era

*"O satisfy us early with thy mercy; that we may rejoice
and be glad all our days"* (Psalm 90:14).

Radak observes this verse as "a reference to the
dawn of the Messianic era, which will shine as
brilliantly as the morning sun. At that time, we
will be sated [gratified with more than enough] by
God's kindness and we will never again experience any misery. Then we shall sing out and rejoice all our days."[14]

*"Make us glad according to the days wherein thou
hast afflicted us, and the years wherein we have seen
evil"* (Psalm 90:15).

Rashi comments, "Make us glad in the Messianic era of the future for a duration of time
which will equal the length of time that we suffered in exile in this world." Many opinions are
offered by the Talmud (Sanhedrin 99a) to
determine the duration of the Messianic era. Some
say that it will last forty years corresponding to the
number of years the Jews suffered in the
wilderness, ... or 400 years corresponding to the
years of the Egyptian bondage, ... or 365 years
corresponding to the days of the solar year, for the

---

[14] Feuer, *Tehillim*, p. 1129.

burning sun is a symbol of fiery Divine retribution, ... or 7000 years like the days of the week, and each day of God is 1000 years."[15]

Jewish theologians have been hard at work for centuries trying to determine the time for the coming of the Messiah. Psalm 90 appears to be one of those special passages studied by the rabbis. They seem to be convinced that it refers to the conclusion of the sixth millennium!

A Call to Rebuild the Temple

"Let thy work appear unto thy servants, and thy glory unto their children.

"And let the beauty of the LORD our God be upon us: and establish thou the work of our hands upon us; yea, the work of our hands establish thou it" (Psalm 90:16-17).

Rabbi Avrohom Chaim Feuer, in his commentary on the Psalms, wrote:

"Specifically, we await the most monumental accomplishment of Jewish history: the final reconstruction of the third Beis HaMikdash [Temple]. Actually, since the destruction of the second Temple, God has been slowly reconstructing the edifice in heaven. When it is completed, God will display His works by bringing the celestial Temple down to earth (Dorash Moshe).

"After God returns His presence to earth, we ask that He continue to dwell here for future generations so that our children and descendants will enjoy His glory. Indeed, we hope that His glory will be apparent soon!" [16]

---

[15] Ibid., p. 1130.

[16] Ibid.

Dorash Moshe observes that "after the Temple is reconstructed, God will gather in the scattered exiles, and Israel will return to the Holy Land."[17]

Moses prays for God to establish *"the work of our hands."* The rabbinical interpretation says, "The blessing of the Temple and the Tabernacle is not confined to Israel. Rather, it is the factor which lends solidarity and prosperity to the entire world. We pray that God return to this world and establish His blessed presence for all time (Dorash Moshe).[18]

This verse-by-verse commentary on Psalm 90, quoting rabbinical theology, offers us a rare opportunity to see this stanza of the Song of Moses in a special prophetic light. We may, indeed, be the generation targeted by the prophecies of this outstanding psalm. More than that, we may be living in the decade of destiny. Every phrase of every verse appears to give a prophetic view of a Chosen People who are approaching the end of 6,000 years and the beginning of the millennial reign of Christ!

---

[17] Ibid., p. 1131.

[18] Ibid.

Chapter Six

Psalm 91
Dedicated to Levi

"He that dwelleth in the secret place of the Most High shall abide under the shadow of the Almighty.

"I will say of the LORD, He is my refuge and my fortress: my God; in him will I trust" (Psalm 91:1-2).

Though Moses composed this psalm, his name is not given. Rabbis say that, because of his humility, Moses submerged himself in God and, therefore, gave himself no credit. He secreted himself *"in the secret place ... under the shadow of the Almighty,"* therefore this psalm does not mention his name—nor do the rest of these Mosaic Psalms (91-100).

A Call to Rebuild the Temple

The last verses of the previous Psalm (90:16-17), call for a rebuilding of the Temple. Moses composed both them and Psalm 91 on the day "he completed construction of the Tabernacle."[1] The juxtaposition of Psalms 90-91, following the Leviticus Psalms (73-89), indicate a continuation of this

---

[1] Feuer, *Tehillim*, p. 1133.

series of prophecies designed to lead Israel toward a return to Temple liturgy.

Furthermore, Psalm 91 was dedicated to Levi as a prophetic reference to the priests who will restore Temple worship. Various implements of Temple worship have been under construction over the past few years, and we may assume the Jews have plans for the erection of a portable sanctuary in the near future. Whether a place of worship is erected by 1991 or not cannot be predicted. According to Amos, the *"Tabernacle of David"* will be raised up in the last days:

> *"In that day will I raise up the tabernacle of David that is fallen, and close up the breaches thereof; and raise up its ruins as in the days of old:*
>
> *"That they may possess the remnant of Edom, and of all the heathen* [Gentiles], *which are called by my name, saith the LORD that doeth this"* (Amos 9:11-12).

The future Jewish sanctuary may not be a building made of stone, but a tent—one that could be erected in a matter of hours. Amos called it the *"Tabernacle of David."*

Most religious Jews deny that a Jewish sanctuary could be built near to the Moslem Dome of the Rock. They say that the Mosque must first be removed from the sacred site. Since 1967, at least six attempts to blow up the hexagon-shaped building have failed. Eventually, religious Jews may be forced to accept a compromise with the Moslems and be content with using only the northern half of the Temple Mount. Ezekiel predicted the erection of a Jewish tent next to a *"profane place:"*

> *"I ... will set my sanctuary in the midst of them ... My tabernacle [tent] also shall be with them ..."(Ezekiel 37:26-27).*

> *"Afterward he brought me to the temple, and measured the posts, six cubits broad on the one side, and six cubits broad on the other side, which was the breadth of the tabernacle [tent]"* (Ezekiel 41:1).

> *"... it had a wall round about, five hundred reeds long, and five hundred broad, to make a separation between the sanctuary and the **profane place"** (Ezekiel 42:20).

Is the Mosque of Omar the *"profane place"* mentioned by Ezekiel? The Moslem site, along with the El Aksa Mosque at the south end of the compound, are both situated in that part of the Temple Mount referred to as the "Court of the Gentiles." A future Jewish Temple may have to share the mountain with the Moslem Mosque. John was given a similar vision in Revelation 11:1-2:

> *"And there was given me a reed like unto a rod: and the angel stood, saying, Rise, and measure the temple of God, and the altar, and them that worship therein.*

> *"But the **court** which is without the temple leave out, and measure it not; for it is given unto the **Gentiles:** and the holy city shall they tread under foot forty and two months"* (Revelation 11:1-2).

The entire southern half of the Temple Mount is historically designated as the "Court of the Gentiles." This may be observed on most maps in Bible dictionaries showing Jerusalem as it was in the days of Herod's Temple.

Rabbi Feuer designated Psalm 91 as the psalm used for cleansing the Temple Mount:

"The Talmud (Shavuos 15b) explains that it was possible to expand the territory of ... the Temple courtyards by following a carefully detailed ritual: The Song of Thanksgiving [Psalm 100] was recited to the accompaniment of musical instruments in every corner of the city and upon every large rock. Then they would recite this psalm [91].... This psalm was recited in order to cleanse the hitherto unsanctified area of all impure and evil forces." [2]

The Mosaic Blessing to Levi

The prophetic importance of Psalm 91 is thus established. Without this psalm, Temple worship cannot be restored. Furthermore, the descendants of the tribe of Levi will be designated as priests in the future Jewish sanctuary. It is fitting, therefore, that Psalm 91 is dedicated to Levi. Moses said of Levi in Deuteronomy 33:8-11:

"Let thy Thummim and thy Urim be with thy holy one, whom thou didst prove at Massah, and with whom thou didst strive at the waters of Meribah;

"Who said unto his father and to his mother, I have not seen him; neither did he acknowledge his brethren, nor knew his own children: for they have observed thy word, and kept thy covenant.

"They shall teach Jacob thy judgments, and Israel thy law: they shall put incense before thee, and whole burnt sacrifice upon thine altar.

"Bless, LORD, his substance, and accept the work of his hands: smite through the loins of them that rise against him, and of them that hate him, that they rise not again" (Deuteronomy 33:8-11).

---

[2] Feuer, *Tehillim*, p. 1138.

Many things are predicted in this passage:

First, this Mosaic blessing in Deuteronomy 33 corresponds with what I call the third stanza in the Song of Moses, which was placed in Psalm 91. In fact, each of the eleven blessings in Deuteronomy 33 corresponds to Psalms (90-100). Deuteronomy 32 is the first in a series of twelve stanzas that make up the Song of Moses and the other eleven were evidently laid aside by Moses for inclusion in Israel's future songbook. The eleven blessings in Deuteronomy 33 are each a synopsis of one of the Psalms dedicated to a particular tribe.

Second, the above passage gives not only an overview of Psalm 91, but a prophecy of Levi's position in the last days and their connection with a restored Jewish Temple. The passage, *"Let thy Thummim and thy Urim be with thy holy one, whom thou didst prove at Massah, and with whom thou didst strive at the waters of Meribah"* appears to be a message about the rejected Messiah—the smitten rock at the waters of Meribah!

Just as Moses smote the rock, so Israel has smitten Christ. The *"holy one"* not only refers to the High Priest, but is also a prophetic reference to Israel's greater High Priest, Jesus Christ. According to the prophecy, the long-lost Urim and Thummim will not be recovered for use in the restored sanctuary. Israel will have to leave it in the hands of their coming Messiah.

Third, the passage, *"Who said unto his father and to his mother, I have not seen him; neither did he acknowledge his brethren, nor knew his* *own children: for they have observed thy word, and kept thy covenant"* refers primarily to the High Priest, who became so involved in his priestly duties he apparently neglected his own people; and prophetically to Christ who turned from Israel to a world full of Gentiles with His offer of eternal life. Yet, orthodox Judaism has faithfully observed the Mosaic Law to this day.

Fourth, the passage, *"They shall teach Jacob thy judgments, and Israel thy law: they shall put incense before thee, and whole burnt sacrifice upon thine altar"* offers a prophecy that during the Tribulation Period, the tribe of Levi will restore Temple worship, which will include the burning of incense and the offering of sacrifices.

Fifth, the passage, *"Bless, LORD, his substance, and accept the work of his hands: smite through the loins of them that rise against him, and of them that hate him, that they rise not again"* asks God for help against the antichrist during the future Tribulation Period. The *"work of his hands"* alludes to a reconstructed Temple. The verse portrays what seems to be a restored priesthood offering their sacrifices. When confronted with the claims of a false messiah, they will reject the usurper and turn to Israel's true Messiah!

Psalm 91 opens with a rebuilt Temple (however portable it might be). The Levites will feel protected at the Tabernacle, in whose *"secret place"* or Holy of Holies dwells the Shekinah glory. They shall worship *"in the shadow of the Almighty."*

This verse also may allude to those who dwell in heaven—in the presence of God. Could this be a reference to the Rapture and Resurrection? I do not think we can afford to suggest any more than a simple allusion to that *"blessed hope"* for *"no man knoweth the day nor the hour."*

Verse 16, which says, *"With long life will I satisfy him, and show him my salvation,"* also appears to be a reference to the resurrection. Radak commented, "He will witness the salvation I will bring about at the advent of the Messiah, at the time of the revival of the dead, and at the salvation of the World to Come." [3]

The builder of the Mosaic Tabernacle was Bezalel of the tribe of Judah. The word, Bezalel, means "in the shadow of God." It is said that "Bezalel anticipated aspects of the Divine blueprint even before Moses gave him the necessary information. So amazed was Moses that he asked Bezalel, 'Perhaps you reside in the shadow of God?' " [4]

The Snare of the Fowler

"Surely he shall deliver thee from the snare of the fowler, and from the noisome pestilence.

"He shall cover thee with his feathers and under his wings shall thou trust: his truth shall be thy shield and buckler.

"Thou shalt not be afraid for the terror by night; nor for the arrow that flieth by day" (Psalm 91:3-5).

---

[3] Ibid., p. 1143.

[4] Ibid.

God promises to deliver Israel from *"the snare of the fowler."* The Chosen People will be ensnared in a trap set by their enemy and only God will be able to deliver them. The *"fowler"* could either be satan, the antichrist or the Palestinians.

Satan and his "man of the hour" could have woven a political web in the Middle East that eventually engulfs the region in war. This psalm uses such terms as *"the arrow that flieth by day"* and *"the destruction that wasteth at noonday"* to predict some dreadful war unleashed in the Middle East. Several Arab states may be involved, but the target will ultimately be Israel. Only God will be able to deliver Israel from the *"snare."*

For the past few years, the Palestinians living in Israel have been creating unrest by throwing rocks at the Jews. This "intifada" has been encouraged by the PLO. It appears to be a trap or dilemma with no easy answers. If Israel annexes the occupied areas the Palestinians will become citizens endowed with the power to vote. At some time in the future, they could outnumber the Jews and vote in their own government. On the other hand, if Israel does not annex the territories, the present system of apartheid could bring down the same international condemnation presently imposed upon South Africa.

The Noisome Pestilence

Not only will the LORD save the Jewish remnant from the *"snare* [trap] *of the fowler,"* He will also save them from the *"noisome pestilence."* There

are several possible interpretations of this term.
Some suggest it means *"sudden destruction."* The
following verses seem to reveal a tragic war.

In I Thessalonians 5:3 the apostle Paul warned:

> *"For when they shall say, Peace and safety; then*
> ***sudden destruction*** *cometh upon them, as travail upon*
> *a woman with child; and they shall not escape"*
> (I Thessalonians 5:3).

Could this *"noisome pestilence"* be referring to
the same cataclysmic devastation referred to as a
"sudden destruction" by Paul? The meaning of the
original Hebrew term refers to a sudden event of
catastrophic proportions. It is like seeing a large
object falling from a tall building upon a person on
the street below. By the time you yell, "Look out!"
it's too late. That is the intent of the meaning in
both the New Testament passage and in this
psalm. In any event, both will occur in the latter
days, prior to the Second Advent of Christ.

The term *"noisome pestilence"* has also been
translated as a raging epidemic. Hebrew scholars
say that it refers to "a pestilence that causes such
destruction that the world order is betrayed ... a
sudden pestilence which comes at this moment,
without warning."[5] In the end-time there will be
several world-wide epidemics raging out of control. Disease is one of the major signs of the end-
time cited by Jesus in Matthew 24:7: *"For nation
shall rise against nation, and kingdom against
kingdom: and there shall be famines, and **pesti-***

---

[5] Feuer, *Tehillim*, p. 1135.

lences, and earthquakes, in divers places."

In Psalm 91 Moses explains that the *"noisome pestilence"* is *"a terror by night"* (v. 5) and that it *"walketh in darkness"* (v. 6). God promises the remnant safety from the disease saying, *"Only with thine eyes shalt thou see the reward of the wicked"* (v. 8). The passage seems somewhat descriptive of a new disease, first diagnosed in 1981 called "Acquired Immune Deficiency Syndrome" (AIDS). Some say AIDS could decimate the population by the year 2000. According to an Associated Press report, "By 1991 everyone will know someone with AIDS." The AP reporter was not aware of Psalm 91 when he wrote his story. In a TIME magazine article dated February 17, 1986, it was reported that 17,000 Americans had contracted the disease and that half of them had died.[6] But on November 3, some eight and one half months later, TIME reported 15,000 dead.

The disease had doubled its death toll and was continuing to grow on an exponential curve. The TIME report said, "the figure is expected to rise to nearly 180,000 in five years"[7] By 1989, TIME reported that some 44,000 Americans with AIDS needed health and other services costing $3.75 billion. "By 1992 the figure is likely to more than double."[8] The average health cost per AIDS victim in 1989 was estimated at $83,000. Most hospital stays for an average patient is 7 days, but AIDS patients

---

[6] *Time,* February 17, 1986, p. 90.

[7] *Time,* November 3, 1986, p. 76.

[8] *Time,* October 16, 1989, p. 88.

usually stay 20 to 30 days.

I am not suggesting that this psalm demands fulfillment in 1991, but the date of 1991 was cited by the Associated Press, ABC-TV and by TIME magazine who, in turn, were quoting then U. S. Surgeon General, C. Everett Koop. I believe this prophecy will come to pass as it is predicted in Psalm 91 and that it may be already under development. AIDS is a fatal disease which travels in *"darkness"* and *"at night"* and appears to be *"a reward of the wicked."* It can only be considered as the judgment of an offended Holy God.

More than half of all diagnosed victims are dead and there is little hope for the other half. It is running rampant among homosexuals, prostitutes and drug users. The number of victims is doubling every year. If that continues, then theoretically, the entire population of the world could be dead within a few short years. Some have suggested that the disease will affect only a certain group. If so, once all the people who are going to be affected are dead, the epidemic will subside. One sad note: Many innocent children and young people have also been infected through tainted blood transfusions.

Chemical Weapons

Since a Middle East war appears to be one of the themes of this psalm, the *"noisome pestilence"* could be some kind of chemical weapon or nerve gas inflicted upon the populace. Gas masks have been readied for all Jewish citizens in Israel. Iraq has already used such weapons against Iran as well as some of their own people in recent uprisings.

Song of Demons

"Nor for the pestilence that walketh in darkness; nor for the destruction that wasteth at noonday.

"A thousand shall fall at thy side and ten thousand at thy right hand; but it shall not come nigh thee.

"Only with thine eyes shalt thou behold and see the reward of the wicked" (Psalm 91:6-8).

Some Jewish theologians interpret the *"destruction that wasteth at noonday"* to be by demonic forces. The Talmud (Shavuos 15b) records that the psalm was used to drive out demons when the Temple Mount was cleansed or expanded. Some call it the "Song of Demons" because verse 7 reads that thousands and ten thousands of demons will fall. Others call it the "Song of Plagues" because verse 10 promises protection from any plague. This psalm was also recited by the Levites during the Temple period in order to "cleanse the hitherto unsanctified area of all impure and evil forces."[9] Used as it was for cleansing the Temple site centuries ago, one can see how a priesthood could prepare the site for Temple worship.

"Because thou hast made the LORD which is my refuge, even the Most High, thy habitation;

"There shall no evil befall thee, neither shall any plague come nigh thy dwelling.

---

[9] Feuer, *Tehillim*, p. 1138.

> *"For he shall give his angels charge over thee, to keep thee in all thy ways.*
>
> *"They shall bear thee up in their hands, lest thou dash thy foot against a stone* (Psalm 91:9-12).

Since this is considered a "Song of Demons," it is easy to understand how the prince of demons could take Jesus to the pinnacle of the Temple and urge him to jump off. The devil, himself, recited a portion of this psalm. He must have been especially familiar with it.

A Promise of Resurrection

> *"With long life will I satisfy him, and shew him my salvation* (Psalm 91:16).

Radak, believed that this verse will be fulfilled "at the advent of the Messiah, at the time of the revival of the dead, and at the salvation of the world to come."[10] This is a resurrection verse, which adds to the prophetic nature of the psalm. These things will happen in the future as the Messianic Era approaches.

The number 91 is made up of two Hebrew letters, "tzade" and "aleph." They comprise part of a root word, "tsaw," meaning "to go out, or to be cast out."[11] When the Temple site is cleansed, demons will, indeed, be cast out! Then the Temple will be erected.

---

[10] Ibid., p. 1143.

[11] *Gesenius' Lexicon*, p. 698.

Chapter Seven

Psalm 92
Dedicated to Judah

"A psalm or song for the sabbath day" (Psalm 92: introduction).

Rabbinic sources agree that the future redemption of Israel approaches at this point. The Messianic Era is about to begin. Therefore, this psalm was dedicated to the future world, a "day which is completely Sabbath, for ordinary weekdays will not exist in that totally sacred world."[1] Talmudic scholars have commented on this psalm with the following assessment:

"Human history is God's masterpiece. Physical creation was completed at the end of the sixth day, but the spiritual development of mankind will continue until this world ends, at the close of the sixth millennium ... When the panorama of human history is completed, the seventh millennium will be ushered in as the day of everlasting Sabbath. At that time all Adam's descendants will look back and admire God's completed masterpiece."[2]

---

[1] Feuer, *Tehillim*, p. 1146.
[2] Ibid., p. 1145.

This psalm is designated as the Song of the Day for the Sabbath. Christian theologians are not alone in believing the world will welcome the kingdom of heaven at the end of six thousand years of history. Jewish scholars believe it, too. The evidence is overwhelming for a promise of Divine intervention into human affairs. The Son of God will soon appear to establish a heavenly throne on earth. The next thousand years will be paradise!

Praises Will Be Given
In Israel's New Future Temple

"It is a good thing to give thanks unto the LORD, and to sing praises unto thy name, O most High" (Psalm 92:1).

Just as Psalms 73-89 demonstrate a prophetic scenario for restoring the priesthood, and Psalms 90-91 call for a new future Temple, Psalm 92 "describes the priests and Levites who flourish in the service which they render to God in the Temple courtyards.... Similarly, in the future, the righteous and true scholars will dwell in the environs of the Holy Temple, where their comprehension of the Divine design will blossom (Radak)."[3] Obviously, the reconstruction of a Temple in Jerusalem is the central theme around which the fulfillment of these prophecies revolve.

The first verse, which says, *"It is a good thing to give thanks unto the Lord, and to sing praises unto thy name, O most High,"* reveals that the

___

[3] Ibid., p. 1154.

psalm is dedicated to Judah,[4] because at his birth, Leah said, *"Now I will praise the Lord: therefore she called his name Judah"* (Genesis 29:35). The name Judah means "praise" and is the tribe through which the Messiah was promised.

The Dawn of the Messianic Era

"... to show forth thy loving-kindness in the morning, and thy faithfulness every night" (Psalm 92:2).

This verse shows the "contrast between the gloom of exile and the bright dawn of redemption.... Subsequent generations of Jewish exiles are encouraged to maintain their faith in God, Who will surely usher in the light of redemption in the glorious Messianic age (Rashi)."[5] The term for "every night" is plural, indicating that the exile of Israel will cover many nights, but the term "dawn" is singular, indicating a specific time in the future when Messiah will come!

"... upon an instrument of ten strings, and upon the psaltry; upon the harp with a solemn sound" (Psalm 92:3).

The instrument referred to is an assor or neivel. "According to the Talmud, the harp of the Temple had seven strings, but in Messianic times the harp will have eight strings, and in the World to Come, it will have ten."[6] Over the past few years,

[4] Ibid., p. 1147.

[5] Ibid.

[6] Ibid., p. 1148.

religious Jews have been manufacturing a thousand harps for use in Israel's future Temple. Those harps have twenty-two strings, perhaps one for each letter of the Hebrew alphabet.

"For thou, LORD, hast made me glad through thy work: I will triumph in the works of thy hands.

"O LORD, how great are thy works! And thy thoughts are very deep" (Psalm 92:4-5).

According to Jewish theologians, these verses were recited when the construction of the Mosaic Tabernacle was completed, because it was regarded as God's work. The Jewish Midrash explains that the construction of a future Temple will also be God's handiwork, and that Israel will also rejoice at that time.

The Antichrist

Such a Temple will be necessary, according to Daniel and others, because the antichrist will commit the *"abomination of desolation"* there. The following verse may refer to him:

"A brutish man knoweth not; neither doth a fool understand this" (Psalm 92:6).

Though he does not understand, the antichrist will incur the wrath of the world when he moves his throne to Jerusalem and demands to be worshiped as God. He will commit the predicted "abomination of desolation" and demand that all men accept a mark in the flesh of the right hand or forehead. Those who have not been brain-

washed by his propaganda machine will balk. I
believe the *"kings of the east"* (Revelation 16:12)
will rebel. They will marshall their forces against
the antichrist and his crumbling government. The
greatest war of history will be in the making—
Armageddon!

> *"When the wicked spring as the grass, and when all the
> workers of iniquity do flourish; it is that they shall be
> destroyed for ever...*
>
> *"But thou, LORD, art most high for evermore.*
>
> *"For, lo, thine enemies, O LORD, for, lo, thine enemies
> shall perish; all the workers of iniquity shall be scattered.*
>
> *"But my horn shalt thou exalt like the horn of a unicorn:
> I shall be anointed with fresh oil.*
>
> *"Mine eye also shall see my desire on mine enemies, and
> mine ears shall hear my desire of the wicked that rise up
> against me.*
>
> *"The righteous shall flourish like the palm tree: he shall
> grow like a cedar in Lebanon"* (Psalm 92:7-12).

The wicked flourish like *"grass"* and are soon
withered. On the other hand, *"the righteous flourish like the palm tree"* and the *"cedar in
Lebanon."* God allows the wicked to prosper so
they will suffer all the more when they are punished. An example is Haman. Jewish folktales say
that his original treachery occurred when he ad-
vised Ahasuerus to halt the construction of the
Second Temple. At that time he was only a minor
official. If God had punished him then, no one
would have noticed. Therefore God "caused
Haman to prosper and succeed so that he could
hang and teach the world a lesson in Divine retri-

bution."[7] That reflects the thinking of scholars about the antichrist as well. The world ruler will be allowed enough proverbial rope to hang himself.

Moses gave a synopsis of this psalm and a promise of the conquering Messiah in his blessing to Judah in Deuteronomy 33:7.

> *"And this is the blessing of Judah: and he said, Hear, LORD, the voice of Judah, and bring him unto his people: let his hands be sufficient for him; and be thou a help to him from his enemies"* (Deuteronomy 33:7).

In keeping with the theme of Israel's rescue at the Advent of Messiah, Psalm 92:9 says:

> *"For, lo, thine enemies, O LORD, for lo, thine enemies shall perish; all the workers of iniquity shall be scattered"* (Psalm 92:9).

Jewish theologians set the time for the fulfillment of this psalm, along with Psalm 93, which they say is a continuation of the theme, at the Battle of Gog and Magog.

> *"Those that be planted in the house of the LORD will flourish in the courts of our God.*
>
> *"They shall still bring forth fruit in old age; they shall be fat and flourishing;*
>
> *"To show that the LORD is upright: he is my rock, and there is no unrighteousness in him"* (Psalm 92:13-15).

Radak (12th century) commented that this passage describes the Messianic age, when men will

---

[7] Ibid., p. 1151.

achieve longevity. What is now considered old age will then be regarded as youth. Isaiah (65:20) indicated that if someone dies at the age of one hundred, people will say that he died young.[8]

The *"Rock"* was used as a metaphor of the Messiah by both Moses and David. It is said that both men died on the Sabbath. They await the resurrection of that future Sabbath, the seventh millennium. Therefore, Psalm 92 was designated as a song for the Sabbath. Both men used the metaphor of the *"Rock"* to declare their confidence in God's judgment. *"There is no unrighteousness in Him."*

The theme continues in Psalm 93.

---

[8] Ibid., p. 1155.

Chapter Eight

Psalm 93
Dedicated to Benjamin

> *"The LORD reigneth, he is clothed with majesty: the Lord is clothed with strength, wherewith he hath girded himself: the world also is stablished, that it cannot be moved.*
>
> *"Thy throne is established of old: thou art from everlasting"* (Psalm 93:1-2).

Psalm 93 fits very nicely with this decade, as we approach the end of the sixth millennium. Its theme projects one into the future to the end of Israel's exile and the beginning of what Jewish theologians call the "Messianic era." For example, Rashi wrote that this psalm is dedicated to "the Messianic era, when all men will again recognize God's majesty."[1]

Psalm 93 continues the theme of Psalm 92 which concludes with the prediction that in the "Messianic era," men will declare that God is just and that only He deserves to be *clothed with majesty* and *strength.*

This psalm is the Song of the Day for the sixth

---

[1] Feuer, *Tehillim*, p. 1157.

day of the week in Jewish liturgy because on that day God completed His work and donned the grandeur of His creation.[2] Thus, this song was designated as the Song of Friday when the "footsteps of Sabbath" could be heard. In like manner, near the end of the sixth millennium the footsteps of the Messiah and His great Sabbath (the seventh millennium) can be felt. The psalm echoes the pronouncements that will be made at the end of Israel's exile when the golden age has arrived. God's throne was prepared in ages past, but will be recognized when the world is set firm in the "Messianic era." Rabbi Feuer writes:

"All we see of God is the physical garment He donned when time began at the dawn of Creation. No matter how much of God's greatness we think we understand, our limited intellect grasps but the minutest fraction of His infinite and eternal greatness, which transcends time and space."[3]

The Floods of War

"The floods have lifted up, O LORD, the floods have lifted up their voice; the floods lift up their waves.

"The LORD on high is mightier than the noise of many waters, yea, than the mighty waves of the sea" (Psalm 93:3-4).

There are two possibilities for the fulfillment of these verses. Either or both could be under development at the present time.

---

[2] Ibid.

[3] Ibid., p. 1159.

First, the *"flood"* could be indicative of the world's most overwhelming war. Rashi wrote that the term is a metaphor for the "enemy hordes who seek to sweep Israel away. They raise their voices and threaten Israel with extinction."[4] Even today, Jewish scholars say this refers to the Gentile nations; who will gather outside the gates of Jerusalem for the final war of Gog and Magog.[5]

"The LORD ... is mightier than the noise of many waters," is the same metaphor given in Isaiah's prophecy concerning that future war. In describing the battle which threatens Israel's existence, Isaiah wrote,

> *"Woe to the multitude of many people, which make a noise like the noise of the seas; and to the rushing of nations, that make a rushing like the rushing of mighty waters!*
>
> *"The nations shall rush like the rushing of many waters: but God shall rebuke them, and they shall flee far off ..."* (Isaiah 17:12-13).

The Isaiah passage appears to be describing an invasion by the mighty Magog. It will be so massive, it is likened to a flood. Ezekiel described the Battle of Gog and Magog in a similar manner:

> *"Thou shalt ascend and come like a storm, thou shalt be like a cloud to cover the land, thou, and all thy bands, and many people with thee"* (Ezekiel 38:9).

---

[4] Ibid.

[5] Ibid.

The description is certainly prophetic and concerns the days just prior to the "Messianic era."

Second, the description could be that of an actual worldwide flood—perhaps not as devastating as Noah's deluge, but global, nevertheless. Such a flood may occur during the Tribulation Period when God pours out His seven vials of wrath upon an unbelieving world. An explosion in the sun could melt the polar caps. Jesus might have been referring to a flood when He said:

"But as the days of Noe [Noah] *were, so shall also the coming of the Son of man be"* (Matthew 24:37).

Furthermore, Gabriel spoke of an end-time flood:

"... and the end thereof shall be with a flood ..." (Daniel 9:26).

The Revelation account of seven angels pouring out seven vials of God's wrath could produce a flood capable of inundating all of the coastal areas of the world. As the fourth angel pours out his vial of wrath upon the sun, men are scorched with fire. This could be describing even a small explosion in our sun. If such a thing were to occur, rising temperatures could melt the polar caps and raise the levels of the oceans some fifteen to twenty feet. This could produce a worldwide flood.

As the fifth angel pours out his vial of wrath, darkness covers the earth. Were our sun to experience a small explosion, the brilliance might last only a short time, then darkness could result. Joel described such a scene:

"The sun shall be turned into darkness, and the moon into blood, before the great and the terrible day of the LORD come" (Joel 2:31).

Isaiah put it this way:

"The light of the moon shall be as the light of the sun, and the light of the sun shall be sevenfold ..." (Isaiah 30:26).

Yet, Isaiah also depicted the opposite:

"... the sun shall be darkened in his going forth, and the moon shall not cause her light to shine" (Isaiah 13:10).

Thus the fourth and fifth vials become clear. If the sun experienced an unusually large solar flare, a short period of heating could melt the polar caps, dry out the rivers (including the Euphrates), and create huge clouds around the world producing hurricanes, tornadoes and hailstones weighing a hundred pounds apiece. Tectonic pressures could cause earthquakes, level mountains, and move coastlines as described in Revelation 16. One thing is certain, Psalm 93 prepares the world for the day of God's vengeance.

The Temple Stands

"Thy testimonies are very sure: holiness becometh thine house, O LORD, for ever" (Psalm 93:5).

This psalm closes with a plea that when these "exceedingly trustworthy prophecies about the

Third Temple are finally fulfilled, may it stand for all time."[6] Indeed, the Jewish Temple will be rebuilt—perhaps in the near future. Moses introduced that theme in the blessing he delivered to Benjamin, the one to whom this psalm is dedicated:

> "And of Benjamin, the beloved of the LORD shall dwell in safety by him; and the LORD shall cover him all the day long, and he shall dwell between his shoulders" (Deuteronomy 33:12).

Benjamin dwelt in the "shelter of God," the Temple having been built in their city. The border between Judah and Benjamin was the Tyropeon valley where today the Western Wall of the Temple Mount is located. The Temple site itself lies on Benjamin's land. With this psalm dedicated to Benjamin and its last verse making another reference to the Temple, I am convinced that Temple worship will be restored soon.

The Mosaic blessing also says, "*he* [Benjamin] *shall dwell between his* [Judah's] *shoulders*." The two Psalms (92 and 93) are linked together just as the territories of Benjamin and Judah meet in Jerusalem at the Temple Mount. Judah is the royal tribe, from whom the Messiah will come. Benjamin is a part of the prophetic profile of the Messiah because of the meanings of his names.

Rachel died giving birth to Benjamin. Her hard labor pains became a prophetic metaphor for the birth of the Messianic Era. As she died, Rachel

[6] Ibid., p. 1161.

named the baby "Benoni" (son of my sorrow), but Jacob changed his name to Benjamin (son of my right hand). These two names became prophetic profiles of the Messiah. When Christ came the first time, he was *"a man of sorrows, and acquainted with grief"* (Isaiah 53:3). Upon His ancension, Christ sat down at the *"right hand of God"* (Colossians 3:1). Someday, he will return to establish His throne in Jerusalem on the Temple Mount at the border between the territories of Benjamin and Judah. Therefore, I believe the link between Psalms 92 and 93 emerges as a prophetic statement about the Second Coming of Christ.

Chapter Nine

Psalm 94
Dedicated to Gad

"O Lord God, to whom vengeance belongeth; O God, to whom vengeance belongeth, show thyself.

"Lift up thyself, thou judge of the earth: render a reward to the proud" (Psalm 94:1-2).

This is a prophecy about the *"day of vengeance,"* when Christ will appear in power and great glory. According to Jewish theology, this psalm predicts the "worldwide war of Gog and Magog," which will "herald the Messianic era." At that time, "God will appear in order to punish His foes as we read here, 'O God of vengeance, appear!' "[1]

The term *"vengeance"* is the key to the understanding of God's plan for a sinful world. It is a word used often in prophetic passages which describe God's judgment upon the world at the end of this present age. For example, the term was used by Isaiah to describe events attending the Advent of the Messiah:

"The Spirit of the Lord GOD is upon me; because the LORD hath anointed me to preach good tidings unto the

---

[1] Feuer, *Tehillim*, p. 1164.

meek; he hath sent me to bind up the brokenhearted, to proclaim liberty to the captives, and the opening of the prison to them that are bound;

"To proclaim the acceptable year of the Lord and the day of vengeance of our God; to comfort all who mourn" (Isaiah 61:1-2).

This is also the term used by Isaiah to describe the glorious appearing of Christ on that day when He comes to judge the world and save Israel:

"Who is this that cometh from Edom, with dyed garments from Bozrah? this that is glorious in his apparel, travelling in the greatness of his strength? I that speak in righteousness, mighty to save.

"Wherefore art thou red in thine apparel, and thy garments like him that treadeth in the winevat?

"I have trodden the winepress alone; ...

"For the day of vengeance is in mine heart, and the year of my redeemed is come" (Isaiah 63:1-4).

Isaiah wrote about the coming of Christ to tread the *"winepress of the fierceness and wrath of Almighty God"* (Revelation 19:15).

How Long?

"LORD, how long shall the wicked, how long shall the wicked triumph?

"How long shall they utter and speak hard things? and all the workers of iniquity boast themselves?" (Psalm 94:3-4).

The question *"How long?"* is asked eighteen times in the Psalms. We have finally arrived at the last one, perhaps because the day is approaching!

The answer is imminent! The Son of God is soon to appear in the clouds of glory to judge the world and establish His kingdom.

Whether this will occur in 1994 is by no means certain. We cannot set dates for future events. It is important to note, however, that the first five psalms in this Song of Moses (90-94) offer a set of recurring themes—the restoration of Temple worship, the coming of Elijah, the war of Gog and Magog, and the coming of the Messiah to judge the wicked. They may not necessarily draw a chronological scenario in each successive psalm as appears to be the case in the previous 89 psalms. Even if they do appear to be chronological, it is not our intent to suggest a series of specific dates for these predicted events.

How long? It was asked first by the Lord in Psalm 4:2, then was taken up by God's Chosen People in Psalms 6:3 and repeated over and over until the question reaches a heart-rending climax in Psalm 94. It never appears again in the Psalms. If the question is to be asked at all, it is at least the prerogative of the Jews. They are the Chosen People. The promise of deliverance will come. Messiah will appear to establish a millennium of peace. God will keep His promise.

War Is Raging

"*They break in pieces thy people, O LORD, and afflict thine heritage.*

"*They slay the widow and the stranger, and murder the fatherless.*

"*Yet they say, The LORD shall not see, neither shall*

the God of Jacob regard it.

"Understand, ye brutish among the people: and ye fools, when will ye be wise?

"He that planted the ear, shall he not hear? He that formed the eye, shall he not see?

"He that chastiseth the heathen, shall not he correct? He that teacheth man knowledge, shall he not know?

"The LORD knoweth the thoughts of man, that they are vanity" (Psalm 94:5-11).

As the end of the Tribulation Period approaches, the Gentile nations will seek to destroy the Jewish race. What Hitler attempted, the world will try to finish. Why? Perhaps the entire Jewish race will be accused of conspiring to enslave the world.

It is not out of reason to consider the possibility that the antichrist may be of Israelite descent. Since the Son of God came from the tribe of Judah, the man of sin could emerge from one of the other tribes. Even the rabbis, some 2,150 years ago, speculated that the lost tribe of Dan might produce the antichrist.[2] If so, then the world may try to blame all of the Jews with a blanket condemnation. Mankind will finally believe the devil's lie that all of the world's ills are caused by the Jews.

The Jews have always been the whipping boy of nations. The only plausible reason for such action by the Gentiles is that satan has them deceived. He is determined to destroy God's plan for paradise on this planet. The devil has been trying to usurp the throne of God ever since his fall. But his final

---

[2] James H. Charlesworth, Editor, *The Old Testament Pseudepigrapha*, (Garden City, NY: Doubleday and Company, Inc., 1983) p. 809.

hour will arrive at the end of the Tribulation.

The Trap Backfires

"Blessed is the man whom thou chastenest, O LORD, and teachest him out of thy law;

"That thou mayest give him rest from the days of adversity, until the pit be digged for the wicked" (Psalm 94:12-13).

The pit or trap laid by the antichrist to enslave the human race will lead to his own undoing. In this psalm the trap backfires. Those who prepared the pit, fall into it themselves.

"For the LORD will not cast off his people, neither will he forsake his inheritance.

"But judgment shall return unto righteousness: and all the upright in heart shall follow it.

"Who will rise up for me against the evildoers? or who will stand up for me against the workers of iniquity?

"Unless the LORD had been my help, my soul had almost dwelt in silence.

"When I said, My foot slippeth; thy mercy, O LORD, held me up.

"In the multitude of my thoughts within me thy comforts delight my soul.

"Shall the throne of iniquity have fellowship with thee, which frameth mischief by a law?" (Psalm 94:14-20).

Israel is not forever forsaken. God's Chosen People were set aside only temporarily, that the Gospel might be taken to the Gentiles. If the Lord had not offered salvation to the Gentiles, what would have happened to those millions of people over the past twenty centuries? One day Israel will have to face that question.

Because so much wickedness has been perpetrated upon Jews in the name of Christ, the Jews have a tendency to blame all Christians for the sins of a few who, under the guise of Christianity, committed those crimes. Those who are quick to condemn all Christians are themselves victims of the same delusion that causes Gentiles to blame all Jews for the sins of a few. Paul explained:

> *"For I would not, brethren, that ye should be ignorant of this mystery, lest ye should be wise in your own conceits; that blindness in part is happened to Israel, until the fulness of the Gentiles be come in.*
>
> *"And so all Israel shall be saved: as it is written, There shall come out of Zion the Deliverer, and shall turn away ungodliness from Jacob:*
>
> *"For this is my covenant unto them, when I shall take away their sins"* (Romans 11:25-27).

God has made certain covenants with Israel which He will not forsake. The Abrahamic Covenant is just as viable today as it ever was. The Jew has been promised the heritage of Eretz (the land of) Israel, and God will keep His promise. Furthermore, the Davidic Covenant will also be fulfilled. The Scion (offspring) of David will sit upon a throne in Jerusalem and rule the world. Gentile Christianity may not understand all of the spiritual ramifications of God's covenants, but neither do the Jews understand the New Covenant (New Testament) made by Jesus Christ. One day soon, however, we all will understand.

This psalm, the fifth written by Moses, was dedicated to the tribe of Gad. The word Gad means "troop." It is a reference to military prowess and envisions an invasion of the holy city. Moses referred to it in Deuteronomy 33:20 in this manner:

> *"And of Gad, blessed be he that enlargeth Gad: he dwelleth as a lion, he teareth the arm with the crown of the head. And he provideth the first part for himself, because there, in a portion of the lawgiver, was he seated; and he came with the heads of the people, he executed the justice of the LORD, and his judgments with Israel"* (Deuteronomy 33:20).

Gad draws a prophetic picture of armies while the reference to a *"lion"* may imply the coming of Christ (the lion) to execute judgment and set up the kingdom. In like manner, Psalm 94 pleads for divine relief from an invading army. In keeping with Deuteronomy 33:20, Moses promised an answer to their cry for help.

> *"They gather themselves together against the soul of the righteous, and condemn the innocent blood.*
>
> *"But the LORD is my defence; and my God is the rock of my refuge.*
>
> *"And he shall bring upon them their own iniquity, and shall cut them off in their own wickedness; yea, the LORD our God shall cut them off"* (Psalm 94:21-23).

According to Jewish tradition, Elijah descended from the tribe of Gad. It is Elijah who is expected to come as a forerunner of Christ to prepare the Chosen People for their King. Radak commented, "Elijah will herald the advent of the Messianic era, when God will appear as the God of vengeance, who will punish the proud and cruel nations."[3] It is said that Moses composed this psalm as "a prayer to bring that day of Messianic redemption and retribution closer."[4] The Talmud designates this psalm as the Song of the Day for the fourth day of the week. Why the fourth? According to Jewish theologians, Wednesday was the day God created the sun and moon. In the future, the God of vengeance will punish the idolators who worshiped these celestial bodies."[5]

As the armies of the nations gather for the world's worst war, Christ will come to save the day. Jesus said, *"... except those days should be shortened, there should no flesh be saved; ..."* (Matthew 24:22). Without the intervention of Jesus Christ, the Jewish race would be brutally eliminated from among the nations. Furthermore, so fierce will be the battle, that if left to themselves, the armies would destroy all humanity. With the advent of the nuclear age it is easy to see how such a thing would be possible.

---

[3] Feuer, Tehillim, p. 1163.

[4] Ibid.

[5] Ibid.

Chapter Ten

Psalm 95
Dedicated to Issachar

"O come, let us sing unto the LORD: let us make a joyful noise to the rock of our salvation.

"Let us come before his presence with thanksgiving, and make a joyful noise unto him with psalms" (Psalm 95:1-2).

The mood changes with Psalm 95 from tribulation to rejoicing. Psalms 95-100 foreshadow setting up the kingdom. They reflect upon the time when Christ will judge the nations, rid the world of war, remove the curse, and return paradise to the planet.

Used to Welcome the Sabbath

Beginning with this psalm, the next five (95-99) along with Psalm 29 are used in synagogues on Friday night to "Welcome the Sabbath."

"Every week, on the eve of the Sabbath, the Jew abandons his pursuit of and preoccupation with the material world and envelops himself in the spirit of the Sabbath. The Sages of Talmudic times would don their finest clothing and get up with the approach of the Sabbath, saying, 'Let us go out to greet the Sabbath queen' (Shabbos 119a).

"The custom of reciting the six mizmorim (Psalms 95-99 and Psalm 29), the Friday night service of Welcoming the Sabbath—was instituted by Rabbi Moshe Cordovero (1522-1570). The new liturgy spread gradually until it was adopted in virtually all Jewish communities. The common theme of these six psalms is that God is King of the universe; indeed, this echoes the theme of the Sabbath, which reminds us that God created heaven and earth in six days and rested on the seventh. Someone who recognizes God as Master of the material world during the six working days is prepared to welcome His intense spiritual presence on the holy Sabbath." [1]

The "queen of the Sabbath" could be the bride of Christ who will be at His side when He returns at the close of the Tribulation Period. These past six thousand years correspond with the six days of creation. Therefore, we suggest that the next five Psalms (95-99) along with Psalm 29, not only welcome the Sabbath, but the seventh millennium as well—a time when God shall rest gloriously in His kingdom established on earth.

Our English translation of verse 1 uses the term *"joyful noise."* In Hebrew, the verse reads, "let us blow the shofar to the Rock of our salvation." Jewish commentators say that the shofar trumpet is sounded publicly to announce the coronation of a new king. In His coming kingdom, Christ will be the King of kings.

"For the LORD is a great God, and a great King above all gods" (Psalm 95:3).

---

[1] Feuer, Tehillim, p. 1175.

Radak explains that this psalm refers to the Messianic era when Israel will achieve a deeper awareness of God's power and omnipresence. Then every Jew will arouse his neighbor with the words of this psalm, urging him to praise the Almighty for the wonders he wrought during the epoch of Messianic triumph and redemption."[2]

God Is Maker of All

This is the sixth of eleven psalms composed by Moses. He dedicated it to Issachar. In Psalm 95, we can see the coming Redeemer as the same one who made the heavens and the earth.

"In his hand are the deep places of the earth: the strength of the hills is his also.

"The sea is his, and he made it: and his hands formed the dry land.

"O come, let us worship and bow down: let us kneel before the LORD our maker" (Psalm 95:4-6).

Rabbi Feuer makes the following observation:

"In the future, the exiles will be gathered in because they will prostrate themselves, as Isaiah (27:13) states: 'And they will prostrate themselves before Hashem [God] at the holy mountain in Jerusalem.' The Holy Temple will be rebuilt in this merit, as 99:9 states: 'Exalt Hashem, our God, and prostrate before His holy mountain.' The dead are also destined to be resurrected in this merit, as this verse states: 'Come! Let us prostrate ourselves and bow ... before Hashem, our Maker.' "[3]

---

[2] Ibid., p. 1176.

[3] Ibid., p. 1179.

Harden Not Your Hearts

The psalmist implores Israel not to be guilty of doing what their forefathers did.

"For he is our God; and we are the people of his pasture, and the sheep of his hand. Today if ye will hear his voice,

"Harden not your heart, as in the provocation, and as in the day of temptation in the wilderness:

"When your fathers tempted me, proved me, and saw my work.

"Forty years long was I grieved with this generation, and said, It is a people that do err in their heart, and they have not known my ways:

"Unto whom I sware in my wrath that they should not enter into my rest" (Psalm 95:7-11).

The Jewish Talmud says:

"If all of Israel would repent even for one day, the son of David would immediately arrive, as this verse attests: 'Even today, if we but heed His call.' If all of Israel would observe a single Sabbath properly, the son of David would arrive. Scripture refers to the Sabbath as 'today' [lit. the day, i.e., the day par excellence] and the Psalmist assures Israel: 'Even today [the Messiah will come], if we but heed His call' (Yerushalmi Taanis 1:1).

"Unto whom I sware in my wrath that they should not enter into my rest" says that God will gather from the exiles all the devout ones of Israel who will be redeemed by the Messiah. In the future all of the devout will sing to Hashem and greet Him with intense thanksgiving."[4]

---

[4] Ibid., p. 1183.

The Great Sabbath Rest

These verses are the subject of Hebrews 4:4-10 and are clearly set within the prophetic time frame of the seventh millennium, which corresponds with the seventh day after creation.

"For he spake in a certain place of the seventh day on this wise, And God did rest the seventh day from all his works.

"And in this place again, If they shall enter into my rest.

"Seeing therefore it remaineth that some must enter therein, and they to whom it was first preached entered not in because of unbelief:

"Again, he limiteth a certain day, saying in David, Today, after so long a time; as it is said, Today if ye will hear his voice, harden not your hearts.

"For if Jesus had given them rest, then would he not afterward have spoken of another day.

"There remaineth therefore a rest to the people of God.

"For he that is entered into his rest, he also hath ceased from his own works, as God did from his" (Hebrews 4:4-10).

The *"rest"* referred to in this passage is the millennial reign of Christ. According to the text, the prophecy should come to pass in the seventh millennium. Those in the wilderness were given the promise of a *"rest,"* but it was not the final rest. If it had been, Christ would not have spoken of another *"rest."* What a glorious prospect for the seventh millennium, which should begin soon!

According to the prophetic implications of Psalms 90-100, at the close of the sixth millennium, the world will be enveloped in catastrophic war. The genocide of the Jews will be imminent. Armies from around the world will converge upon Jerusalem to destroy every Jew from the face of the earth. No nation will stand beside Israel. None will come to their defense. In the darkness of the hour, the Israeli people will turn to the one person whom they had rejected. They will pray to the one who was nailed to a cross. When they do, they will be redeemed!

Issachar and Zebulun Rejoice

The theme of Psalms 95 and 96 can be seen in the rejoicing of Issachar and Zebulun recorded in the Mosaic blessing:

"And of Zebulun he said, Rejoice, Zebulun, in thy going out; and, Issachar, in thy tents" (Deuteronomy 33:18).

In keeping with the theme of rejoicing, Psalm 95 opens with, *"O COME, let us sing unto the LORD: let us make a joyful noise to the rock of our salvation"* (Psalm 95:1). May we rejoice with Zebulun and Issachar in these last years before the seventh millennium. If those early theologians who commented on the prophetic nature of the six days of creation are correct, we all have a glorious future just ahead.

Chapter Eleven

Psalm 96
Dedicated to Zebulun

"O sing unto the LORD a new song: sing unto the LORD, all the earth.

"Sing unto the LORD, bless his name; shew forth his salvation from day to day" (Psalm 96:1-2).

David recited this psalm (together with Psalm 105) when he brought up the Ark of the Covenant from the home of Obed Edom and placed it in the Tabernacle of David, which he had erected for it on the hilltop above the city of Jerusalem—the site where Solomon later built the Temple. This psalm appears in I Chronicles 16:23-33 (with some minor variations) where David appointed Asaph and his brethren to sing praises before the Tabernacle of David and the Ark of the Covenant.

The Ark had been held in captivity by the Philistines until it was returned. For years, it had resided in the home of Abinadab at Kerjath Jearim. Bringing the Ark to Jerusalem was the highlight of David's life. He was filled with joy as he offered this song of praise. Jewish theologians say that it is a prophetic song to be sung by Israel and the Messiah when they are finally released from exile.

The words *"O Sing unto the LORD a new song,"* serve as the introduction to many psalms which speak of the future. See Psalm 33:3, 40:4, 98:1, 149:1, and Isaiah 42:10.

This *"new song"* corresponds with Revelation 5. The Lamb approaches the throne, takes the title deed to earth and breaks the seals. The redeemed sing, *Thou art worthy to take the book, and to open the seals thereof: for thou wast slain, and hast redeemed us to God by thy blood out of every kindred, and tongue, and people, and nation; And hast made us unto our God kings and priests: and we shall reign on the earth* (Revelation 5:9-10).

Revelation 14 may be the prophetic fulfillment of this portion of the Song of Moses. The scene is the Temple site on Mount Zion. One hundred forty four thousand Jews are praising God. They *"follow the Lamb whithersoever he goeth."*

> *"And I looked, and, lo, a Lamb stood on the mount Zion, and with him a hundred forty and four thousand, having his Father's name written in their foreheads.*
>
> *"And I heard a voice from heaven, as the voice of many waters, and as the voice of a great thunder: and I heard the voice of harpers harping with their harps:*
>
> *"And they sung as it were a **new song** ..."* (Revelation 14:1-3).

The setting of Psalm 96, therefore, is future. It describes the praise due to God on that day when Christ returns to the Temple site and to the Ark of the Covenant. The Jewish remnant will rejoice with a *"new song."*

Judgment of the Nations

"Declare his glory among the heathen, his wonders among all people.

"For the LORD is great, and greatly to be praised: he is to be feared above all gods.

"For all the gods of the nations are idols: but the LORD made the heavens" (Psalm 96:3-5).

For centuries, Israel has suffered exile among the Gentile nations. When Christ returns and places Israel at the head of the nations, all Gentiles will see God's glory and grace. All nations will worship Him in that day.

The Babylonian system of idolatry will crumble in that day and all nations will realize that God made the universe. All foolish scientific theories about evolutionary development will be dispelled as all people are made to understand that God *"made the heavens."*

"Honour and majesty are before him: strength and beauty are in his sanctuary" (Psalm 96:6).

Radak made this observation:

"In the future, God's praises will be so widespread that even the majestic and glorious stars will offer praise to the Creator. They will declare that their majesty is a reflection of Divine glory."[1]

"His sanctuary" refers to the Tabernacle of David which will be set up during the Tribulation Period,

---

[1] Feuer, *Tehillim*, p. 1188.

desecrated by the antichrist, but redeemed and cleansed by Christ at His Second Advent.

Christ Will Reign in the Temple

"Give unto the LORD, O ye kindreds of the people, give unto the LORD glory and strength.

"Give unto the LORD the glory due unto his name: bring an offering, and come into his courts.

"O worship the LORD in the beauty of holiness: fear before him, all the earth.

"Say among the heathen that the LORD reigneth: the world also shall be established that it shall not be moved: he shall judge the people righteously" (Psalm 96:7-10).

Midrash Shocher Tov says that this is a reference to the future redemption, when all the Gentile nations will bring gifts to the Messiah. All Jews will return from their long exile.

"Come into his courts" refers to the courtyard of the restored Temple. *"Fear before him"* means that all the nations that failed to fear God throughout history will recognize His greatness in the Messianic era and will tremble before Him. *"The world also shall be established"* means that in the Messianic era the world will be fixed so that it cannot falter. Before the arrival of Messiah, earth will be in a state of chaos. Isaiah wrote,

"The foundations of the earth do shake. The earth is utterly broken down, the earth is clean dissolved, the earth is moved exceedingly. The earth shall reel to and fro like a drunkard, and shall be removed like a cottage ..." (Isaiah 24:18-20).

"Let the heavens rejoice, and let the earth be glad; let the sea roar, and the fulness thereof.

"Let the field be joyful, and all that is therein: then shall all the trees of the wood rejoice

"Before the LORD: for he cometh, for he cometh to judge the earth: he shall judge the world with righteousness, and the people with his truth" (Psalm 96:11-13).

Jewish theologians say that Moses' seventh psalm was dedicated to Zebulun, who rejoiced when he went out to earn a livelihood so that he could support his brother Issachar, who studied the Torah. After the arrival of Messiah, both tribes will praise the Lord. *"The heavens rejoice"* refers to all celestial bodies reflecting the glory of God. *"Let the earth be glad"* refers to the happiness evoked by that which is established and familiar. Radak says these verses are a "figurative allusion to the happiness which will sweep the universe at the advent of the Messianic era of eternal peace."[2]

"For he cometh, for he cometh ..." is a reference to two comings. Jewish theologians offer varied opinions about this. Rabbi Feuer writes:

"Malbim offers ... [an] interpretation of the two arrivals: First, He will manifest Himself in the functioning of nature when people recognize that the so-called Law of Nature is truly the concealed Hand of God. Second, God will be perceived as the One Who judges the deed of mankind."[3]

I wish to offer another interpretation as to why

---

[2] Ibid., p. 1190.

[3] Ibid., p. 1191.

"for he cometh" is given twice. I think it clearly shows that Christ will come twice: First, he came 2,000 years ago to provide eternal life, and second, he will return to ... *judge the world with righteousness, and the people with his truth* (Psalm 96:13).

The theme of Psalms 95 and 96 can be seen in the rejoicing of Issachar and Zebulun recorded in the Mosaic blessing:

> *"And of Zebulun he said, **Rejoice,** Zebulun, in thy going out; and, Issachar, in thy tents"* (Deuteronomy 33:18).

In keeping with that theme, Psalm 95:1 says:

> *"O COME, let us **sing** unto the LORD: let us make a **joyful noise** to the rock of our salvation"* (Psalm 95:1).

Psalm 96, following the same theme, is dedicated to Zebulun and opens with:

> *"O SING unto the LORD a new song: **sing** unto the LORD, all the earth"* (Psalm 96:1).

Rabbi Avrohom Chaim Feuer, in his commentary TEHILLIM, says, "At that time, all men will unite to form a community of faith dedicated to proclaiming their belief in the One and Only God Who created heaven and earth and Who controls nature and history."[4]

---

[4] Ibid., p. 1192.

Dedication of the Tabernacle of David

One final note: Psalm 91 was written for the dedication of the Mosaic Tabernacle. Psalm 96 was used for the dedication of the Tabernacle of David. Both of these psalms being positioned as they are—following the Leviticus Psalms (73-89), which predict the restoration of Temple liturgy, are powerful prophecies that religious Jews in Israel will surely soon restore Temple worship. Such a Temple or Tabernacle must be in operation during the future Tribulation Period in order for the antichrist to commit the abomination of desolation— *"... so that he as God sitteth in the temple of God, showing himself that he is God"* (II Thessalonians 2:4).

Chapter Twelve

Psalm 97
Dedicated to Joseph

"The LORD reigneth; let the earth rejoice; let the multitude of isles be glad thereof" (Psalm 97:1).

According to Rabbi Avrohom Chaim Feuer, Moses dedicated this psalm to the tribe of Joseph (Ephraim and Manasseh), "from whom Joshua is descended. Joshua would conquer the land of Canaan in God's Name, and this victory is described in verse 1. *'The hills* (the mighty monarchs of Canaan) *melted like wax ...'* (verse 5) before Joshua. This psalm also alludes to the future ..."[1]

This rabbinical interpretation names Joshua as the one of whom this psalm speaks and states that it "also alludes to the future ..." Messiah. I would point out that the name Joshua in the Hebrew language comes from the same root word translated "Jesus" in the New Testament. In this psalm, the greater Joshua (Jesus Christ) is actually praised as Redeemer and King. The psalm describes the battle of Armageddon and the glorious appearing of Christ.

---

[1] Feuer, *Tehillim*, p. 1193

"Clouds and darkness are round about him: righteousness and judgment are the habitation of his throne.

"A fire goeth before him, and burneth up his enemies round about.

"His lightnings enlightened the world: the earth saw, and trembled.

"The hills melted like wax at the presence of the LORD, at the presence of the LORD of the whole earth.

"The heavens declare his righteousness, and all the people see his glory" (Psalm 97:2-6).

Rabbi Rashi wrote, "This alludes to the outbreak of the war of Gog and Magog (which precedes the advent of Messiah), as described in Ezekiel 38:22: 'And I will punish him with pestilence and with blood. Torrential rain, hailstones, and sulfurous fire I will rain upon him.'"[2]

Jewish theologians do not accept the New Testament book of Revelation and do not call the end-time war, *"Armageddon."* They call it by the Old Testament description, *"Gog and Magog."* Christian theologians, however, see two wars, Gog and Magog, which I believe will introduce the Tribulation Period, and Armageddon, which will follow seven years later at the close of the Tribulation Period. Russia will be the main enemy in the Battle of Gog and Magog and *"the kings of the east"* will be the main enemy in the Battle of Armageddon.

In the final analysis, no one knows the precise chronology of events. However, I am inclined to believe that the war described in Psalm 97 is that of

[2] Ibid., p. 1194

Armageddon rather than Gog and Magog.

This Song of Moses (Psalms 90-100) cannot be viewed as giving a year-by-year account of the Tribulation Period because the themes of war, restoring Temple worship, and the coming of Messiah are spread throughout these psalms. No one psalm deals with just one event. The Book of Revelation gives more of a chronological description of end-time events.

Let us be reminded, at this point, that this Song of Moses is sung in Revelation 15 at a time when seven angels are preparing to pour out bowls of God's wrath upon the earth:

> *"And I saw another sign in heaven, great and marvellous, seven angels having the seven last plagues; for in them is filled up the wrath of God.*
>
> *"And I saw as it were a sea of glass mingled with fire: and them that had gotten the victory over the beast, and over his image, and over his mark, and over the number of his name, stand on the sea of glass, having the harps of God.*
>
> *"And they sing the song of Moses the servant of God"* (Revelation 15:1-3).

The Second Advent of Christ is in view in Psalm 97. It corresponds with John's account in Revelation:

> *"And I saw heaven opened, and behold a white horse; and he that sat upon him was called Faithful and True, and in righteousness he doth judge and make war;*
>
> *"His eyes were as a flame of fire, and on his head were many crowns; and he had a name written, that no man knew, but he himself.*

"And he was clothed with a vesture dipped in blood: and his name is called the Word of God.

"And the armies which were in heaven followed him upon white horses, clothed in fine linen, white and clean.

"And out of his mouth goeth a sharp sword, that with it he should smite the nations: and he shall rule them with a rod of iron: and he treadeth the winepress of the fierceness and wrath of Almighty God.

"And he hath on his vesture and on his thigh a name written, KING OF KINGS, AND LORD OF LORDS" (Revelation 19:11-16).

Daniel also saw this event in his vision recorded in Daniel 7. Following his description of four beasts (kingdoms) which will rise up out of the sea (humanity) and the final kingdom consisting of ten horns (kings) with a little horn (antichrist), Daniel writes:

"I beheld till the thrones were cast down, and the Ancient of days did sit, whose garment was white as snow, and the hair of his head like the pure wool: his throne was like the fiery flame, and his wheels as burning fire.

"A fiery stream issued and came forth from before him: thousand thousands ministered unto him, and ten thousand times ten thousand stood before him: the judgment was set and the books were opened.

"I beheld then because of the voice of the great words which the horn spake: I beheld even till the beast was slain, and his body destroyed, and given to the burning flame.

"As concerning the rest of the beasts, they had their dominion taken away: yet their lives were prolonged for a season and time.

"I saw in the night visions, and behold, one like the Son of man came with the clouds of heaven, and came to the Ancient of days, and they brought him near before him.

"And there was given him dominion, and glory, and a kingdom, that all people, nations, and languages, should serve him: his dominion is an everlasting dominion, which shall not pass away, and his kingdom that which shall not be destroyed" (Daniel 7:9-14).

Zechariah also gives a magnificent description of that final glorious event:

"Behold, the day of the LORD cometh, and thy spoil shall be divided in the midst of thee.

"For I will gather all nations against Jerusalem to battle; and the city shall be taken, and the houses rifled, and the women ravished; and half of the city shall go forth into captivity, and the residue of the people shall not be cut off from the city.

"Then shall the LORD go forth and fight against those nations, as when he fought in the day of battle.

"And his feet shall stand in that day upon the mount of Olives, which is before Jerusalem on the east, and the mount of Olives shall cleave in the midst thereof toward the east and toward the west, and there shall be a very great valley; and half of the mountain shall remove toward the north, and half of it toward the south ...

"And this shall be the plague wherewith the LORD will smite all the people that have fought against Jerusalem; Their flesh shall consume away while they stand upon their feet, and their eyes shall consume away in their holes, and their tongue shall consume away in their mouth" (Zechariah 14:1-4,12).

When the final war gathers momentum and the nations converge against Israel for their proposed

genocide of the Jews, the Chosen People will realize that death looms upon their posterity and that
no other messiah has appeared to save them. With
no nation coming to their aid, with their armed
forces running out of ammunition, with their
backs against the wall, and having no where else
to turn, they will pray for deliverance to the one
whom their forefathers had rejected. They will cry
out to Jesus Christ, accepting Him as their long-
awaited Messiah.

That is just what the Lord is waiting to hear. He
will immediately muster the forces of heaven and
come to the rescue of Israel.

The Nations Will Be Ashamed

*"Confounded be all they that serve graven images,
that boast themselves of idols: worship him, all ye gods.*

*"Zion heard, and was glad; and the daughters of
Judah rejoiced because of thy judgments, O LORD.*

*"For thou, LORD, art high above all the earth: thou art
exalted far above all gods"* (Psalm 97:7-9).

On that day, all people who refused to believe in
Christ will be ashamed. Jewish theologians say
that "in the future every idol will come before its
worshipers and contemptuously spit in their
faces. The worshipers will be shamed and the
idols (having completed their mission) will vanish
from the earth."[3] It appears as if these idols are
really demons who have tricked mankind into
turning their affections from the true God. A man

---

[3] Ibid., p. 1196.

couldn't be fooled, however, if he wasn't first filled with pride. Man's desire to become a god has filled him with contempt for his Creator.

"The daughters of Judah rejoiced," because Christ is the offspring of David, of the tribe of Judah. Even the rabbis recognize that the daughters of Judah will rejoice because the Messiah will be from that tribe. "The Messiah's relatives will have special reason to rejoice, upon his arrival (Chazah Zion)."[4]

The Saints Will Rejoice

"Ye that love the LORD, hate evil: he preserveth the souls of his saints; he delivereth them out of the hand of the wicked.

"Light is sown for the righteous, and gladness for the upright in heart.

"Rejoice in the LORD, ye righteous; and give thanks at the remembrance of his holiness" (Psalm 97:10-12).

As the world converges upon Jerusalem for their deadly work, the sun will turn as "black as sackcloth of hair" (Revelation 6:12). In the darkened sky above Jerusalem, the clouds will roll back "as a scroll" (Revelation 6:14), like a mighty curtain upon a stage—to reveal the majesty and glory of the ruler of the universe. Angels will attend His grand entrance. The armies of heaven will be gathered on His right and on His left. An angry world will be astounded to see the mighty God of creation come to the defense of Israel.

---

[4] Ibid.

Messiah Ben Joseph

The theme of Psalm 97 can be seen in the Mosaic blessing given to Joseph:

> *"And of Joseph he said, Blessed of the LORD be his land, for the precious things of heaven, for the dew, and for the deep that coucheth beneath,*
>
> *"And for the precious fruits brought forth by the sun, and for the precious things put forth by the moon,*
>
> *"And for the chief things of the ancient mountains, and for the precious things of the lasting hills,*
>
> *"And for the precious things of the earth and fullness thereof, and for the good will of him that dwelt in the bush: let the blessing come upon the head of Joseph, and upon the top of the head of him that was separated from his brethren.*
>
> *"His glory is like the firstling of his bullock, and his horns are like the horns of unicorns: with them he shall push the people together to the ends of the earth: and they are the ten thousands of Ephraim, and they are the thousands of Manasseh"* (Deuteronomy 33:13-17).

This lengthy blessing presents God's plans for the whole earth. The kingdom is declared! Joseph is compared to the one whom the rabbis call "Messiah Ben Joseph." We are reminded that Joseph was rejected by his brethren and sold for a few shekels of silver. But though they "thought it for evil, God meant it unto good" (Genesis 50:20). The prophetic scenario of being rejected by his brothers points us to Christ, once rejected by Israel, only to return and be crowned King of kings. It is a magnificent description of the Second Coming of Christ, of whom Joseph was a type.

Chapter Thirteen

Psalm 98
Dedicated to Naphtali

Psalm 98 is dedicated to Naphtali. Its theme is found in the Mosaic blessing:

> *"And of Naphtali he said, O Naphtali, satisfied with favour, and full with the blessing of the LORD: possess thou the west and the south"* (Deuteronomy 33:23).

The verse implies a setting up of the world kingdom by the Messiah, especially seen in the phrase, *"possess thou ..."* In keeping with this theme, Psalm 98 says:

> *"O sing unto the LORD a new song; for he hath done marvellous things: his right hand, and his holy arm, hath gotten him the victory"* (Psalm 98:1).

Indeed, as the Mosaic blessing declares, Israel is *"satisfied with favour, and full with the blessing of the LORD!"* In Psalm 98, Christ has come to save Israel and rule the world!

This psalm is very similar to Psalm 96, which was used by David when the Ark of the Covenant was brought to Jerusalem. This psalm, on the other hand, was first sung when the Ark was returned from Philistine territory by two milk cows.

Jewish folklore says that the two cows turned their faces toward the Holy Ark and this psalm burst forth from their lips![1] Well, legends will be legends, but the fact that this psalm is so similar to the one used at the dedication of the Tabernacle of David, we feel assured that it is connected to the future return of the Ark to Jerusalem.

The *"new song"* is thought by some to be this very psalm. It is believed that when the Messiah comes to redeem Israel they will sing Psalm 98.

The *"victory"* alludes to the coming of Christ to conquer and judge the world. It is not used in Psalm 96. Therefore, these two psalms (96 and 98), being so similar and flanking Psalm 97 on either side, appear to point to Psalm 97 as the all-important description of the coming of Christ. With His coming in Psalm 97, we can move straight into Psalm 98 with its declaration of *"victory!"*

> *"The LORD hath made known his salvation: his righteousness hath he openly showed in the sight of the heathen.*
>
> *"He hath remembered his mercy and his truth toward the house of Israel: all the ends of the earth have seen the salvation of our God"* (Psalm 98:2-3).

Jewish theologians say that the statement, *"The Lord hath made known his salvation,"* means that "at the time of redemption, God will finally make known the precise date of the advent of the Messiah." Until then, the time has been shrouded in mystery. They cite Deuteronomy 32:34, the first

---

[1] Feuer, *Tehillim*, p. 1202.

stanza of the Song of Moses, which says, *"Is not this laid up in store with me, and sealed up among my treasures?"* Rabbis also quote Daniel 12:4, *"But thou, O Daniel, shut up the words, and seal the book, even to the time of the end: many shall run to and fro, and knowledge shall be increased."* This verse also has a parallel passage in Isaiah 56:1 which reads, *"Keep ye judgment, and do justice: for my salvation is near to come, and my righteousness to be revealed."* Therefore, the rabbis say that this prophecy will be fulfilled by the Messiah. When He is about to come, he will reveal the "precise time" to the Jews.[2]

The *"heathen"* in verse 2 refers to Gentile nations. And though Jewish theologians do not like to consider it, the Jewish Messiah did come 2,000 years ago to provide "salvation" for Gentiles. Israel was given an opportunity to receive Jesus as Messiah, but were blind to His position. Because of Israel's unbelief, God turned to the Gentiles with His offer of eternal life. Paul discussed the matter in Romans 9-11.

However, God did not forever forsake Israel, as some would have us believe. Verse 3 explains that God will remember His promises to Israel—*"He hath remembered his mercy and his truth toward the house of Israel."* At the Second Advent of Christ, Israel will realize that God *"made known his salvation"* to Gentiles and Gentiles will realize that God *"remembered ... Israel."* Paul explains this in the eleventh chapter of Romans:

---

[2] Ibid., p. 1203.

"What then? Israel hath not obtained that which he seeketh for; but the election hath obtained it, and the rest were blinded.

"(According as it is written, God hath given them the spirit of slumber, eyes that they should not see, and ears that they should not hear;) unto this day....

"I say then, Have they stumbled that they should fall? God forbid: but rather through their fall salvation is come unto the Gentiles, for to provoke them to jealousy.

"Now if the fall of them be the riches of the world, and the diminishing of them the riches of the Gentiles: how much more their fulness? ...

"For if the casting away of them be the reconciling of the world, what shall the receiving of them be, but life from the dead?" (Romans 11:7-8,11-12,15).

Yes, Israel was *"cast away"* but not forever. God turned to the Gentiles with the gospel, but one day, a wonderful thing will happen. Paul put the question this way, *"For if the casting away of them* [Israel] *be the reconciling of the world* [salvation for Gentiles] *what shall the receiving of them* [Israel] *be, but **life from the dead**?"* *"Life from the dead"* is what we have been waiting for. That is the *"Blessed Hope!"* One day, soon, Israel will be saved and resurrection day will arrive!

The verse, *"all the ends of the earth have seen the salvation of our God,"* corresponds with John's salutation to the Apocalypse. *"Behold, he cometh with clouds; and every eye shall see him, and they also which pierced him: and all kindreds of the earth shall wail because of him"* (Revelation 1:7).

Psalm 98 also describes His spectacular appearance, *"... all the ends of the earth have seen the salvation of our God"* (Psalm 98:3).

> *"Make a joyful noise unto the LORD, all the earth: make a loud noise, and rejoice, and sing praise.*
>
> *"Sing unto the LORD with the harp; with the harp, and the voice of a psalm.*
>
> *"With trumpets and sound of cornet make a joyful noise before the LORD, the King.*
>
> *"Let the sea roar, and the fullness thereof; the world, and they that dwell therein.*
>
> *"Let the floods clap their hands: let the hills be joyful together*
>
> *"Before the LORD; for he cometh to judge the earth: with righteousness shall he judge the world, and the people with equity"* (Psalm 98:4-9).

Verse nine is almost identical to the concluding verse of Psalm 96, with this difference: In Psalm 96 the words, *"for he cometh"* is repeated twice. In Psalm 98, it is given only one time. In Psalm 96, the first phrase alludes to the coming of Christ 2,000 years ago and the second use of the phrase refers to the return of Christ, which apparently had not yet occurred. However, its use only one time in Psalm 98 refers only to the Second Coming of Christ, which, by this time, has already taken place. His Second Coming is graphically described in Psalm 97.

When He comes, the Savior will establish His throne on Mount Moriah, site of the great Jewish Temples. There Christ will bring all nations before His bar of justice.

Chapter Fourteen

Psalm 99
Dedicated to Dan

"The Lord reigneth; let the people tremble: he sitteth between the cherubim; let the earth be moved.

"The LORD is great in Zion; and he is high above all the people.

"Let them Praise thy great and terrible name; for it is holy.

"The king's strength also loveth judgment; thou dost establish equity, thou executest judgment and righteousness in Jacob.

"Exalt ye the LORD our God, and worship at his footstool; for he is holy" (Psalm 99:1-5).

Moses dedicated his tenth psalm to the tribe of Dan, whose name means "judge." Psalm 99 speaks of the future Day of Judgment, "when God will call all of the depraved nations to task."[1]

The symbol of a snake (a many-headed Hydra) was attributed to Dan. It is the symbol used in Revelation to describe the kingdom of the antichrist. It is "Rahab" the dragon of Psalm 87:4 and 89:10.

---

[1] Feuer, *Tehillim*, p. 1207

What is so remarkable about the number 99 is that 9 is derived from the ninth letter of the Hebrew alphebet "teth," meaning "a serpent." Two of them (9 and 9) represent a two-headed serpent! Or they could represent 99 heads! Though the number 99 has no meaning in the Lexicon, the number 9, itself, still has a definite symbolic and prophetic significance. The symbol of the serpent can be found in the opening chapters of Genesis and the closing chapters of Revelation.

The promise was made to Eve that the *"seed of the woman would bruise the serpent's head"* (Genesis 3:15). To Dan (the serpent tribe) was given the awesome task of bringing judgment upon the house of Israel. In fact, early Jewish theologians have speculated that Dan would produce the antichrist. It is noted in a commentary on an apocryphal writing entitled, "The Testaments of The Twelve Patriarchs." In this ancient writing, dating back to at least 150 B. C., the last words of each of the twelve sons of Jacob are supposedly recorded. In the portion on the last words of Dan, the dying patriarch is reported to have said:

> "For I know that in the last days you will defect from the Lord, you will be offended at Levi, and revolt against Judah; but you will not prevail over them ... To the extent that you abandon the Lord, you will live by every evil deed ... and you are motivated to all wickedness by the spirits of deceit among you. For I read in the Book of Enoch the Righteous that your prince is Satan ..."[2]

---

[2] H. C. Key, "Testaments Of The Twelve Patriarchs," *The Old Testament Pseudepigrapha*, Vol. 1, ed. James H. Charlesworth (Garden City, NY: Doubleday, 1983), p. 809

"The Testaments of the Twelve Patriarchs" is preserved in a volume entitled, PSEUDEPIGRAPHA. In a footnote, the editor, James H. Charlesworth wrote:

> "No known Enochic text supports this, although Jewish and patristic speculation linked Dan and the Antichrist, possible on the basis of the idolatry attributed to Dan in Judges 18:11-31 and the prophecies of judgment linked to Dan in Jeremiah 8:16-17."[3]

Dan, the judge, receives a Mosaic blessing which corresponds with Psalm 99:

> *"And of Dan he said, Dan is a lion's whelp: he shall leap from Bashan"* (Deuteronomy 33:22).

The tribe actually moved into the territory of Bashan above the Sea of Galilee and captured the city of Laish (meaning "lion") changing the name of the village to Dan. By the time of the reign of David, however, most of the tribe had disappeared. Around 1050 B.C. the book of I Chronicles listed the genealogies of the other eleven tribes, excluding Dan! Furthermore, Dan is not given in the list of tribes recorded in Revelation 7. The tribe made that mysterious *"leap from Bashan,"* leaving no obvious trail. They are regarded as a "lost tribe." Will they produce the antichrist? Have they been the guiding force behind all of Israel's troubles down through history? As the dying Jacob gave his last words he said of Dan:

---

[3] Ibid.

"Dan shall judge his people, as one of the tribes of Israel.

*"Dan shall be a **serpent** by the way, an **adder** in the path, that biteth the horse heels, so that his rider shall fall backward"* (Genesis 49:16-17).

What happened to the tribe of Dan? Where did they migrate. What family dynasty may have roots in that tribe? For further details, may I suggest you obtain a copy of our book, GUARDIANS OF THE GRAIL (see ad in back of this volume).

Psalm 99 heralds the reign of Christ, as He comes to execute judgment upon the wicked antichrist and restore the kingdom to Israel.

"Moses and Aaron among his priests, and Samuel among them that call upon his name; they called upon the LORD, and he answered them.

"He spake unto them in the cloudy pillar: they kept his testimonies, and the ordinance that he gave them.

"Thou answeredst them, O LORD our God: thou wast a God that forgavest them, though thou tookest vengeance of their inventions.

"Exalt the LORD our God, and worship at his holy hill; for the LORD our God is holy" (Psalm 99:6-9).

We have no indication why Samuel is included in a psalm ascribed to Moses. His name must have been added at a later date. Jewish theologians offer no suggestions as to how he became part of this Mosaic psalm, but say that Samuel is listed because he was regarded as a great prophet before God for his ministry in the Mosaic Tabernacle. Some say that Samuel, a Levite, and descendant of the same family as Moses and Aaron, was also responsible for sanctifying the Tabernacle at Shiloh. His stature matched that of Moses and Aaron in certain respects. Samuel was considered to be one of the greatest prophets of all time. Ibn Ezra suggested that a pillar of cloud hovered over the home of Samuel just as it did over the Mosaic Tabernacle—so great was Samuel.[4]

Jeremiah may give us a clue as to the prophetic nature of Psalm 99. In Jeremiah 15, God tells the prophet that the Chosen People are about to be taken into Babylonian captivity. The Lord was so determined to scatter the Jews that He tells Jeremiah:

> *"Though Moses and Samuel stood before me, yet my mind could not be toward this people: cast them out of my sight, and let them go forth"* (Jeremiah 15:1).

The people complain that they don't deserve this punishment because:

> *"I have neither let on usury, nor men have lent to me on usury; yet every one of them doth curse me"* (Jeremiah 15:10).

This may be a clue to Israel's problems in the end-time. The Chosen People will be blamed by Gentile nations for using interest rates to gain monetary control of nations. Yet they complain, *"I have neither lent on usury, nor men have lent to me on usury."* This practice was condemned by God. However, the tribe of Dan was foretold by the dying Jacob that they would be as a *"serpent by the*

---

[4] Feuer, *Tehillim*, p. 1211.

way, an adder in the path, that biteth the horse heels, so that his rider shall fall backward" (Genesis 49:17). The Hebrew term translated, *"usury"* is "nashak," meaning "bite of the serpent."

One of the major problems besetting our world today is the accumulation of national debts acquired by all nations as a result of borrowing huge amounts from the international banking cartel. The U. S. national debt soared past $3 trillion in the decade of the 1980's.

Many people blame all the Jews for our monetary woes. That was Hitler's complaint in the 1930's and the issue continues to cloud the true picture of world conditions today. This "blanket condemnation" of World Zionism actually diverts our attention from the real problem. The "Jews" are not guilty as a race any more than the Germans were guilty for the sins of Adolf Hitler.

The lost tribe of Dan may have produced a family dynasty who is now in control of international banking. The infamous antichrist could rise out of that tribe. He may even now be in control of international banking. One day, he is destined to offer himself as Israel's messiah on the Temple Mount in Jerusalem. He will take over the city, establish his throne and commit the *"abomination of desolation"* (Matthew 24:15). He will establish monetary control over every human on the planet and demand a mark be taken in the right hand or forehead of all who would participate in the marketplace. Yes, Israel's "serpent" tribe will most likely produce the one to bring God's final judgment upon the world. The name Dan means "judge."

In Psalm 99, we are told that God will listen to Moses, Aaron and Samuel, who are among those *"that call upon his name; they called upon the LORD, and he answered them."* At the end of Israel's long exile among the Gentile nations, we are told that God forgives Israel, though he took *"vengeance of their inventions."* They will *"worship at his footstool,"* and *"exalt the LORD our God, and worship at his holy hill,"* for the long-awaited Messiah has arrived and *"sits between the cherubim"* (a reference to the Ark of the Covenant).

Israel's long exile is over. The war of Gog and Magog (and/or Armageddon) is concluded. Christ has returned and His kingdom is established!

Chapter Fifteen

Psalm 100
Dedicated to Asher

"Make a joyful noise unto the LORD, all ye lands.

"Serve the Lord with gladness: come before his presence with singing.

"Know ye that the LORD he is God: it is he that hath made us, and not we ourselves; we are his people, and the sheep of his pasture.

"Enter into his gates with thanksgiving, and into his courts with praise: be thankful unto him, and bless his name.

"For the Lord is good; his mercy is everlasting; and his truth endureth to all generations" (Psalm 100:1-5).

According to Jewish theologians, this psalm was sung in the Temple during the service of a Thanksgiving offering; an offering that one would bring "after having survived great danger."[1] That insight into Jewish thinking certainly fits with the conclusion of the Tribulation Period. During Armageddon, Israel will experience the greatest danger it has ever faced. Jesus predicted, *"except those days be shortened, there should no flesh be saved: but for the elect's sake those days shall be*

---

[1] Feuer, *Tehillim*, p. 1215.

shortened" (Matthew 24:22). The glorious return of Christ at the climax of Armageddon will herald the salvation of Israel. Then this song of Thanksgiving will be appropriate, for Israel will have "survived great danger," indeed!

> "Rabbi Hirsch explains that this song of thanksgiving deals with the gratitude that will be due to God in the Messianic Age, when the world has reached perfection. Psalm 100 serves as a finale to the previous psalms concerning the approach of the Messianic Era."[2]

This statement by rabbinical authorities concurs with our independent research—that the Psalms are prophetic and depict a year-by-year account of the restoration of Israel in this century. "Psalm 100 serves as a finale to the previous psalms ..." which start at Psalm 1 and the opening of this century in 1901. Psalm 48 describes the birth of Israel in 1948. In fact, each psalm seems to correspond generally with events which befell the Jewish people in each year of this century. In our book, HIDDEN PROPHECIES IN THE PSALMS, we have outlined the modern history of Israel and have documented historical events, comparing them with the prophetic nature of each psalm which is numbered according to the year. At least the first 89 years (1901-1989) are described in the first 89 psalms.

When we come to Psalm 90, we cannot conclude that the Song of Moses is chronological as the previous 89 are. The first 89 psalms are only introduc-

---

[2] Ibid., p. 1215.

tory to the Song of Moses (Psalms 90-100). The Song of Moses, itself, may not necessarily be chronological. But when we come to Psalm 100, we are reminded by early Jewish theologians that we have arrived at the "FINALE TO THE PREVIOUS PSALMS CONCERNING THE APPROACH OF THE MESSIANIC ERA!"

These verses declare the Kingship of Christ and the blessings of the kingdom age. Messiah sits upon the throne of this world to establish a golden age for mankind. Furthermore, early theologians say that this should come at the end of six thousand years—as the rabbis said, "when the world has reached perfection."

At the close of the sixth day of creation, God reviewed all that He had created, *"and behold, it was very good"* (Genesis 1:31). In like manner, at the close of six thousand years, God will be pleased with all that has transpired. The wicked will have been judged and the righteous will enter into God's Sabbath rest—the seventh millennium.

The number 100 happens to be the 19th letter of the Hebrew alphabet. Does it conclude the 1900's? (Don't miss that combination of 19 and 100 which makes nineteen-hundred.) By the way, please note that Christ's appearance in the book of Revelation happens to be in chapter number 19! Could that also refer to the conclusion of the 1900's?

Psalm 100 is filled with praise and blessing, indicative of the name Asher, (which means "blessed, happy"). Moses blessed the tribe saying,

"Let Asher be blessed with children; let him be accept-able to his brethren, and let him dip his foot in oil.

"Thy shoes shall be iron and brass; and as thy days, so shall thy strength be" (Deuteronomy 33:24-25).

The thrust of this blessing is that the Chosen People will be blessed with material blessings for a very long period of time—a thousand years. The rejoicing of Psalm 100 follows the theme as the kingdom is established and God's judgment of mankind is concluded!

There is nothing in this psalm about judgment. The previous psalms contain descriptions of judgment. Nothing negative, however, is recorded in Psalm 100. All is happiness and joy. The Messiah reigns in Jerusalem as King of kings and Lord of lords.

This psalm takes us to the story of Anna, the daughter of Phanuel, of the tribe of Asher, who approached Simeon, Joseph, Mary and the Christ child in the Temple. Simeon had just uttered the prophecy:

"This child is set for the fall and rising again of many in Israel....

"Anna, coming in at that instant gave thanks likewise unto the Lord, and spake of him to all them that looked for redemption in Jerusalem" (Luke 2:34,38).

These two people represent a prophetic scenario hidden in the Song of Moses. The first stanza of the Song of Moses (located in Deuteronomy 32) was dedicated to the tribe of Simeon (whose name means "hearing") and predicts the *"fall"* of Israel. This first stanza was kept under the LAW in the book of Deuteronomy (a prediction of Israel's spiritual deafness) while the other eleven stanzas were removed to the Psalms, which is characterized by GRACE. They were placed in Psalms 90-100 because they represent the *"rising again"* of Israel. The return of Israel to their Promised Land is an act of GRACE and shows God's redemption of Israel from the curse of the LAW.

The first stanza of the Song of Moses was dedicated to Simeon and the last stanza was dedicated to Asher. This scenario is depicted in Luke 2, through the actions of Simeon (named after the tribe of Simeon) and Anna (of the tribe of Asher). The name Asher means "blessed," and in keeping with the prophetic nature of her name, Anna *"gave thanks"* and *"spake of him to all them that looked for redemption in Jerusalem."* At the Second Advent of Christ, Israel will finally be redeemed, placed at the head of the nations, and enjoy the Millennial reign—utopia at last!

Chapter Sixteen

The Great Sabbath Rest

According to early theologians, seven millennia of world history are somehow related to the seven days of creation. Those seven days were thought to prophetically represent seven one thousand year periods of human history. That is precisely the theme set by Moses in Psalm 90:

"For a thousand years in thy sight are but as yesterday when it is past, and as a watch in the night" (Psalm 90:4).

Listed Six Times in Revelation 20

In Revelation, the millennial reign of Christ is stated six times to be 1,000 years in length:

"And he laid hold on the dragon, that old serpent, which is the Devil, and Satan, and bound him a thousand years [number 1],

"And cast him into the bottomless pit, and shut him up, and set a seal upon him, that he should deceive the nations no more, till the thousand years should be fulfilled [number 2]: *and after that he must be loosed a little season.*

"And I saw thrones, and they sat upon them, and judgment was given unto them: and I saw the souls of them that were beheaded for the witness of Jesus, and for the word of God, and which had not worshiped the beast, neither his image, neither had received his mark upon their foreheads, or in their hands; and they lived and reigned with Christ a thousand years [number 3].

"But the rest of the dead lived not again until the thousand years were finished [number 4]. *This is the first resurrection.*

"Blessed and holy is he that hath part in the first resurrection: on such the second death hath no power, but they shall be priests of God and of Christ and shall reign with him a thousand years [number 5].

"And when the thousand years are expired, Satan shall be loosed out of his prison [number 6]*"* (Revelation 20:2-7).

It must be more than a coincidence that the millennial reign of Christ is repeated **six** times. The implication seems obvious. From the creation of Adam to the second coming of Christ, God has determined six 1,000 year periods of human history. The reference of Peter to the *"day of the Lord"* is also used by the Old Testament prophets— Zechariah, Joel, Isaiah, Ezekiel, and others:

"Behold the day of the LORD cometh" (Zechariah 14:1).

"Blow ye the trumpet in Zion, and sound an alarm in my holy mountain: let all the inhabitants of the land tremble: for the day of the LORD cometh, for it is nigh at hand" (Joel 2:1).

"Behold, the day of the LORD cometh, cruel both with wrath and fierce anger, to lay the land desolate: and he shall destroy the sinners thereof out of it" (Isaiah 13:9).

"For the day is near, even the day of the LORD is near, a cloudy day; it shall be the time of the heathen" (Ezekiel 30:3).

In Hebrews 4:4-6 this future millennium is referred to as a *"sabbath"* rest:

"For he spake in a certain place of the seventh day on this wise, And God did rest the seventh day from all his works.

"And in this place again, If they shall enter into my rest.

"Seeing therefore it remaineth that some must enter therein, and they to whom it was first preached entered not in because of unbelief" (Hebrews 4:4-6).

According to these verses, the millennial reign is considered to be more than just a rest. It is a *"sabbath"* rest. Furthermore, the Jewish people in Jesus' day were not allowed to enter into that rest because of their unbelief:

"For if Jesus had given them rest, then would he not afterward have spoken of another day" (Hebrews 4:8).

According to these verses, Israel was not allowed to enter into that *"rest"* when Jesus came the first time. They must await the duration of what the Bible calls *"the last days."* That would be at least two millennial days—the "Dispensation of Grace." Days FIVE and SIX must transpire before day SEVEN can be implemented. Bear in mind, each of these days are considered to be 1,000 years in length. Hebrews 4 leads us to only one conclusion—from the time of the creation of Adam until the end of the *"day of the Lord,"* must be 7,000 years. That great *"sabbath"* rest is implied to be the SEVENTH millennium.

Seven Days of Creation

Let us, therefore, consider the six days of creation recorded in the first chapters of Genesis to see what kind of prophetic scenario is taught by the events of each day. If those early theologians were correct, we should be able to point out a prophetic overview of each millennium of history.

The First Day
4,000 B. C. to 3,000 B. C.

"And the earth was without form, and void; and darkness was upon the face of the deep, And the Spirit of God moved upon the face of the waters.

"And God said, Let there be light: and there was light.

"And God saw the light, that it was good: and God divided the light from the darkness.

"And God called the light Day, and the darkness he called Night. And the evening and the morning were the first day" (Genesis 1:2-5).

There are two things about this first day of creation of which we should take note. First, God said, *"Let there be light,"* and second, He divided the light from the darkness. He called the light good, implying that the darkness represented evil.

God put man in the Garden of Eden, and gave him a choice between the tree of life and the tree of the knowledge of good and evil. The scenario fits. A distinction was made between good and evil.

The events of the first day of creation correspond with the fall of Adam in the first millennium.

Light Represents Good

Consider the definition of "light." I think it will explain why light is a type of good and why darkness is a type of evil.

The entrance of light into the universe came at the instant God spoke. It was an ACTIVITY issuing from the voice of God. According to scientific definition, there are two possible explanations: First, light could a disturbance of the continuum. Perhaps it can best be described as the effect one gets when a pebble is dropped into a pond of water. The impact of the pebble upon the pond creates a set of waves, issuing from the point of impact. It is a disturbance of the continuum.

Another theory is that light is made up of particles with each little package being jostled against the other creating a domino effect—as one domino would fall against the other and so on down the line. Perhaps, it can best be understood by saying that the dominoes represent the continuum and the entrance of light creates a disturbance. Perhaps the dominoes do not represent the light, they simply represent the continuum.

In either case, light is the result of energy. As long as the continuum remains undisturbed, there is no light. Once the continuum is disturbed, however, that energy source, becomes measurable. Perhaps that is why the scripture says, *"The entrance of thy word giveth light."* That is why Jesus, who is the logos, the Word of God, said, *"I am the light of the world."* John puts it this way:

> *"In him was life; and the life was the light of men. And the light shineth in darkness; and the darkness comprehended it not"* (John 1:4-5).

In the beginning of creation, the earth was without form and void. Darkness was upon the face of the deep. There was no disturbance for the continuum of the universe, when suddenly God spoke! and the very entrance of His word gave light! It was a disturbance of the continuum, the entrance of an energy source—and it was good!

This teaches us that good is active and the opposite of good (evil) is a lack of activity. For example, if you are active, you are happy and productive. But if you are lazy, then you are neither happy nor productive. When God spoke on that first creation day, the entrance of His word into the universe created an active energy. The Bible calls it *"light."*

Therefore, God could make the first day of creation to represent the first millennium of human history. *"Let there be light* [the entrance of activity] *and it was good."*

In like manner, God created Adam and Eve and told them to tend the garden. Just as God divided the light from the darkness, He gave Adam and Eve a choice between good and evil. Over the course of the first millennium (of which Adam lived 930 years) mankind grappled with the question of good and evil.

The Second Day
3,000 B. C. to 2,000 B. C.

The second day of creation represents those events which occurred in the second millennium of history. God divided the waters from the waters. In this prophetic scenario, we can see Noah's flood:

> "And God said, Let there be a firmament in the midst of the waters, and let it divide the waters from the waters.
>
> "And God made the firmament, and divided the waters which were under the firmament from the waters which were above the firmament: and it was so.
>
> "And God called the firmament Heaven. And the evening and the morning were the second day" (Genesis 1:6-8).

God divided the firmament, and it rained for forty days. Please note that God did not say that it was good. It came as a judgment upon an unbelieving human race. May I suggest that the great flood of Noah's day was predicted by the events of the second day of creation.

The Third Day
2,000 B. C. to 1,000 B. C.

That brings us to the third day of creation when God called forth the dry land:

> "And God said, Let the water under the heaven be gathered together into one place, and let the dry land appear: and it was so.

"And God called the dry land Earth; and the gathering together of the waters called he Seas: and God saw that it was good.

"And God said, Let the earth bring forth grass, the herb yielding seed, and the fruit tree yielding fruit after his kind, whose seed is in itself, upon the earth: and it was so.

"And the earth brought forth grass, and herb yielding seed after his kind, and the tree yielding fruit, whose seed was in itself, after his kind: and God saw that it was good.

"And the evening and the morning were the third day" (Genesis 1:9-13).

He caused the land to be fruitful and multiply. In like manner, God caused the waters of the great deluge to be abated and gave to Noah the command to *"be fruitful and multiply and replenish the earth."* Just as on that third day of creation the earth brought forth vegetation, in like manner, during the third millennium the earth again produced vegetation to replace that which was destroyed in the flood.

Furthermore, God gave Noah and his family the command to be fruitful and multiply, to bring forth a human race who would love and serve God. This also represents an organized system of religion—a way by which the human race can be spiritually fruitful. We can see it at Sinai during the third millennium when God established the Mosaic Covenant with the descendants of Abraham, Isaac, and Jacob.

The Fourth Day
1,000 B. C. to 1 A. D.

The fourth day of creation gives a prophetic overview of the fourth millennium of history.

"And God said, Let there be lights in the firmament of the heaven to divide the day from the night; and let them be for signs, and for seasons, and for days, and years:

"And let them be for lights in the firmament of the heaven to give light upon the earth: and it was so.

"And God made two great lights; the greater light to rule the day, and the lesser light to rule the night: he made the stars also.

"And God set them in the firmament of the heaven to give light upon the earth,

"And to rule over the day and over the night, and to divide the light from the darkness: and God saw that it was good.

"And the evening and the morning were the fourth day" (Genesis 1:14-19).

God created lights in the firmament of the heaven. He created stars and set them in the heavens for signs. This is a prophetic picture of those days which began with the building of Solomon's Temple. And in the years following, most of the Old Testament books were written. Isaiah, Jeremiah, Ezekiel, Daniel, Micah, Joel, Amos, Zechariah, and others were surely lights set in the firmament of human history to give us prophetic signs of the times.

It was also on the fourth day that God made two great lights. The greater light to rule the day and the lesser light to rule the night. In like manner, the fourth millennium introduced another great light. *"When the fullness of time was come* (thus ending day four) *God sent His son, made of a woman, made under the law, that He might redeem them that were under the law"* (Galatians 4:4-5). Yes, God sent forth the greater light (Christ) and the lesser light (Christians).

It was Jesus who said, *"I am the light of the world"* (John 8:12). The sun is a commonly known symbol of Jesus Christ. But then Jesus turned to His disciples, who represented New Testament Christianity, and said, *"Ye are the light of the world"* (Matthew 5:14). Just as the moon reflects the light of the sun, New Testament Christianity should reflect the glory of our Savior.

The Fifth Day
1 A. D. to 1,000 A. D.

The fifth day of creation represents the pouring out of the Holy Spirit (typified by water) and the development of Christianity in the fifth millennium.

"And God said, Let the waters bring forth abundantly the moving creature that hath life, and fowl that may fly above the earth in the open firmament of heaven.

"And God created great whales, and every living creature that moveth, which the waters brought forth abundantly, after their kind, and every winged fowl after his kind: and God saw that it was good.

"And God blessed them, saying, Be fruitful, and multiply, and fill the waters in the seas, and let fowl multiply in the earth.

"And the evening and the morning were the fifth day" (Genesis 1:20-23).

The *"water"* appears to be a type of the Holy Spirit and the term, *"bring forth abundantly,"* seems to be a picture of the great commission. On this fifth day God called forth the fish.

Jesus told His disciples that He would make them to be *"fishers of men."* The insignia of the early church was a fish. The term *"be fruitful and multiply"* is a prophetic picture of our responsibility as New Testament Christians. We are to take the message of the gospel to every creature.

The Sixth Day
1,000 A. D. to 2,000 A. D.

The great commission spills over into the sixth day of creation where the Lord brought forth the *"living creature after his kind."* The events of the sixth day correspond with the growth of Christianity in the sixth millennium.

"And God said, Let the earth bring forth the living creature after his kind, cattle, and creeping thing, and beast of the earth after his kind: and it was so.

"And God made the beast of the earth after his kind, and cattle after their kind, and everything that creepeth upon the earth after his kind: and God saw that it was good.

"And God said, Let us make man in our image, after our likeness: and let them have dominion over the fish of the sea, and over the fowl of the air, and over the cattle, and over all the earth, and over every creeping thing that creepeth upon the earth.

> *"So God created man in his own image, in the image of God created he him; male and female created he them."*
>
> *"And God blessed them, and God said unto them, Be fruitful, and multiply ...*
>
> *"And God saw everything that he had made, and, behold, it was very good. And the evening and the morning were the sixth day"* (Genesis 1:24-27).

On the fifth and sixth days of creation God said, *"Be fruitful and multiply."* It was also on the sixth day of creation that God made man in His own image. In like manner, I think, it will be at the end of the sixth millennium that all who have received Christ as Savior will be resurrected or raptured—to be made again like unto His image.

Also, the fall of Adam and Eve appears to be a prophetic picture of the Battle of Armageddon when an unbelieving human race will be judged of God. After the fall, God predicted that Eve would travail in childbirth.

In like manner, this sixth millennium will conclude with the prophetic *"birthpangs of travail."* These birthpangs, however, will bring forth a new humanity recreated in the image of God. For you see, *"this corruptible must put on incorruption, and this mortal must put on immortality"* (I Corinthians 15:53). That's what the rapture and the resurrection is all about.

The Seventh Day
2,000 A. D.? and Counting ...

That brings us to the seventh day, when God ended His work and rested. Here is a prophetic picture of the great sabbath rest—the seventh millennium of human history. Wow! What a picture! And we can follow God's plan of the ages through the Genesis account of creation.

Sabbath Days in the New Testament

Let's consider the possibility that certain events in the gospel narratives take on prophetic implications when viewed with respect to the "millennial day" concept. The number of days listed in various stories may have prophetic implications.

Several events occurred on a sabbath day, lending support to the implication that these events are prophetic scenarios, which will be ultimately fulfilled during a future millennial sabbath.

Christ Announced His Ministry on a Sabbath Day

In Luke's gospel Jesus enters the synagogue at Nazareth to announce the beginning of His ministry. It was on a sabbath that He took the scroll of Isaiah and read the words,

"The Spirit of the Lord is upon me, because he hath anointed me to preach the gospel to the poor; he hath sent me to heal the brokenhearted, to preach deliverance to the captives, and recovering of sight to the blind, to set at liberty them that are bruised,

"To preach the acceptable year of the Lord" (Luke 4:18-19).

Then He closed the book. Had He continued to read, He would have read the words *"and the day of vengeance of our God."* Perhaps the fact that He announced His mission on a sabbath day offers a prophetic implication that the *"day of vengeance"* will be fulfilled during the seventh millennium.

Christ Plucked Corn on a Sabbath Day

On another sabbath, our Savior plucked ears of corn—a seeming violation of rabbinical law:

> *"And it came to pass on the second sabbath after the first, that he went through the corn fields; and his disciples plucked the ears of corn, and did eat, rubbing them in their hands.*
>
> *"And certain of the Pharisees said unto them, Why do ye that which is not lawful to do on the sabbath days? ...*
>
> *"And he said unto them, That the Son of man is Lord also of the sabbath"* (Luke 6:1-2,5).

It seems the Savior was saying that the future millennial reign of Christ would be a time of planting and harvest. It would be a time of activity and progress. Though it is considered to be a sabbath rest, that rest will be spiritual rather than physical. It will be a rest from evil—a rest from the temptations of Satan.

Notice the reply of Christ to the priests in Luke 6:5, *"And he said unto them, That the Son of man is Lord also of the sabbath."*

Here, He implies that He will bear the title of "Lord of lords" during that future 1,000 year reign.

Christ Healed the Withered Hand
on a Sabbath Day

Then there was the time Christ healed a man with a withered right hand on the sabbath day:

> *"And it came to pass also on another sabbath, that he entered into the synagogue and taught: and there was a man whose right hand was withered.*

> *"And the scribes and Pharisees watched him, whether he would heal on the sabbath day; and they might find an accusation against him.*

> *"But he knew their thoughts, and said to the man which had the withered hand, Rise up, and stand forth in the midst. And he arose and stood forth.*

> *"Then said Jesus unto them, I will ask you one thing; Is it lawful on the sabbath days to do good, or to do evil? to save life, or to destroy it?*

> *"And looking round about upon them all, he said unto the man, Stretch forth thy hand. And he did so: and his hand was restored whole as the other"* (Luke 6:6-10).

By healing on the sabbath, Jesus implied that the kingdom would be a time for healing. During the seventh millennium mankind will see the eradication of all diseases.

Christ Healed a Woman

In Luke 13, Jesus performed another healing on the sabbath day. This time it was a woman who had a spirit of infirmity for eighteen years. The Savior loosed her from her infirmity, and implied that Satan had been the cause of her problem.

"And ought not this woman, being a daughter of Abraham, whom Satan hath bound, lo, these eighteen years, be loosed from this bond on the sabbath day?" (Luke 13:16).

The implication is at once apparent: During the future "Day of the Lord" all will be healed.

Christ Healed a Man With Dropsy

Luke records yet another healing on the sabbath.

"And it came to pass, as he went into the house of one of the chief Pharisees to eat bread on the sabbath day, that they watched him.

"And behold, there was a certain man before him which had the dropsy.

"And Jesus answering spake unto the lawyers and the Pharisees, saying, Is it lawful to heal on the sabbath day:

"And they held their peace. And he took him and healed him, and let him go;

"And answered them, saying, Which of you shall have an ass or an ox fallen into a pit, and will not straightway pull him out on the sabbath day?

"And they could not answer him again to these things" (Luke 14:1-6).

Jesus healed the man of his infirmity in the presence of the lawyers and the Pharisees. In doing so, it seems that Jesus implied, prophetically, that such would be the case during the great sabbath rest—the seventh millennium of history.

The Parables

In the verses following, He told the parable of a wedding. By doing so, He seemed to imply, prophetically, that during the seventh millennium, there would be a wedding:

"And he put forth a parable to those which were bidden, when he marked how they chose out the chief rooms; saying unto them,

"When thou art bidden of any man to a wedding, sit not down in the highest room; lest a more honourable man than thou be bidden of him ..." (Luke 14:7-8).

Following that, Jesus gave the parable of a great supper, implying that in the future kingdom, the Marriage Supper of the Lamb would be celebrated:

"Then said he unto him, A certain man made a great supper, and bade many ...

"And the lord said unto the servant, Go out into the highways and hedges, and compel them to come in, that my house may be filled" (Luke 14:16,23).

It is amazing that all of these incidents appear to have a prophetic implication when viewed in the context of the great sabbath—that seventh 1,000 year period of human history.

The Pool of Bethesda

Another sabbath healing took place in Jerusalem at the pool of Bethesda. Jesus healed a man who had been sick for 38 years. The religious authorities became angry and confronted Jesus with an accusation that He should not heal on the sabbath day. Jesus replied:

> *"For the Father judgeth no man, but hath committed all judgment unto the Son:*
>
> *"That all men should honour the Son, even as they honour the Father. He that honoureth not the Son honoureth not the Father which hath sent him.*
>
> *"Verily, verily, I say unto you, He that heareth my word, and believeth on him that sent me, hath everlasting life, and shall not come into condemnation; but is passed from death unto life"* (John 5:22-25).

Christ spoke of those attributes which He possessed, and which would be manifested during His millennial reign. Since these events occurred on a sabbath day, Jesus seemed to imply that His reign would be a time of sabbatical rest—the seventh millennium.

Christ Healed a Blind Man

Another healing took place on a sabbath day, recorded in John 9. Jesus made clay, put it upon the eyes of a blind man and told him to go wash in the pool of Siloam. When he did, he was healed.

> *"And it was the sabbath day when Jesus made the clay, and opened his eyes"* (John 9:14).

This healing took place on the sabbath day, and is another reminder of that which shall occur during the millennial reign of Christ. Blind eyes will be made to see, withered limbs will be made whole, leprous diseases will be made clean, and evil spirits will be cast out. Yes, those events recorded in the gospel narratives which occurred on a sabbath day seem to be a prophetic picture of that which shall occur during the millennial reign of Christ on earth.

A Counting of Days Is Also Important

Also, there are certain events in the Bible which occurred over a period of two or three days.

The Story of Jonah

Jonah spent three days and three nights in the stomach of a whale, and, in like manner, Jesus spent three days and three nights in the heart of the earth. These two events could also be a prophetic picture of three thousand years wherein God has dealt with His Chosen People. Like Jonah, the nation of Israel had refused to take the message of God's judgment and mercy to the Gentiles. As Jonah spent three days in the great fish, so have the Jewish people been judged of God for the past three millennia.

The Story of Saul

There is another story given in the book of Acts which also may portray a prophetic implication. It is the story of Saul on his way to Damascus and seeing the Lord in the midst of a brilliant light. When the light was gone, Saul of Tarsus was blind. He had to be led by the hand into the city of Damascus. Please note, he was blind for three days. This may be a prophecy of the history of Israel over a period of about three millennia. In I

Corinthians Paul referred to this experience:

> "... *last of all he was seen of me also, as of one born out of due time*" (I Corinthians 15:8).

"Born out of due time." According to C. I. Scofield, Paul was representing the nation as a whole. His experience of conversion was a prophetic picture of the future national conversion of Israel. The three days he spent in darkness, then, could well represent the future time when that national conversion would take place.

Joseph and Mary
Searched Three Days

Now let's go back to the gospel narratives and pick up a few more events which seem to have prophetic implication when viewed from a millennial day perspective. In Luke chapter 2, Joseph and Mary searched for the twelve year old Jesus. On the third day, they found Him in the Temple:

> "*And he said unto them, How is it that ye sought me? wist ye not that I must be about my Father's business?*" (Luke 2:49).

If the Dispensation of Grace covers a period of 2,000 years, and if the millennial reign of Christ covers the third 1,000 year period, then the finding of Christ in the Temple on the third day may well represent His being about the Father's business during the coming third millennium.

Feeding the 4,000

The story of the feeding of the 4,000 is recorded in Matthew 15 and Mark 8. Please note that the multitude had followed Him for three days. It was on that third day that Jesus fed the multitude. Prophetically, it may refer to that millennial day when the problem of famine will be solved.

Tell Herod, "... the third day I shall be perfected."

In Luke 13, some Pharisees came saying,

"Get thee out, and depart hence: for Herod will kill thee" (Luke 13:31).

Jesus replied:

"Go ye, and tell that fox, Behold, I cast out devils, and I do cures today and tomorrow, and the third day I shall be perfected" (v. 32).

Three days later, Jesus made His triumphal entry into the city of Jerusalem. These verses seem to have a powerful prophetic implication. They may refer to the third millennium, when Jesus will make yet another triumphal entry into the city of Jerusalem. In the coming millennium, the ministry of Christ will be perfect.

The Wedding in Cana

In the gospel of John, Jesus attended a wedding in Cana of Galilee. This wedding may be a prophetic picture of the future marriage feast which will take place after the Rapture.

"And the third day there was a marriage in Cana of Galilee" (John 2:1).

Please note, that the wedding took place on the third day. Again, this may be a prophetic implication of the future marriage of the Lamb to His bride, New Testament Christianity. The scripture implies that it will take place after two millennia, on the third day!

The Money Changers

In the latter part of that chapter, Jesus went up to Jerusalem. Upon entering the Temple, He found money changers selling oxen, sheep, and doves. He drove the money changers out and said:

"Take these things hence; make not my Father's house an house of merchandise" (John 2:16).

When the Jews asked Him why He had done these things and what sign He could show them that He had the authority to cleanse the sanctuary, Jesus answered:

"Destroy this temple, and in three days I will raise it up" (John 2:19).

Now, to be sure, He was speaking of the Temple of His body, which they did destroy and which He did raise up the third day. Prophetically, however, it may be a picture of the future Temple which the Messiah will *"raise up"* when He comes. It may be that the three days listed in verse 19 represent three millennial days. The statement made by Jesus at the Temple in Jerusalem may be more profound than that which first meets the eye.

When Christ returns, He will cleanse the sanctuary, drive out those future money changers, and will erect a magnificent Temple. Remember please, He said that day, *"Destroy this temple, and in three days I will raise it up."*

That statement, by the way, is also referred to in Mark 14:58. When Jesus was arrested and brought to trial before the Sanhedrin court, certain false witnesses came to testify:

> *"We heard him say, I will destroy this temple that is made with hands, and within three days I will build another made without hands"* (Mark 14:58).

Those people never forgot the statement made by the Savior. In Luke 15:29, we find the Savior hanging upon the cross. Those who passed by:

> *"... railed on him, wagging their heads, and saying, Ah, thou that destroyest the temple, and buildest it in three days, Save thyself, and come down from the cross"* (Luke 15:29).

Even in the last hours of His life the people mocked Him about the promise He made that He could rebuild the Temple in three days. Those three days, however, may refer to three millennia, three 1,000 year periods. The prediction may yet be fulfilled, just as Jesus said it would!

The Story of the Samaritans

There is another story given in John 4, which may also lend support to the prophetic implication that a day could equal a thousand years:

> "*So when the Samaritans were come unto him, they besought him that he would tarry with them: and he abode there two days.*
>
> "*And many more believed because of his own word;*
>
> "*And said unto the woman, Now we believe, not because of thy saying: for we have heard him ourselves, and know that this is indeed the Christ, the Savior of the world.*
>
> "*Now after two days he departed thence, and went into Galilee*" (John 4:40-43).

Jesus spent two days among the Samaritans. This may represent two millennial days we call the Dispensation of Grace. It has been a time of Gentile conversion. The New Testament church, which is pictured in the Bible as the Bride of Christ is, for the most part, a Gentile bride. We may be prophetically typified by the Samaritans, among whom Jesus stayed for two days.

The story begins with Jesus and His disciples passing through the country of Samaria. As they came near to a city called Sychar, Jesus stopped at a well and sent his disciples into town to buy bread. While He was there, a Samaritan woman came out to draw water. Jesus asked her for a drink and then told her how she could receive living water to quench her spiritual thirst. This is a prophetic picture of the Dispensation of Grace. When the woman replied that Jews worship at Jerusalem and the Samaritans worship at Mt. Gerizim, Jesus said:

> *"Woman, believe me, the hour cometh, when ye shall neither in this mountain, nor yet at Jerusalem, worship the Father.*
>
> *"But the hour cometh, and now is, when the true worshipers shall worship the Father in spirit and in truth"* (John 4: 21,23).

Jesus introduces the Dispensation of Grace. It began with the first coming of Christ and shall be concluded when He comes back the second time. Meanwhile, just as He spent two days with the Samaritans, He has spent two millennia among the Gentiles.

The Story of Lazarus

There is another story recorded in John's gospel which seems to agree with the teaching that one day equals a thousand years.

It is the story of Lazarus. When he came down with the illness, his sisters, Mary and Martha, sent word to Jesus that he was sick:

> *"When he had heard therefore that he was sick, he abode two days still in the same place where he was.*
>
> *"Then after that saith he to his disciples, Let us go into Judea again"* (John 11:6-7).

Jesus delayed His trip to Bethany for two days. When He finally came, Lazarus was already in the grave. Obviously, He planned it that way. Prophetically, it may imply two millennial days before He comes again. Just as Jesus raised Lazarus from the dead, He is coming to raise all believers from the dead.

The Transfiguration

Finally, the story of the Transfiguration is given in Matthew 17. Jesus met with Moses and Elijah. The event was a prophetic picture of the Second Coming of Christ:

> *"And after six days Jesus taketh Peter, James, and John his brother, and bringeth them up into an high mountain apart"* (Matthew 17:1).

Please note, the event took place *"after six days."* It may represent a prophetic scenario of that which shall occur at the end of the sixth millennium of human history!

It is amazing! Time after time, throughout the gospel narrative, we find prophetic implications which lend support to the teaching that a day equals a thousand years, and that after six thousand years of human history, the Savior will return to this earth, raise the dead, eradicate disease, feed the hungry, establish His promised kingdom, and rule over the earth during the seventh 1,000 years. That is the doctrine of the great Sabbath Rest!

Chapter Seventeen

Moses and the Messiah

"The Lord thy God will raise up unto thee a Prophet from the midst of thee, of thy brethren, like unto me; unto him ye shall hearken ..." (Deuteronomy 18:15).

"... like unto me," said Moses, *"... like unto me!"* Now, we know that Moses was looking forward to the promised Messiah, but for him to say that Christ would demonstrate certain traits or characteristics found in himself is most important. The statement gave me a desire to take a closer look at Moses' life. I wanted to find out how and why Christ can be compared to Moses. Peter quoted the prophecy while preaching in the Temple during the days following Pentecost:

"For Moses truly said unto the fathers, A prophet shall the Lord your God raise up unto you of your brethren, like unto me; him shall ye hear in all things whatsoever he shall say unto you" (Acts 3:22).

As I studied the life and ministry of Moses, I became convinced that Moses offers a fascinating prophetic profile of the Messiah. Peter was right when he said, *"For Moses TRULY said ..."* It was no flight of fancy. Moses could humbly say that Christ would bear certain characteristics demonstrated in his own life.

For instance, Moses was born in a time when Jewish male children were being slaughtered. Pharaoh was trying to abort the birth of a Jewish deliverer. Likewise, in the days of Jesus' birth, Herod the Great had the male children of Bethlehem slaughtered—an attempt to kill the coming King. Moses was born in Egypt and returned to Egypt to lead his people out. In like manner, Jesus was taken to Egypt as an infant in order that the prophecy might be fulfilled, *"Out of Egypt have I called my son"* (Matthew 2:15).

This prophecy was originally given by Hosea. *"When Israel was a child, then I loved him, and called my son out of Egypt"* (Hosea 11:1). Hosea was referring to the Exodus led by Moses. Yet, Matthew gave a prophetic meaning to the Hosea passage and specifically related it to Christ. The life of Moses is a prophetic profile of Jesus Christ. These are only a few of the many comparisons that can be made between Moses and Christ.

Grant R. Jeffrey, in his book, HEAVEN—THE LAST FRONTIER, suggested,

> "At least fifty elements and events are parallel in both lives. Both filled the roles of prophet, priest, lawgiver, teacher, and leader of men. Both confirmed their teaching with miracles. Both spent their early years in Egypt, miraculously protected from those who sought their lives.

> "Moses' family initially did not accept his role, but later his brother, Aaron, and sister, Miriam, helped him.

Jesus' mother and brothers initially failed to follow Jesus, but later his brother James became the leader in the church in Jerusalem. Both confronted demonic powers and successfully subdued them.

"As Moses appointed seventy rulers over Israel, Jesus anointed seventy disciples to teach the nation. Moses sent twelve spies to explore Canaan, Jesus sent twelve apostles to reach the world. Both fasted for forty days and faced spiritual crises on mountain tops.

"As Moses stretched his hand over the Red Sea to divide it, Jesus rebuked the Sea of Galilee and quieted the waves. Both of their faces shone with the glory—Moses on Mount Sinai and Jesus on the Mount of Transfiguration. Moses lifted up a brazen serpent in the wilderness and Jesus was lifted up on the cross. The people were ungrateful and rebelled against the leadership of both men. The generations that rebelled against them died in their lack of faith, one in the wilderness and one in the siege of Jerusalem in 70 A.D." [1]

Now let us consider several experiences from the Sinai drama and compare the ministry of Moses with that of Christ.

Seven Dispensations

To begin with, Moses made seven trips into the presence of God. Notice how they correspond to the great dispensations of history. The term "dispensation" refers to a unique time wherein God deals with man in seemingly altogether different ways. The seven dispensations of history, as determined by theologians, are as follows:

[1] Grant R. Jeffrey, *Heaven—The Last Frontier*, (Toronto, Frontier Research Publications, 1990), p.78.

1. The Dispensation of **Innocence,** from the Creation to the Fall.

2. The Dispensation of **Conscience,** from the expulsion out of Eden to the Flood.

3. The Dispensation of **Human Government,** from the Flood to the Tower of Babel.

4. The Dispensation of **Promise,** from the call of Abraham to the Exodus from Egypt.

5. The Dispensation of **Law,** from Sinai to Calvary.

6. The Dispensation of **Grace,** from Calvary to the Second Coming.

7. The Dispensation of the **Kingdom**, wherein the Messiah will reign as King of kings and Lord of lords.

Moses' First Encounter:
The Dispensation of Innocence

Let us examine Moses' first ascent into the presence of God and compare it with the Dispensation of Innocence:

"And Moses went up unto God, and the Lord called unto him out of the mountain, saying, Thus shalt thou say to the house of Jacob, and tell the children of Israel;

"Ye have seen what I did unto the Egyptians, and how I bare you on eagles' wings, and brought you unto myself.

*"Now therefore, **if ye will obey my voice indeed, and keep my covenant, then ye shall be a peculiar treasure unto me above all people: for all the earth is mine:***

*"**And ye shall be unto me a kingdom of priests, and***

an holy nation. These are the words which thou shalt speak unto the children of Israel.

"And Moses came and called for the elders of the people, and laid before their faces all these words which the Lord commanded him" (Exodus 19:3-7).

This is similar to the message given to Adam and Eve in the Garden of Eden:

*"And God blessed them, and God said unto them, Be fruitful, and multiply, and **replenish the earth, and subdue it: and have dominion** over the fish of the sea, and over the fowl of the air, and over every living thing that moveth upon the earth"* (Genesis 1:28).

A comparison can be made between God's promises to Adam and His later message to Israel. To *"have dominion"* corresponds with the statements *"a peculiar treasure ... above all people"* and *"a kingdom of priests ... an holy nation."*

For God to say that Israel will become a kingdom of priests implies a responsibility to guide the world in its worship of God. This requires a leadership position. When Israel finally becomes *"a kingdom of priests"* the human race will be restored. Therefore, the message to Adam in the Dispensation of Innocence appears to be repeated here, following Moses' first ascent.

Moses' Second Encounter:
The Dispensation of Conscience

Moses' second ascent is given in Exodus 19:8-14:

"...And Moses returned the words of the people unto the Lord.

"And the Lord said unto Moses, Lo, I come unto thee in a thick cloud, that the people may hear when I speak with thee, and believe thee for ever. And Moses told the words of the people unto the Lord.

"And the Lord said unto Moses, Go unto the people, and sanctify them today and tomorrow, and let them wash their clothes,

"And be ready against the third day: for the third day the Lord will come down in the sight of all the people upon mount Sinai.

"And thou shalt set bounds unto the people round about, saying, Take heed to yourselves, that ye go not up into the mount, or touch the border of it: whosoever toucheth the mount shall be surely put to death:

"There shall not an hand touch it, but he shall surely be stoned, or shot through; whether it be beast or man, it shall not live: when the trumpet soundeth long, they shall come up to the mount.

"And Moses went down from the mount unto the people ..." (Exodus 19:8-14).

This corresponds to the Dispensation of Conscience—from the expulsion to the Flood.

First, God told Moses to *"sanctify them ... let them wash their clothes."* Before the Fall of Adam there was no need for sanctifying. After the Fall, however, there was then a need for cleansing—sin had entered the human race. The era was called "conscience" because Adam became knowledgeable on the subject of sin. He learned the difference between good and evil. This corresponds with the command at Sinai to have the people to wash their clothes—a metaphor for spiritual cleansing.

Secondly, The LORD instructed Moses to *"set bounds ... go not up into the mount, or touch the border of it."* This compares with the story of the expulsion from Eden:

> *"Therefore, the LORD God sent him forth from the garden of Eden, to till the ground from whence he was taken.*
>
> *"So he drove out the man; and he placed at the east of the garden of Eden cherubim, and a flaming sword which turned every way, to keep the way of the tree of life"* (Genesis 3:23-24).

Adam was forbidden to enter the garden and Israel was forbidden to touch the mountain.

Thirdly, God descended to the summit of Sinai for a meeting with His People on the third day.

> *"And it came to pass on the third day in the morning, that there were thunders and lightnings, and a thick cloud upon the mount..."* (Exodus 19:16).

According to Flavius Josephus, it rained:

> "So they passed two days in this way of feasting, but on the third day before the sun was up, the cloud spread itself over the whole camp of the Hebrews, such a one as none had seen before and encompassed the place where they had pitched their tents. And while all the rest of the air was clear, there came strong winds that raised up large showers of rain which became a mighty tempest. There was also such lightning—terrible to those that saw it. And thunder, with its thunder bolts, declared God to be there."[2]

---

[2] Flavius Josephus, *"Antiquities of the Jews,"* Book 3, Chapter 5, paragraph 2, p. 70.

Just as the second era ended with a great flood, in like manner, this second encounter was concluded with a great rain—perhaps to remind them of the flood which came in the days of Noah. Because of these comparisons, I feel that the scenario represented a picture of the Dispensation of Conscience—from the Fall to the Flood.

Moses' Third Encounter:
The Dispensation of Human Government

Moses' third trip to the summit of Mount Sinai is recorded in Exodus 19:17-20:

> *"And Moses brought forth the people out of the camp to meet with God; and they stood at the nether part of the mount.*
>
> *"And mount Sinai was altogether on a smoke, because the Lord descended upon it in fire: and the smoke thereof ascended as the smoke of a furnace, and the whole mount quaked greatly.*
>
> *"And when the voice of the trumpet sounded long, and waxed louder and louder, Moses spake, and* **God answered him by a voice.**
>
> *"And the Lord came down upon mount Sinai, on the top of the mount: and the Lord called Moses up to the top of the mount; and Moses went up"* (Exodus 19:17-20).

It is here that the story corresponds with the Dispensation of Human Government:

> *"And the Lord said unto Moses, Go down, charge the people, lest they break through unto the Lord to gaze, and many of them perish.*
>
> *"And let* **the priests** *also, which come near to the Lord, sanctify themselves, lest the Lord break forth upon them.*

> "And Moses said unto the Lord, The people cannot come up to mount Sinai: for thou chargedst us, saying, **Set bounds** about the mount, and sanctify it.
>
> "And the Lord said unto him, Away, get thee down, and thou shalt come up, thou, and Aaron with thee: but let not the priest and the people break through to come up unto the Lord, lest he break forth upon them.
>
> "So Moses went down unto the people, and spake unto them" (Exodus 19:21-25).

First, the Scriptures inform us of a division between the people and the priesthood. This division corresponds to events during the postdiluvian era. This Dispensation of Human Government witnessed a separation of the languages and of the three basic divisions of the human race.

Second, at the Tower of Babel the various lineages of Shem, Ham, and Japheth were scattered, and the bounds were set. Likewise, God told Moses to set bounds about the Mount and sanctify it.

Third, God spoke audibly to the people of Israel and gave to them the most profound set of laws in human history—the Ten Commandments. No nation or group of nations has ever been able to improve upon these laws. With the Ten Commandments, God established a governing covenant for Israel—corresponding to the Dispensation of Human Government.

The third Dispensation is called "Human Government," because of events surrounding the building of the Tower of Babel. The people established a form of government and built the city with its monument to human ingenuity.

"*And the whole earth was of one language, and of one speech.*

"*And it came to pass, as they journeyed from the east, that they found a plain in the land of Shinar; and they dwelt there.*

"*And they said one to another, Go to, let us make brick, and burn them thoroughly. And they had brick for stone, and slime had they for mortar.*

"*And they said, Go to, let us build us a city and a tower, whose top may reach unto heaven; and let us make us a name, lest we be scattered abroad upon the face of the whole earth.*

"*And the LORD came down to see the city and the tower, which the children of men builded.*

"*And the LORD said, Behold, the people is one, and they have all one language; and this they begin to do: and now nothing will be restrained from them, which they have imagined to do.*

"*Go to, let us go down, and there confound their language, that they may not understand one another's speech.*

"*So the LORD scattered them abroad from thence upon the face of all the earth: and they left off to build the city.*

"*Therefore is the name of it called Babel; because the LORD did there confound the language of all the earth: and from thence did the LORD scatter them abroad upon the face of all the earth*" (Genesis 11:1-9).

Babel was not a skyscraper that stretched into the stratosphere. It was a temple of worship. At its top was a "holy of holies" of sorts, where the people erected images of idolatry—the sun (Baal), the moon (Ishtar), and other signs of the zodiac which the people regarded as gods. No wonder God said in the first and second commandments:

"Thou shalt have no other gods before me.

"Thou shalt not make unto thee any graven image, or any likeness of any thing that is in heaven above ..." (Exodus 20:3-4).

These commandments appear to be a direct reference to the Tower of Babel and the Dispensation of Human Government.

Fourthly, The languages were changed at Babel. This compares with an unusual event that occurred when God spoke from the summit of Sinai. Joseph Good, author of ROSH HASHANAH AND THE MESSIANIC KINGDOM TO COME writes,

"The Revelation at Sinai, it was taught, was given in desert territory, which belongs to no one nation exclusively; and it was heard not by Israel alone, but by the inhabitants of all the earth. The Divine Voice divided itself into the seventy tongues then spoken on earth, so that all the children of men might understand its world embracing and man-redeeming message." [3]

The Jewish commentary, Exodus, Rabba says,

"When G-d[4] gave the Torah on Sinai, He displayed untold marvels to Israel with His voice. What happened? G-d spoke and the Voice reverberated throughout the world.... It says, *'And all the people witnessed the thunderings'* (Exodus. 20:15). Note that it does not say 'the thunder,' but *'the thunderings;'* wherefore, R. Johanan said that G-d's voice, as it was uttered, split up into sev-

---

[3] Joseph Good, *Rosh Hashanah and the Messianic Kingdom to Come*, (Port Arthur, Texas: Hatikva Ministry, 1989), p. 30, quoting Rabbi Joseph Hertz, in his *Authorized Daily Prayer Book* (p. 791).

[4] Jewish theologians leave out the vowel in the names of God out of reverence, to insure that they do not take the name of God in vain.

enty voices, in seventy languages, so that all the nations should understand. When each nation heard the Voice in their own vernacular, their souls departed [i.e. they were in fear], save Israel, who heard but who were not hurt." [5]

Rabbi Moshe Weissman, in THE MIDRASH SAYS, writes,

"On the occasion of matan Torah (the giving of the Torah), the Bnai Yisrael (the children of Israel) not only heard Hashem's (the L-rd's) Voice but actually saw the sound waves as they emerged from Hashem's (the L-rd's) mouth. They visualized them as a fiery substance. Each commandment that left Hashem's (the L-rd's) mouth traveled around the entire camp and then came back to every Jew individually, asking him, "Do you accept upon yourself this Commandment with all halachot (Jewish law) pertaining to it?" Every Jew answered, "Yes," after each Commandment. Finally, the fiery substance which they saw, engraved itself on the luchot (tablets)." [6]

As a reference to Babel, when all languages were established, God is said to have spoken in every language at the same time. By giving the Torah (Law), God was establishing a divine government to counter "human government." Yes, Moses' third ascent to the summit of Mt. Sinai corresponded to the Dispensation of Human Government. A side note: the voice of God came from His mouth as if they were "tongues" (languages) of fire speaking every language. This

---

[5] Exodus, Rabba 5.9

[6] Rabbi Moshe Weissman, *The Midrash Says* (Benei Yakov Publications, 1980), p. 182.

Sinai experience occurred on the very same calendar day that later became known as Pentecost! Both the Dispensation of Law and the Dispensation of Grace were inaugurated on the same day! Both occasions witnessed the voice of God as *"tongues of fire,"* in which all languages were heard simultaneously!

Moses' Fourth Encounter:
The Dispensation of Promise

Moses' fourth ascent to the summit is recorded in Exodus 20:21 to 24:3. The account can be divided into three basic categories:

1. God told Moses to make an altar of earth.
2. God elaborated upon the Ten Commandments.
3. God promised to bring them into the Land.

> *"An altar of earth thou shalt make unto me, and shalt sacrifice thereon thy burnt-offerings, and thy peace-offerings, thy sheep, and thine oxen: in all places where I record my name I will come unto thee, and I will bless thee"* (Exodus 20:24).

First, the *"altar of earth"* appears to be a temporary place of worship until the Tabernacle could be constructed. It was not to be the final form of worship. It represented the *"promise"* of a better thing. It is typical of the Dispensation of Promise wherein God called Abraham to leave his home and move to a land of *"promise"*—a land which *"flowed with milk and honey"*—to look for a city *"whose Builder and Maker is God."*

> *"By faith Abraham, when he was called to go out into a place which he should after receive for an inheritance, obeyed; and he went out, not knowing whither he went.*
>
> *"By faith he sojourned in the land of promise, as in a strange country, dwelling in tabernacles with Isaac and Jacob, the heirs with him of the same promise:*
>
> *"For he looked for a city which hath foundations, whose builder and maker is God"* (Hebrews 11:8-10).

The word *"promise"* is used twice in the above passage, indicating the theme of the dispensation. God dealt with Abraham, Isaac, and Jacob by a promise—the Abrahamic Covenant. The account is given in Genesis 15.

> *"And he brought him forth abroad, and said, Look now toward heaven, and tell the stars, if thou be able to number them: and he said unto him, So shall thy seed be.*
>
> *"And he believed in the LORD; and he counted it to him for righteousness.*
>
> *"And he said unto him, I am the LORD that brought thee out of Ur of the Chaldees, to give thee this land to inherit it"* (Genesis 15:5-7).

The Abrahamic Covenant promised a coming *"seed"* and a Promised Land. Furthermore, it was accepted by faith. Now at Sinai, Moses was given the same kind of promise. Just as Abraham wandered and sojourned in the desert areas of the Promised Land, even so Moses and the Chosen People had to wander in the wilderness for forty years. The altar of earth was temporary. Even the Tabernacle was temporary. God eagerly awaited a future Temple to be built on Mt. Moriah in Jerusalem. But, life must continue during this interim period, so God gives further instructions about His moral law:

"Now these are the judgments which thou shalt set before them" (Exodus 21:1).

Secondly, During Moses' second forty days on the summit, God will greatly expand the Law to include 613 commandments. God brings the Dispensation of Promise to a close and opens a new era—the Dispensation of Law.

Thirdly, God proposes to make good on His promise to Abraham. He is about to give Israel their Promised Land.

"I will send hornets before thee which shall drive out the Hivites, and the Canaanites, and the Hittites, from before thee.

"And He said, I will not drive them out from before thee in one year, lest the land become desolate and the beast of the field multiply against thee.

"By little and little I will drive them out from before thee, until thou be increased and inherit the land" (Exodus 23:28-30).

What God promised to Abraham, Isaac and Jacob, He is about to bring to pass through Moses. This will complete the Dispensation of Promise and institute the Dispensation of Law.

Moses' Fifth Encounter:
The Dispensation of Law

Moses' fifth trip to the top of Sinai is recorded in Exodus 24:9-32:14. Moses spends forty days and forty nights in the presence of God—a perfect parallel to the Dispensation of Law.

It begins on a mountain called Sinai and concludes on a mountain called Calvary. It begins with the giving of the Law and concludes with the death of the Lawgiver.

> *"Then went up Moses, and Aaron, Nadab, and Abihu, and seventy of the elders of Israel:*
>
> *"And they saw the God of Israel: and there was under his feet as it were a paved work of a sapphire stone, and as it were the body of heaven in his clearness.*
>
> *"And upon the nobles of the children of Israel he laid not his hand: also they saw God, and did eat and drink.*
>
> *"And the Lord said unto Moses, Come up to me into the mount, and be there: and I will give thee tables of stone, and a law, and commandments which I have written; and thou mayest teach them"* (Exodus 24:9-12).

According to the Scripture, Moses and Joshua, left the elders in the care of Aaron and Hur and went up into the mount. The Shekinah Glory descended upon the mount and hovered there for six days. On the seventh day God called unto Moses out of the midst of the cloud of glory:

> *"And Moses went into the midst of the cloud, and gat him up into the mount: and Moses was in the mount forty days and forty nights"* (v. 18).

During this time God delivered the Ten Commandments on tables of stone, plans for the Tabernacle and the pattern for the priesthood. Also, He instructed Moses in the service of sacrifices.

Forty days! Why forty days? Could these days be a

prophetic picture of the time involved in the Dispensation of Law? If so, then how could forty days fit into the picture? As I pondered this question, I remembered the Jubilee—the fiftieth year. There are forty Jubilees in 1960 years.

According to the Talmud (Sanhedrin 97B), Rabbinical theologians wrote that there should be 2,000 years of desolation, 2,000 years wherein the Torah would flourish; and 2,000 years for the Messianic era—followed by a seventh millennium wherein the Messiah would be exalted.

Therefore, let me suggest that we include the Dispensation of Promise in the overall picture of this period—the Dispensation of Law. The total time given by rabbinical scholars for the "flourishing of the Torah" is 2,000 years, thus combining the Abrahamic Covenant of Promise (500 years) with the Mosaic Covenant of Law (1,500 years).

Likewise, though the tables of stone containing the Ten Commandments were given during this fifth trip of Moses, the Law was spoken orally on the occasion of Moses' fourth trip, which symbolized the Dispensation of the Promise. Therefore, the possibility exists that the forty days spent by Moses in the presence of God were comparable to forty periods of Jubilee, during which time the "Torah flourished."

A Jubilee was commanded to be observed every forty nine years. Therefore, over a period of 1960 years the people should observe forty Jubilees. Some theologians feel the forty days and nights Moses spent in the presence of God may well be symbolic of forty Jubilees. Those forty days ended with a rejection of Moses' efforts, the building of a golden calf, and the breaking of God's law. As a prophetic overview of the Dispensation of Law, the rebellion of Israel fits quite well with the rejection of Christ some 2,000 years later.

What a perfect parallel! How marvelously the ministry of Moses matches the mission of the Messiah. No wonder Moses wrote, *"God shall raise up unto thee a prophet like unto me."*

Transition Between Law and Grace

While Moses was atop Mt. Sinai, Joshua also was nearby. When Moses began his descent, Joshua joined him:

> *"And Moses turned, and went down from the mount, and the two tables of the testimony were in his hand: the tables were written on both their sides; on the one side and on the other were they written.*
>
> *"And the tables were the work of God, and the writing was the writing of God, graven upon the tables.*
>
> *"And when Joshua heard the noise of the people as they shouted, he said unto Moses, There is a noise of war in the camp"* (Exodus 32:15-17).

How prophetic that Joshua accompanied Moses down the mountain at the close of his fifth trip! It is a perfect profile of that prophet whom God would raise up *"like unto Moses!"* The name Joshua in the Old Testament is basically the same as the name Jesus in The New Testament. Furthermore, it was Joshua who succeeded Moses after his death on Mount Nebo. It was Joshua who led the children of Israel into the Promised Land. Surely, the name of the Messiah could have been nothing other than Joshua—the Hebrew counterpart for the Greek word translated Jesus.

As they descend, Moses and Joshua hear a clamor in the camp. They arrive to find a golden calf. At this point, Moses brakes the tables of stone, grinds the golden calf to powder, spreads it upon the water, and makes the people drink. This tragic affair culminates in the deaths of 3,000 men:

> "And he said unto them, Thus saith the Lord God of Israel, Put every man his sword by his side, and go in and out from gate to gate throughout the camp, and slay every man his brother, and every man his companion, and every man his neighbor.
>
> "And the children of Levi did according to the word of Moses: and there fell of the people that day about three thousand men" (Exodus 32:27-28).

The number reminds me of 3,000 converts who submitted to baptism following Peter's sermon. Baptism is a symbol of death, corresponding with the deaths of those who helped build the golden calf. Therefore, the converts at Pentecost correspond to the loss of those who died at Sinai.

Moses' Sixth Encounter:
The Dispensation of Grace

Now, for the sixth time, Moses approaches the Lord on behalf of Israel. This time he offers himself as a substitute—a profile of Christ, the Great Substitute. Moses becomes a mediator:

"*And Moses returned unto the Lord, and said, Oh, this people have sinned a great sin, and have made them gods of gold.*

"*Yet now, if thou wilt, forgive their sin; and if not, blot me, I pray thee, out of thy book which thou hast written*" (Exodus 32:31-32).

It is here that we can see the ministry of Christ. Moses became the "mediator" before the Lord. He said, "*... forgive ... and if not, blot me, I pray thee, out of thy book ...*" Moses offered himself as a substitute for the people. In like manner, Christ became our "Great Substitute." On Calvary He prayed, "*... Father, forgive them; for they know not what they do....*" (Luke 23:34). Then from the cross He prayed, "*... My God, my God, why hast thou forsaken me?*" (Matthew 27:46). The Great Substitute is pictured here as Moses prays, "*Forgive ... and if not, blot me ... out of thy book.*"

This encounter prophetically compares with those transition years which concluded with the Dispensation of Law and instituted the Dispensation of Grace:

"*... Depart, and go up hence, thou and the people which thou hast brought up out of the land of Egypt, unto the land which I sware unto Abraham, to Isaac, and to Jacob, saying, Unto thy seed will I give it:*

"*And I will send an angel before thee; and I will drive out the Canaanite, the Amorite, and the Hittite, and the Perizzite, the Hivite, and the Jebusite:*

"*Unto a land flowing with milk and honey: for I will not go up in the midst of thee: for thou art a stiffnecked people: lest I consume thee in the way*" (Exodus 33:1-3).

At this point God turns from the Jewish people in the same way He turned from Israel after the crucifixion, setting aside the Jews and taking His message of salvation to the Gentiles. God said that He would not *"go up in the midst"* of Israel. In a symbolic gesture, Moses returned to his home, took his tent:

> *"... and pitched it without the camp, afar off from the camp, and called it the tabernacle of the congregation"* (Exodus 33:7).

This was not the proposed Tabernacle containing a Holy Place and Holy of Holies. This was Moses' own tent. Moses went to his home, dismantled his tent, took it outside the camp, and raised it up. It is a prophetic picture of the Lord Jesus Christ who left the camp of Israel and pitched His Tabernacle, or New Testament Church, outside the camp—among the Gentile nations.

With the children of Israel looking on, Moses and Joshua entered the tent:

> *"And it came to pass, as Moses entered into the tabernacle, the cloudy pillar descended, and stood at the door of the tabernacle, and the Lord talked with Moses.*
>
> *"And all the people saw the cloudy pillar stand at the tabernacle door: and all the people rose up and worshiped, every man in his tent door.*
>
> *"And the Lord spake unto Moses face to face, as a man speaketh unto his friend. And he turned again into the camp: but his servant Joshua, the Son of Nun, a young man, departed not out of the tabernacle"* (Exodus 33:9-11).

When Moses left the tent, Joshua stayed! This is a prophetic picture of the future Messiah who should follow Moses. It is a fulfillment of Moses' prophecy of the Prophet who would be raised up in his likeness. Just as Joshua stayed in the tent, Jesus Christ, the Jewish Messiah, left His people to establish New Testament Gentile Christianity. And Jesus is still in the New Testament Church today. How perfect then, is the parallel—Joshua stayed in the tent!

Moses Finds Grace

In the following encounter, Moses finds grace in God's sight:

> *"And Moses said unto the Lord, See, thou sayest unto me, Bring up this people: and thou hast not let me know whom thou wilt send with me. Yet thou hast said, I know thee by name, and thou hast also found **grace** in my sight.*
>
> *"Now therefore, I pray thee, if I have found **grace** in thy sight, shew me now thy way, that I may know thee, that I may find **grace** in thy sight: and consider that this nation is thy people.*
>
> *"And he said, My presence shall go with thee, and I will give thee rest.*
>
> *"And the Lord said unto Moses, I will do this thing also that thou hast spoken: for thou hast found **grace** in my sight, and I know thee by name"* (Exodus 33:12-14,17).

The word *"grace"* is the key. Just as Moses and the children of Israel found grace (unmerited favor) in the sight of God, even so, after Christ's death on Calvary, a new dispensation was instituted—the Dispensation of Grace:

"For by grace are ye saved through faith; and that not of yourselves, it is the gift of God" (Ephesians 2:8).

This sixth encounter with God, along with its attending events, seems to be a prophetic picture of the First Advent of Christ to establish the Dispensation of Grace. When Christ came that first time, He found Israel filled with unbelief. Instead of setting up the Kingdom, He went to the cross to obtain grace.

Moses' Seventh Encounter:
The Dispensation of the Kingdom

After Moses' sixth encounter, he asked the Lord to show him His glory. It is here that God promised Moses that, though he could not see His face, he would be allowed to see His back side. The preparation began for Moses' seventh and final trip to the top of Sinai:

"And he hewed two tables of stone like unto the first; and Moses rose up early in the morning, and went up unto mount Sinai, as the Lord had commanded him, and took in his hand the two tables of stone.

"And the Lord descended in the cloud, and stood with him there, and proclaimed the name of the Lord.

"And the Lord passed by before him, and proclaimed, The Lord, The Lord God, merciful and gracious, longsuffering, and abundant in goodness and truth" (Exodus 34:4-6).

It is here that Moses appears to follow a prophetic scenario which parallels Pentecost

when tongues like as of fire descended upon the
believers. Moses ascends the mountain where he
will spend a second period of forty days. This
seems to be a prophetic type of Christ, who ascended in clouds of glory. Thus began His long
stay in the presence of God. So far, He has not yet
returned to earth.

These forty days seem to be a prophetic picture of
another set of forty Jubilee periods. If this is the
case, then Jesus should return soon. We may now
be in the countdown for the coming of Messiah!

At this point, Moses illustrated the present work
of Christ before the throne of God:

> *"And Moses made haste, and bowed his head toward
> the earth, and worshiped.*
>
> *"And he said, If now I have found* **grace** *in thy sight, O
> Lord, let my Lord, I pray thee, go among us; for it is a
> stiffnecked people; and pardon our iniquity and our sin,
> and take us for thine inheritance"* (Exodus 34:8-9).

Here Moses acts as a mediator. In like manner,
the Lord Jesus Christ has ascended into heaven to
become our Advocate before the Father. He is our
High Priest who has gone to plead our case.

In response to the prayer of Moses, God agrees to
go. But He also warned of severe punishment
which would befall the Jewish people:

> *"And he said, Behold, I make a covenant: before all thy
> people I will do marvels, such as have not been done in
> all the earth, nor in any nation: and all the people
> among which thou art shall see the work of the Lord: for
> it is a terrible thing that I will do with thee"* (Exodus
> 34:10).

This appears to be a promise that God will bring great judgment and tribulation upon the Jewish people. In direct fulfillment of that prophecy, over the past 2,000 years the Jews have suffered. They suffered in A.D. 70 when Titus and his Roman soldiers destroyed the Temple. They suffered in A.D. 135 under the great Diaspora when the Romans scattered the Jews and sold them on the slave markets of the world.

The Jews have suffered the persecutions of Imperial Rome; the Crusades and Inquisitions of Religious Rome; the pogroms or massacres of the Russian Czars; and the Holocaust of Hitler. One day, they will experience the worst period of suffering they have ever known. God predicted a coming Tribulation Period—referred to in the prophecies of Jeremiah as *"Jacob's trouble."*

God said to Moses, *"... I will do marvels, such as have not been done in all the earth, nor in any nation ... for it is a terrible thing that I will do with thee."* I believe this prophecy includes the future Tribulation Period. Jesus said in Matthew 24:21:

> *"For then shall be great tribulation, such as was not since the beginning of the world to this time, no, nor ever shall be. And except those days should be shortened, there should no flesh be saved ..."* (Matthew 24:21).

Exodus 34:28 tells us that Moses *"... was there with the Lord forty days and forty nights; he did neither eat bread, nor drink water. And he wrote upon the tables the words of the covenant, the Ten Commandments."* Moses fasted forty days.

There were three people in the Bible who fasted

for forty days—Moses, Elijah, and Jesus. Moses fasted on top of Sinai. Elijah spent forty days fasting on Mount Sinai. And Jesus went into the "wilderness" to fast for forty days. Perhaps He fasted at the same place:

> *"Then was Jesus led up of the Spirit into the wilderness to be tempted of the devil.*
>
> *"And when he had fasted forty days and forty nights, he was afterwards ahungered"* (Matthew 4:1-2).

Jesus went into the wilderness. The Scripture does not say which wilderness. It is possible that He went all the way to Sinai and fasted there. It would seem fitting that Jesus follow the footsteps of Moses and Elijah in his forty day fast.

The Second Coming of Moses

Finally, after forty days, Moses came down the mountain. His return to the camp of Israel is a tremendous prophetic picture of the Second Coming of Christ.

> *"And it came to pass, when Moses came down from Mt. Sinai with the two tables of testimony in Moses' hand, when he came down from the mount, that Moses wist not that the skin of his face shone while he talked with him.*
>
> *"And when Aaron and all the children of Israel saw Moses, behold, the skin of his face shone; and they were afraid to come nigh him"* (Exodus 34:29-30).

When Moses made his final descent from Sinai, he returned to the people in power and great glory. Likewise, in perfect prophetic fulfillment, Jesus will return one day in clouds of glory. Moses received that glory at the beginning of the forty days period and revealed it unto his people when he returned. In like manner, Jesus received His glory at the moment of His resurrection and shall reveal it to the world when He returns.

When Moses returned to the people after his seventh trip to the top of Sinai, he began the construction of the Tabernacle. This is exactly what the Messiah will do when He comes to establish His Kingdom. He will build the Millennial Temple. Zechariah predicted it:

> *"And speak unto him, saying, Thus speaketh the Lord of hosts, saying, Behold the man whose name is The Branch; and he shall grow up out of his place, and he shall build the temple of the Lord:*
>
> *"Even he shall build the temple of the Lord; and he shall bear the glory, and shall sit and rule upon his throne; and he shall be a priest upon his throne: and the counsel of peace shall be between them both"* (Zechariah 6:12-13).

According to this prophecy, the Messiah will build the Temple when He comes, just as Moses built the Tabernacle in the wilderness after the conclusion of his final forty days. Christ will return to Earth someday (perhaps at the end of forty Jubilees), in power and great glory to build the Temple and establish His Kingdom on the earth.

Notice that the entire sequence of events began in the third month of the year. According to the book of Jasher (an ancient apocryphal book), the Law was given on the sixth day of the third month. This corresponds with Pentecost. How fascinating to contemplate the possibility that Pentecost marked the introductions of both dispensations— the Dispensation of Law and the Dispensation of Grace!

Moses made his descent in power and great glory on Yom Kippur, the Day of Atonement. That day represents a prophetic picture of another great sacrifice to be made by God in the midst of the Battle of Armageddon. Blood will run as deep as the horses' bridles. The Day of Atonement is also a prophetic picture of the coming of Jesus Christ in power and great glory at the conclusion of Armageddon.

Indeed, the story of the ages is played out prophetically in the life and ministry of Moses. No wonder Moses said in Deuteronomy 18:15: *"The Lord thy God will raise up unto thee a Prophet from the midst of thee, of thy brethren, like unto me; unto him ye shall harken."*

In this study we have noted how these seven divine encounters of Moses correspond to the great dispensations of human history. It is marvelous to note how history compares with these scriptures. Obviously the Bible was not of human origin. Only God could have foreseen the future and could have guided Moses to become a prophetic pattern of those events which should one day bring forth the redemption of man.

Chapter Eighteen

Grace in the Wilderness

"Thus saith the LORD, The people which were left of the sword found grace in the wilderness; even Israel, when I went to cause him to rest" (Jeremiah 31:2).

The Dispensation of Grace was introduced by Jesus Christ. He provided eternal life through His death and resurrection. However, this New Testament (or Covenant) was actually given to Israel at the close of their wilderness journey.

The prophet Jeremiah said that Israel *"found grace in the wilderness."* Please note that this *"grace"* was found by those who *"were left of the sword"* at the conclusion of their 40 years *"when I went to cause him to rest."*

In Deuteronomy 29, the Lord gave Moses and the children of Israel another covenant which would someday supercede the covenant of Law. The passage is prophetic and would await its fulfillment in several stages:

*"These are the words of the covenant, which the Lord commanded Moses to make with the children of Israel in the land of Moab, **beside** the covenant which he made with them in Horeb"* (Deuteronomy 29:1).

Israel is in Moab, at the foot of Mt. Nebo. Moses is about to take his last journey up the mountain to view the Promised Land and die. The Mosaic Covenant was established some 40 years before. It is comprised of 613 laws governing every aspect of Jewish life. The people and their future generations are bound to it.

However, at this point, God gives the promise of a New Covenant which would be fulfilled in several stages, but which would, in time, replace the Mosaic Covenant. As we look at this covenant, we will discover that it is the very covenant established by Jesus Christ on the night of the Last Supper. You may recall, Jesus picked up the cup and said:

"For this is my blood of the new testament, which is shed for many for the remission of sins" (Matthew 26:28).

This *"testament"* is the word used to explain the meaning of the term "covenant." Let us not confuse the use of the word covenant with its meaning today. A covenant usually refers to a contract entered into and agreed upon by two parties. Not so with a testament. A testament is imposed upon the second party by its author. Let me explain.

Our Bible is divided into two sections: the Old Testament and the New Testament. They are called testaments because they were written by God, not by man. Furthermore, they were imposed upon men by their author. They are not covenants in the sense that we would enter into an agreement. They are, instead, the testaments of God, who wishes to give us an inheritance—the inheritance of eternal life.

If you have a Last Will and Testament, it most likely says that you wish to leave your estate to your heirs. It is not an agreement between you and your children. It is not a contract that they helped to draw up. You are the only one who wrote it and you are the one who stipulated who the heirs should be.

Now, here is the most important feature of your Last Will and Testament. You must die before the testament takes effect. In the New Testament book of Hebrews, chapter 9, verses 16 and 17, this New Testament is explained:

> *"For where a testament is, there must also of necessity be the death of the testator.*
>
> *"For a testament is of force after men are dead: otherwise it is of no strength at all while the testator liveth"* (Hebrews 9:16-17).

By the way, here is the reason why some people think that salvation is obtained by works. They confuse the meaning of the New Testament and think that it is a covenant or contract entered into by both parties and therefore can be broken by not living up to its requirements. I am happy to inform you that the New Testament is a legal document providing us with the inheritance of eternal life and came into effect upon the death of Jesus Christ. It is a gift to be received, and not a wage which must be earned.

Provision Number One:
Israel Will Be Blind and Deaf

Now let us return to Deuteronomy 29 and review the provisions of this promised New Testament:

"And Moses called unto all Israel, and said unto them, Ye have seen all that the Lord did before your eyes in the land of Egypt unto Pharaoh, and unto all his servants, and unto all his land;

"The great temptations which thine eyes have seen, the signs, and those great miracles:

"Yet the Lord hath not given you an heart to perceive, and eyes to see, and ears to hear, unto this day" (Deuteronomy 29:2-4).

Here is the first provision of this New Covenant or Testament. Israel must be made blind and deaf to the spiritual program which God has planned. Note very carefully, the terminology of verse 4, *"Yet the Lord hath not given you an heart to perceive, and eyes to see, and ears to hear, unto this day."* We will find that verse quoted by the Apostle Paul in Romans 11:8:

"According as it is written, God hath given them the spirit of slumber, eyes that they should not see, and ears that they should not hear; unto this day" (Romans 11:8).

In this passage, Paul is explaining Israel's position in the New Covenant. Romans 9, 10, and 11 deal with the subject. Paul is explaining that God has turned to the Gentiles, including them in his inheritance of eternal life.

In order to carry out this plan, however, he must

make the children of Israel spiritually blind and deaf. The Author of the Testament must die before the inheritance can be divided.

Jesus died to fulfill the provisions of the Old Testament and at the same time to initiate the provisions of the New Testament. The author of the book of Hebrews explains how the death of Christ covered both covenants:

> *"And for this cause he is the mediator of the new testament, and that by means of death, for the redemption of the transgressions that were under the first testament, they which are called might receive the promise of eternal inheritance"* (Hebrews 9:15).

By His death on Calvary, Christ carried out the provisions of both covenants. He paid the penalty imposed by the first covenant while introducing the provisions of the New Covenant. And provision number one says they must be blind and deaf.

Provision Number Two:
The Abrahamic Covenant Is Incorporated Into This New Covenant

Now let's return to Deuteronomy 29 to review provision number two: This covenant includes and preserves the covenant made with Abraham:

> *"That he may establish thee today for a people unto himself, and that he may be unto thee a God, as he hath said unto thee, and as he hath sworn unto thy fathers, to Abraham, to Isaac, and to Jacob"* (Deuteronomy 29:13).

We cannot forget that God has promised Abraham, Isaac, and Jacob the inheritance of the land of Palestine. There are some theologians who say that God has forever forsaken Israel—that the Christian Church has replaced the Jews. This is not the case. We have been included into the commonwealth of Israel, but we have not replaced God's Chosen People. The provisions of this New Covenant preserves the covenant promises made to Abraham, Isaac, and Jacob and the 1948 birth of Israel is very much a part of this New Covenant.

Let us look at the covenant made with Abraham and note that it is included in this New Covenant:

> *"And he [God] brought him forth abroad, and said, look now toward the heaven, and tell the stars, if thou be able to number them: and he said unto him, so shall thy seed be.*
>
> *"And he believed in the Lord; and he counted to him righteousness.*
>
> *"In the same day the Lord made a covenant with Abraham, saying, unto thy seed have I given this land, from the river of Egypt, to the great river, Euphrates"* (Genesis 15:5,6,18).

God did not give Abraham 613 commandments or even 10 to keep. He promised simply by grace that the seed of Abraham would inherit a portion of land on planet Earth, located between the river of Egypt and the river Euphrates. God promised Abraham a Chosen People and a Promised Land. There were no laws or conditions to keep in this covenant. God did not threaten to take away the land and destroy the people if they did not obey Him. The covenant promised to Abraham was strictly a Covenant of Grace and must therefore be fulfilled. Furthermore, the seed mentioned to Abraham included the promise of a Messiah:

> *"Now to Abraham and his seed were the promises made. He saith not, And to seeds, as of many; but as of one, And to thy seed, which is Christ"* (Galatians 3:16).

So the Abrahamic Covenant provided for a Chosen People, a Promised Land, and a coming Messiah to carry out the provisions of that Covenant.

Now, when God made a New Covenant with the children of Israel, in Deuteronomy 29, he included the provisions of that covenant which he made with Abraham:

> *"That he may establish thee today for a people unto himself, and that he may be unto thee a God, as he hath said unto thee, and as he hath sworn unto thy fathers, to Abraham, to Isaac, and to Jacob"* (Deuteronomy 29:13).

There will be a Chosen People, a Promised Land, and a coming Messiah—so said the covenant made with Abraham and so said the covenant made with the children of Israel at the end of their 40 years in the wilderness.

Provision Number Three:
Gentiles Will Be Included in the New Covenant

Now for provision number three: Gentiles will be included in this New Covenant:

> *"Neither with you only do I make this covenant and this oath"* (Deuteronomy 29:14).

Here is the promise that God will include Gentiles in this New Testament. There are to be two kinds of people involved—not the Jews only, but Gentiles as well. That was a mystery not understood until Cornelius, the Roman centurion, accepted Christ at the city of Caesarea. It was a frustration to Peter and the others at first, until the meeting of the council at Jerusalem. James, the moderator of the meeting addressed the assembly:

> *"Simeon hath declared how God at the first did visit the Gentiles, to take out of them a people for his name"* (Acts 15:14).

This was a mystery to the Jews in the first century and remains a point of contention today.

Provision Number Four:
God Will Evict the Chosen People From Their Promised Land

> *"And the LORD shall separate him unto evil out of all the tribes of Israel, according to all the curses of the covenant that are written in this book of the law:*
>
> *"So that the generation to come of your children that shall rise up after you, and the stranger that shall come from a far land, shall say, when they see the plagues of that land, and the sicknesses which the LORD hath laid upon it;*
>
> *"And that the whole land thereof is brimstone, and salt, and burning, that it is not sown, nor beareth, nor any grass groweth therein, like the overthrow of Sodom, and Gomorrah, Admah, and Zeboim, which the LORD overthrew in his anger, and in his wrath:*
>
> *"Even all nations shall say, Wherefore hath the LORD done thus unto this land: why meaneth the heat of this*

great anger:

"Then men shall say, Because they have forsaken the covenant of the LORD God of their fathers, which he made with them when he brought them forth out of the land of Egypt:

"For they went and served other gods, and worshiped them, gods whom they knew not, and whom he had not given unto them:

"And the anger of the LORD was kindled against this land, to bring upon it all the curses that are written in this book" (Deuteronomy 29: 21-27).

God carried out his judgment upon the children of Israel and their land. In A.D. 70, the Romans burned the city of Jerusalem, destroying the Temple and killing thousands. Sixty five years later, in A.D. 135, the Romans once again destroyed the city, even changed Jerusalem's name to Alia Capitolina and deported all Jews to the slave markets of the world. They literally emptied the Promised Land of its Chosen People. That was one of the provisions of this New Covenant given to Moses at the conclusion of their forty years in the wilderness.

While Gentile Christianity has enjoyed the blessings of this New Testament, Israel has suffered severely. We cannot comprehend all of the reasons for it, nor do the Jews understand why they have been scattered among the nations. And that brings us to provision number five.

Provision Number Five:
There Are Some Secret Things

There are some secret things in this New Covenant. They are mysteries known only to God:

"The secret things belong unto the Lord our God; but those things which are revealed belong unto us and to our children forever, that we may do all the words of this law" (Deuteronomy 29:29).

This leaves room for future relevations, including the blindness of Israel, the Dispensation of Gentile Christianity, and the future Tribulation Period. Paul referred to these *"secret things"* in Romans 11:25 where he called them a *"mystery:"*

"For I would not, brethren, that ye should be ignorant of this mystery, lest ye should be wise in your own conceits; that blindness in part is happened to Israel, until the fullness of the Gentiles be come in" (Romans 11:25).

Provision Number Six:
Israel Will Return to Their Promised Land

"And it shall come to pass, when all these things are come upon thee, the blessing and the curse, which I have set before thee, and thou shalt call them to mind among all the nations, whither the LORD thy God hath driven thee,

"And shalt return unto the LORD thy God, and shalt obey his voice according to all that I command thee this day, thou and thy children, with all thine heart, and with all thy soul;

"That then the LORD thy God will turn thy captivity, and have compassion upon thee, and will return and

*gather thee from all the nations, whither the LORD thy
God hath scattered thee"* (Deuteronomy 30:1-3).

The return of the Jews to their Promised Land is
very much a part of the New Covenant made with
Moses at the conclusion of their 40 years in the
wilderness. The Chosen People were not to be forever forsaken. They were to be punished, yes, but
they were also to be returned to their land. The
reason why Jews from all over the world are going
back to Israel in this generation is that God
promised in this New Covenant that He would
bring them back.

In 1892, the first dozen Jews returned to their
Promised Land. In 1898, Theodore Herzl organized the World Zionist Movement. In 1948, the nation was born. Today, some 3.5 million Jews live in
Israel and immigrants continue to come—from
the USSR and Ethiopia by the thousands every
month. We are watching the fulfillment of this
part of the New Covenant.

Provision Number Seven:
Grace Will Replace the Law.

*"And the LORD thy God will circumcise thine heart,
and the heart of thy seed, to love the LORD thy God with
all thine heart, and with all thy soul, that thou mayest
live"* (Deuteronomy 30:6).

This New Covenant will be characterized by a
circumcision of the heart. Jeremiah explained it
further, letting us know that he was referring to
this Deuteronomy passage by quoting the opening
words of the promised New Covenant:

"Behold, the days come, saith the LORD, that I will make a new covenant with the house of Israel, and with the house of Judah:

"Not according to the covenant that I made with their fathers in the day that I took them by the hand to bring them out of the land of Egypt; which my covenant they brake, although I was an husband unto them, saith the LORD:

"But this shall be the covenant that I will make with the house of Israel; After those days, saith the LORD, I will put my law in their inward parts, and write it in their hearts; and will be their God, and they shall be my people.

"And they shall teach no more every man his neighbour, and every man his brother, saying, Know the LORD: for they shall all know me, from the least of them to the greatest of them, saith the LORD: for I will forgive their iniquity, and I will remember their sin no more" (Jeremiah 31:31-34).

The discussion of this New Covenant in Hebrews 8 and 9 not only refers back to the Deuteronomy passage, but quotes the Jeremiah passage as well:

"For this is the covenant that I will make with the House of Israel after those days, saith the LORD; I will put my laws into their mind, and write them in their heart: and I will be to them a God and they shall be to me a people:

"And they shall not teach every man his neighbor, and every man his brother, saying, Know the LORD: for all shall know me, from the least to the greatest.

"For I will be merciful to their unrighteousness, and their sins and their iniquities will I remember no more.

"In that he saith, a new covenant, he hath made the first old. Now that which decayeth and waxeth old is ready to vanish away" (Hebrews 8:10-13).

Here is Provision Number Seven: Grace will replace the Law. God will write his laws into their
hearts. We are already partakers of this Covenant
of Grace, but someday soon, the Jews will have
their spiritual eyes opened, and their spiritual ears
unstopped. Then they will enter into this Covenant
of Grace presently enjoyed by Gentiles.

With the first six provisions of this New Covenant already fulfilled and the Jewish people returning to their Promised Land, we are convinced
the future provisions of this Covenant of Grace will
soon come to pass. God is about to write His laws in
the hearts of the Jews—as He has already done in
the hearts of Gentile Christianity.

There are many more events which will attend
this final provision—among them, seven years of
tribulation, the abomination of desolation, and the
Battle of Armageddon. But the most glorious part
of this New Covenant or Testament of Grace is
given in Hebrews 9:28:

> *"So Christ was once offered to bear the sins of many; and
> unto them that look for him shall he appear the second
> time without sin unto salvation"* (Hebrews 9:28).

Yes, this New Covenant of Grace will be con-
cluded with the glorious Second Coming of Jesus
Christ. With the return of the Jews to the land of
Israel, we have only a few more provisions of this
New Covenant to be fulfilled.

When Was This Covenant Given?

Notice the timing of this New Covenant. It came at the conclusion of Israel's forty years in the wilderness. In those ancient days, after forty years of wandering, they entered the land under the spiritual leadership of Joshua. Their conquest of the land came after Moses' call to spiritual commitment.

What is so amazing to me is that this Covenant of Grace is spelled out by Moses at the end of his career. It is given in Deuteronomy 29-30, just before Moses presented his prophetic "Song of Moses." Even Christian theologians have overlooked the powerful message of Deuteronomy 29-30, and have failed to understand that it is the very covenant which came into effect with the death and resurrection of Jesus Christ and will be given to Israel at His Second Coming. Christian theologians have a tendency to think that the New Testament includes only the gospel of the death, burial and resurrection. But it contains far more than that.

Let us briefly review these seven provisions of the New Covenant, as stated in Deuteronomy 29-30:

1. Israel must be made blind and deaf to God's plan.

2. The Abrahamic Covenant is preserved in this covenant.

3. God will make this covenant with Gentiles as well as Israel.

4. Israel will be evicted from their Promised

Land for a prolonged period of time.

5. This covenant has room for some secret things—to be revealed later.

6. Israel will be returned to their land in the last days.

7. This New Covenant of GRACE will replace the old Covenant of LAW. God will write His law in their hearts.

The first six provisions of this NEW Covenant (or New Testament) have already come to pass. Israel was made blind and deaf to the message of Jesus, thus leading to his crucifixion. They were, subsequently, evicted from their land and have remained in exile for 2,000 years. But in this century, according to the provisions of the covenant, they were returned to their Promised Land. And in 1948, the new state of Israel was born!

Jeremiah Called It
A Covenant of Grace

We are now awaiting the fulfillment of the seventh provision of this NEW Covenant. God has promised to someday write His law in their hearts, showing this covenant to be a Covenant of Grace. In fact, Jeremiah called it just that—a Covenant of Grace:

> *"Thus saith the LORD, The people which were left of the sword found grace in the wilderness; even Israel, when I went to cause him to rest"* (Jeremiah 31:2).

This covenant, described at the end of their wilderness journey, was to be a Covenant of Grace.

Jeremiah said they found *"grace in the wilderness."* The prophet also prefaced his remark with the preceding two verses. Jeremiah 30:24 and Jeremiah 31:1 sets the time frame in which Israel will recognize this Covenant of Grace.

"The fierce anger of the LORD shall not return, until he have done it, and until he have performed the intents of his heart: in the latter days ye shall consider it" (Jeremiah 30:24).

"At the same time, saith the LORD, will I be the God of all the families of Israel, and they shall be my people" (Jeremiah 31:1).

"... in the latter days ye shall consider it."

Though the covenant was predicted in the last chapters of the Mosaic Law, the Jewish people were to be blind and deaf to its provisions until the latter days. And when will those latter days arrive? Jeremiah tells us:

*"For thus saith the LORD; Sing with gladness for Jacob, and shout among the **chief** of the nations: publish ye, praise ye, and say, O LORD, save thy people, the remnant of Israel.*

*"Behold, I will bring them from the **north country**, and gather them from the coasts of the earth, and with them the blind and the lame, the woman with child and her that travaileth with child together: a great company shall return thither"* (Jeremiah 31:7-8).

This is the predicted return of the Chosen People to their Promised Land. God will bring them from the north country (Russia) and from nations all over the world. Even the term *"chief of the nations"* in verse 7 refers to Russia. The Hebrew term for *"chief"* contains the root word "ROSH"— meaning Russia. This *"chief of the nations"* corresponds with the *"chief prince"* in Ezekiel 38:2. We now live in the generation predicted to see this miracle. And the birth of Israel in 1948 proves that these are Jeremiah's predicted *"latter days."*

Jeremiah's New Covenant

God is about to confirm this New Covenant with Israel, just as Jeremiah predicted. The prophet explains the New Covenant which was first given at the end of Israel's 40 years in the wilderness. He places the time frame for this New Covenant into the far future—*"in the latter days."*

When the Chosen People recognize and embrace this New Covenant of Grace, they will realize that it is not a NEW Covenant at all, but one which has been around for thousands of years. Israel will realize that the covenant was available all the time, but they were too blind to see it:

> *"For this commandment which I command thee this day, it is not hidden from thee, neither is it far off.*
>
> *"It is not in heaven, that thou shouldest say, Who shall go up for us to heaven, and bring it unto us, that we may hear it, and do it?*
>
> *"Neither is it beyond the sea, that thou shouldest say, Who shall go over the sea for us, and bring it unto us, that we may hear it and do it?*
>
> *"But the word is very nigh unto thee, in thy mouth, and in thy heart, that thou mayest do it"* (Deuteronomy 30:11-14).

This powerful passage is the subject of Romans 9, 10, and 11. In these New Testament scriptures, we are told about Israel's place in this New Covenant. Romans 10:4-8 is a commentary of this New Covenant given to Moses. The words of Moses are quoted, and they show that the covenant was provided by none other than Jesus Christ Himself:

> *"For Christ is the end of the law for righteousness to every one that believeth.*
>
> *"But the righteousness which is of faith speaketh on this wise, Say not in thine heart, who shall ascend into heaven? (that is, to bring Christ down from above:)*
>
> *"Or, Who shall descend into the deep? (that is, to bring up Christ again from the dead.)*
>
> *"But what saith it? The word is nigh thee, even in thy mouth, and in thy heart: that is the word of faith, which we preach ..."* (Romans 10:4-8).

Someday soon, when Israel recognizes and accepts this New Covenant, they will realize that it is not a NEW Covenant after all. They will not find it in heaven above or in the depths of the sea, but right in front of their eyes. This New Covenant has been in force for 2,000 years, only they could not see it. In fact, this New Covenant has been in their mouths, repeated year after year by Jewish lips, only they could not hear it.

On the Sabbath
Before Rosh Hashanah

Every year, on the Sabbath before Rosh Hashanah, this New Covenant is read aloud in synagogues all over the world. According to the

AMERICAN JEWISH YEAR BOOK, published by the American Jewish Committee, this New Covenant in Deuteronomy 29:9 through Deuteronomy 30:20 is read on the Sabbath day just preceding the Feast of Trumpets.

This text begins with the words, *"Keep therefore the words of this covenant...,"* and ends by saying, *"That thou mayest love the Lord thy God, and that thou mayest obey his voice, and that thou mayest cleave unto him: for he is thy life, and the length of thy days: that thou mayest dwell in the land which the Lord sware unto thy fathers, to Abraham, to Isaac, and to Jacob, to give them."*[1]

Yes, when the time comes to open the eyes and ears of Israel, the words of the covenant won't be in the heavens above, across the sea or under the earth. They will be in the mouths of the Jews around the world, just as they have been for millenia! As Moses said, *"The word is very nigh unto thee, in thy mouth, and in thy heart, that thou mayest do it."*

We must also note at this point that the Jewish recitation of this covenant takes place at a time of prophetic importance: Namely, just before the blowing of the trumpet on Rosh Hashanah! The trumpet blast at the Jewish New Year festival signifies that future time when Israel will have to enter a seven-year period of tribulation. It is to be the time of Jacob's Trouble in which Israel must face the antichrist, the abomination of desolation,

---

[1] Harry Schneiderman, Ed., American Jewish Year Book, (Philadelphia: The American Jewish Committee, 1948), p. 771.

the Battle of Armageddon, and the coming of Messiah to save the day. Every year the covenant is read just before the trumpet is blown!

The Order of Events

This is the prophetic order of events that we expect. **First**, the return of the Jews to their Promised Land; **second**, the suffering of seven years of tribulation; and **third**, the return of Christ to sit upon the throne of David.

After quoting Moses' summation of the covenant in Romans 10, Paul explains at length that Israel, though set aside for a period of time, is not totally rejected. Romans 11:25-29 speak of Israel's restoration in terms of this Covenant of Grace given in Deuteronomy 29:

> "For I would not, brethren, that ye should be ignorant of this mystery, lest ye should be wise in your own conceits; that blindness in part is happened to Israel, until the fullness of the Gentiles be come in.
>
> "And so all Israel shall be saved: as it is written, There shall come out of Zion the Deliverer, and shall turn away ungodliness from Jacob:
>
> "*For this is my covenant unto them*, when I shall take away their sins.
>
> "As concerning the gospel, they are enemies for your sakes: but as touching the election, they are beloved for the fathers' sakes.
>
> "For the gifts and calling of God are without repentance" (Romans 11:25-29).

The message is clear in this passage. The covenant proceeds on the basis of God's grace. It is without limit or condition. Because God is faithful, its provisions have remained in force since the death of Jesus Christ.

Today, there are some theologians who believe that God has forever forsaken Israel—that under this New Testament of Grace, the Church has become heir to all of the promises once given to Israel. This concept is breeding a new form of anti-semitism and Jew-hatred. "Kingdom Now Theology" says that Palestine is filled with a group of Zionist cutthroats. They say that all prophecy was fulfilled in the first century with the destruction of Jerusalem.

What they don't understand is that Israel will never be destroyed again. All of the Arab nations combined cannot rid the Promised Land of its Chosen People. Even the mighty Soviet Union will not be able to drive the Jew from the Middle East. Israel is back to stay. Jeremiah said that the children of Israel will never again be evicted from their land:

> *"Thus saith the LORD, which giveth the sun for a light by day, and the ordinances of the moon and of the stars for a light by night, which divideth the sea when the waves thereof roar; The LORD of hosts is his name:*
>
> *"If those ordinances depart from before me, saith the LORD, then the seed of Israel also shall cease from being a nation before me for ever.*
>
> *"Thus saith the LORD; If heaven above can be measured, and the foundations of the earth searched out beneath, I will also cast off all the seed of Israel for all that they have done, saith the LORD"* (Jeremiah 31:35-37).

God has not forever forsaken Israel. As long as

there is a sun and moon, God will remember His covenant with Israel. As long as there are stars in heaven above, God will keep His promise to Israel. These "Dominion" theologians who would curse the return of the Jew to his land are in gross violation of plain Scripture. God not only promises in Jeremiah's passage that He will return the Jews to Jerusalem, He spells it out very carefully.

Jerusalem's Modern City Limits Predicted by Jeremiah

"Behold, the days come, saith the LORD, that the city shall be built to the LORD from the tower of Hananeel unto the gate of the corner.

"And the measuring line shall yet go forth over against it upon the hill Gareb, and shall compass about to Goath.

"And the whole valley of the dead bodies, and of the ashes, and all the fields unto the brook of Kidron, unto the corner of the horse gate toward the east, shall be holy unto the LORD; it shall not be plucked up, nor thrown down any more for ever" (Jeremiah 31:38-40).

In the day that Jeremiah wrote these words, the city of Jerusalem occupied only a small area along the southern slope of the Temple Mount. It is believed that at the northwest corner of the Temple area stood the tower of Hananeel, where later the fortress of Antonia was built. According to the prophecy, the city limits should expand to the southwest to include the gate of the corner. That should be near the southwestern corner of the old city walls. As it happened, this was exactly the direction of city expansion in the days of Herod and the first century.

Jeremiah's prophecy could not have been describing only the Jerusalem of Jesus' day, for the westward expansion covered roughly the perimeters of the present day walled city. In this century, however, the development of Jerusalem has proceeded in a southwesterly direction from the gate of the corner, culminating at what is today called Mount Herzl, which is most likely the location of the Hill Gareb. The term Gareb means, "scabby." Geologically, we might describe it as layered or stratified deposits of limestone.

Jeremiah's next location covers a wide area, for the Scripture says that it will *"compass about to Goah."* In Hebrew, the word "Goah" refers to the lowing of cattle and implies a vast area of pasture land sweeping around the western and northwestern sides of today's Jerusalem. This description of a future Jerusalem is exactly as the city appears today.

According to Jeremiah, this area also includes *"the whole valley of the dead bodies and of the ashes."* This appears to be a reference to the tombs which have been discovered at the northern reach of the present city of Jerusalem. Today, they are called the Tombs of the Sanhedrin.

The ashes mentioned here are probably the many layers of ashes that accumulated from centuries of Temple sacrifices. They were discovered at the turn of the century by returning settlers who used them to make mortar for their new buildings. These ashes have long since been removed or built upon, so they are no longer visible,

but their location is well documented. The homes
of the Orthodox Jewish Community in the Meah
Shearim are built over those ashes!

Jeremiah's description of the city next moves
eastward to the brook Kidron, then south to the
"corner of the horse gate." Just as prophesied,
Jerusalem has developed along both sides of the
Kidron Valley, from the tombs on the north side of
the city, east and south to the pinnacle of the Temple, at about the spot described by Jeremiah as *"the
horse gate"* which may likely be the place known
today as Solomon's Stables.

In our day, we can see the complete fulfillment
of this prophecy! Please note that Jeremiah's
prophecy did not include the original site of the
city in his day. He was only describing the expansion of the city. The modern city limits of Jerusalem represents a fulfillment of the prophetic
picture given in Jeremiah's prediction.

But we must remember what Jeremiah said
about this modern city. It *"shall be holy unto the
Lord; it shall not be plucked up, nor thrown down
any more forever."* The modern city of Jerusalem
is to stand forever! Through all the agonizing days
to come, we know that this city will remain intact,
ultimately becoming the seat of government for
the entire world.

It is vital, at this point, to note that this prophetic
picture of latter-day Jerusalem is preceded by
Jeremiah's statement concerning this New
Covenant that would be made. We have already
read this in verses 31-34.

This New Covenant Is 3500 Years Old!

This *"new covenant"* is clearly the same covenant given to Moses in Deuteronomy 29, which is a Covenant of Grace, given *"beside the covenant"* of the Law. Of this covenant, we have noted that its language is remarkably similar to the words of the New Covenant which we call the "New Testament." Deuteronomy 30:5-6 says:

> *"And the Lord thy God will bring thee into the land which thy fathers possessed, and thou shalt possess it; and he will do thee good, and multiply thee above thy fathers.*
>
> *"And the Lord thy God will circumcise thine heart, and the heart of thy seed, to love the Lord thy God with all thine heart, and with all thy soul, that thou mayest live"* (Deuteronomy 30:5-6).

This is the centerpiece of the covenant. It not only states that God will give the land to the people, but that their heart of understanding will be opened. Please note: the future spiritual awakening of the Jewish people is secured through the same blood covenant that has awarded salvation to individual believers throughout the Church Age. Hebrews 9:16-17 (quoting the Jeremiah passage) makes this crystal clear. The author of the treatise to the Hebrews writes of this latter-day covenant that God will make with Judah and Israel:

> *"This is the covenant that I will make with them after those days, saith the lord, I will put my laws into their hearts, and in their minds will I write them;*
>
> *"And their sins and iniquities will I remember no more"* (Hebrews 9:16-17).

By grace, God will someday bring the Jewish people under this New Covenant. And we are now awaiting the fulfillment of this prophecy.

When Will This New Covenant Be Made With Israel?

The question now remains. When will this final provision of the covenant take place? When will they be converted to Jesus Christ and under what circumstances? To answer that question we must consider two other covenants which were included in this Covenant of Grace. They are the Abrahamic Covenant and the Davidic Covenant. Both of those covenants were Covenants of Grace. They were divine promises made without any conditions required by either Abraham or David. We have already discussed the Abrahamic Covenant, showing that it was a Covenant of Grace and that it was incorporated into the promises made in Deuteronomy 29-30.

Abraham's Covenant of Grace

While discussing the differences between the Old Testament of Law and the New Testament of Grace, the apostle Paul made a distinct reference to the Abrahamic Covenant:

"What shall we say that Abraham our father, as pertaining to the flesh, hath found?

"For if Abraham were justified by works, he hath whereof to glory; but not before God.

"For what sayeth the scripture? Abraham believed

God, and it was counted unto him for righteous.

"Now to him that worketh is the reward not reckoned of grace, but of debt" (Romans 4:1-4).

Paul went on to explain that Abraham received his covenant long before there was a law and he compares that covenant to the New Covenant or New Testament of Grace.

This is a most important provision of the New Testament. There must be a Chosen People, a Promised Land, and a coming Messiah to carry out the provisions of the covenants. Even though the Jewish people were to be scattered among the nations of the world for a prolonged period of time, our New Covenant or New Testament provides for the latter-day return of the Jewish people to their Promised Land.

David's Covenant of Grace

The next covenant which has been included in our New Covenant is the one made with David:

"Moreover I will appoint a place for my people Israel, and will plant them, that they may dwell in a place of their own, and move no more; neither shall the children of wickedness afflict them anymore, as beforetime,

"And as since the time that I commanded judges to be over my people Israel, and have caused thee to rest from all thine enemies. Also the Lord telleth thee that he will make thee an house.

"And when thy days be fulfilled, and thou shalt sleep with thy fathers, I will set up thy seed after thee, which shall proceed out of thy bowels, and I will establish His kingdom.

"He shall build an house for my name, and I will establish his throne of his kingdom forever.

"I will be his father, and he shall be my son. If he commit iniquity, I will chasten him with the rod of men, and with the stripes of the children of men:

"But my mercy shall not depart away from him, as I took it away from Saul, whom I put away before thee.

"And thine house and thine kingdom shall be established, forever before thee: thy throne shall be established forever" (II Samuel 7:10-16).

There are two basic provisions of this Davidic Covenant. The Chosen People must have a Promised Land, a provision which was made in the Abrahamic Covenant. And second, the seed of David will sit upon the throne of Israel forever. They are two magnificient provisions which are definitely included in the New Covenant which we call the New Testament.

Jesus Christ was from the offspring of King David, and now that the Chosen People are back in their Promised Land, we have the prediction that Jesus will soon come and establish his throne.

Please note that the covenant made with David was a Covenant of Grace with no pre-conditions. The return of the Chosen People to their Promised Land is a promise which cannot be abrogated. Though He has chastised them as He said in verse 14, He also promised David that His mercy would not depart from the *"seed of David."*

After 2,000 years of dispersion among the nations, a Jewish return to the Promised Land in this century fulfills the promise made to David. In spite of Jewish sins, of national iniquity, or of the fact that Israel did not keep the Covenant of Law, God promised the Chosen People a homeland and a Messiah from the lineage of David—by grace, and grace alone. Now let me repeat. The Abrahamic Covenant and the Davidic Covenant were both Covenants of Grace, promised by a loving God, in spite of Israel's sin. And they are both included in the New Covenant or New Testament. In fact, the New Testament opens with this new declaration:

> *"The book of the generation of Jesus Christ, the son of David, the son of Abraham"* (Matthew 1:1).

In this verse which opens the New Testament we are reminded that Jesus Christ is both the Son of Abraham and Son of David, fulfilling both the covenant made with Abraham and the covenant made with David.

When the apostle Paul introduced his epistle to the Romans in which he was to discuss the Covenant of Law and the Covenant of Grace, he reminds us that Jesus Christ is the fulfillment of the covenant made to David:

> *"Concerning his son Jesus Christ, our Lord, which was made of the seed of David according to the flesh"* (Romans 1:3).

Jesus Christ, then, is the fulfillment of both the Abrahamic and Davidic Covenant as well as the fulfillment of the New Covenant made with Moses and the children of Israel in Deuteronomy 29-30.

In Revelation 5:5 we are reminded that Jesus is the fulfillment of the covenant made with David:

*"And one of the elders saith unto me, weep not: Behold,
the lion of the tribe of Judah, the root of David, hath pre-
vailed to open the book and loose the seven seals thereof"*
(Revelation 5:5).

According to the prophecies given in the book of
Revelation, when history reaches its ultimate cli-
max and the world is about to be judged by a holy
God and Christ is about to come to establish His
kingdom, we are reminded that He is the *"root of
David."*

Over and over again, throughout the New Testament, Jesus Christ is presented as the fulfillment of
both the Abrahamic Covenant and the Davidic
Covenant, as well as the New Covenant of Grace
which we call the New Testament. And in each
case, whether it be in Matthew or Romans or
Galatians or the book of the Revelation, these
covenants are distinguished as Covenants of Grace
as opposed to the Covenant of Law which was made
with Israel at Mt. Sinai.

The Ark of the "Old" Covenant

Now let us go back to the Davidic Covenant and
see the occasion of God's promise. David had
brought the Ark of the Covenant to Jerusalem and
had set it up in the Tabernacle of David. Please
understand that the Ark of the Covenant represented a Covenant of Law—the Old Covenant or
the Old Testament. It included the Ten Commandments, along with a total of 613 laws for the children of Israel to keep. On this Ark of the Covenant,
however, there was a Mercy Seat upon which Israel

could find grace.

It was upon the occasion of reestablishing the Old Covenant of Law in Jerusalem that David was given the promise of a New Covenant of Grace. The contrast between the Ark of the Covenant, which represented the throne of God, and the New Covenant upon which the throne of David would be established is evident. And in Revelation 11:15 and 19 the contrast is amplified:

> *"And the seventh angel sounded; and there were great voices in heaven, saying, the kingdoms of this world are become the kingdoms of our Lord, and of his Christ; and he shall reign forever and ever"* (v. 15).
>
> *"And the temple of God was opened in heaven and there was seen in his temple the ark of his testimony: and there were lightnings, and voices, and thunderings, and an earthquake, and great hail"* (v. 19).

Someday, when the seventh angel sounds his trumpet, Christ will establish His kingdom, thus fulfilling the provisions of the New Covenant or New Testament. At that time, *"the temple of God will be open in heaven and there will be seen in his temple the ark of his testimony."* This can only be the Ark of the Old Testament. Now why are both covenants alluded to in Revelation 11? Because when Jesus comes to establish His kingdom, He will fulfill the provisions of the New Covenant or New Testament while at the same time conclude the curses of the Old Covenant or Old Testament.

I believe the Ark of the Covenant has a very important role to be carried out in the future. That brings us to a most important passage of scripture—Psalms 73-89—where we shall consider once again the hidden prophecies in the Psalms.

Psalms 73-89 comprise the third book of the Psalms and correspond with the Mosaic book of Leviticus which deals with the Ark of the Covenant and the establishment of Temple worship. Psalms 73-89 seem to be a prophetic scenario for the return of the Ark of the Covenant to Jerusalem. Remember, David had brought the Ark of the Covenant to Jerusalem just before receiving the Davidic Covenant. The sequence of events fits with the last of the Leviticus Psalms. The theme of Psalm 89 is the Davidic Covenant.

In his procession, David had Asaph, Heman, and Ethan to direct the music, while the sons of Korah carried the Ark of the Covenant on their shoulders. As a prophetic scenario of the return of the Ark to Jerusalem, Psalms 73-83 were written by Asaph, Psalm 88 was written by Heman, and Psalm 89 was written by Ethan. Psalms 84, 85, 87, and 88 were written for the sons of Korah, who carried the Ark of the Covenant upon their shoulders. The Ark itself is typified by Psalm 86.

This leads me to believe that the Ark of the Covenant will be returned to Jerusalem—that the Old Testament or Old Covenant of Law might be reestablished for a period of seven years, wherein Israel will be allowed to make its transition from the Covenant of Law to the Covenant of Grace. If that be so, then it is most important that we understand Psalm 89. It deals with the Davidic Covenant:

"I have made a covenant with my chosen, I have sworn unto David my servant,

"Thy seed will I establish forever, and build up thy throne to all generations. Selah" (Psalm 89:3-4).

For the Covenant of David to be expounded upon in Psalm 89 is most important. Its juxtaposition is prophetically significant. It comes just before the Song of Moses, which is given in Psalms 90-100. The Covenant of David in Psalm 89 is comparable to the juxtaposition of the covenant made with the children of Israel in Deuteronomy 29-30. It is given just prior to the beginning of the Song of Moses in Deuteronomy 32. Both covenants are followed by the Song of Moses. They are evidently related to each other and to the Song of Moses. Someday, Israel will enter into their New Covenant at a time when the prophecies in the Song of Moses began to unfold.

This leads me to believe that the Ark of the Covenant will be returned to Jerusalem and some kind of Temple worship restored. Israel will be brought face to face with the covenant recorded in Deuteronomy 29-30. They will realize that it is the same covenant that Christianity has called the New Testament over these past 2,000 years.

Israel Chose to Live Under the Law

There are some Christian theologians today who say that the Old Testament (Law) was nailed to the Cross and dispensed with—that it does not now exist and never will again. That kind of theology overlooks the fact that God has brought the curses of that Law upon the nation of Israel over the past 2,000 years—to this very day. Let us be reminded that even though Christ was the *"end of the law for righteousness to every one that believeth"* (Romans 10:4), Paul also wrote in the very next verse:

"For Moses describeth the righteousness which is of the law, that the man which doeth those things shall live by them" (Romans 10:5).

And though we live under the provisions of the New Testament of Grace, Israel still lives under the Law. Perhaps that is the covenant which will be confirmed at the beginning of the seven-year Tribulation Period. When the Ark of that Old Testament is returned, we are told in Daniel 9:27 that a covenant will be confirmed for seven years —at the end of which that Old Covenant should finally be concluded:

"And he [the antichrist] *shall confirm the covenant with many for one week: and in the midst of the week he shall cause the sacrifice and the oblation to cease, and for the overspreading of abominations he shall make it desolate, even until the consummation, and that determined shall be poured upon the desolate"* (Daniel 9:27).

The antichrist will establish a covenant. Thus begins the last of the 70 weeks in Daniel's prophecy. The 69th week saw the Messiah cut off. That happened at Calvary. For the past 2,000 years, between the 69th week and the 70th week, we have enjoyed the New Covenant, or New Testament of Grace, while Israel has suffered the curses of the Old Covenant, or Old Testament of

Law. It appears that the Old Covenant must be re-established and the Ark of that Old Covenant returned in order for Israel to make its transition to the New Covenant of Grace.

Ezekiel's Dry Bones

In Ezekiel 37 we are given a prophecy of the return of the Chosen People in order to face the battle of Gog and Magog, welcome the Messiah and set up the kingdom. Ezekiel opens this chapter with the vision of a valley of dry bones. These bones are the whole house of Israel, which will come together just as they have done in 1948. The prophecy continues with the Holy Spirit being breathed upon the nation of Israel. Here is a beautiful promise of God keeping the provisions of the Abrahamic Covenant, the Davidic Covenant, and the New Covenant of Deuteronomy:

"Behold, I will take the children of Israel from among the heathen, whither they be gone, and will gather them on every side, and will bring them into their own land.

"And I will make them one nation in the land upon the mountains of Israel; and one king shall be king to them all: and they shall be no more two nations, neither shall they be divided into two kingdoms any more at all:

"Neither shall they defile themselves any more with their idols, nor with their detestable things, nor with any of their transgressions: but I will save them out of all their dwelling places, wherein they have sinned, and will cleanse them: so shall they be my people, and I will be their God.

"And David my servant shall be king over them and they all shall have one shepherd: they shall also walk in my judgment, and observe my statutes, and do them.

> *"And they shall dwell in the land that I have given unto Jacob my servant wherein your fathers have dwelt; and they shall dwell therein, even they, and their children, and their children's children forever: and my servant David shall be their prince forever.*
>
> *"Moreover I will make a covenant of peace with them; it shall be an everlasting covenant with them: and I will place them, and multiply them, and will set my sanctuary in the midst of them forever more"* (Ezekiel 37:21-26).

Here is the promise fulfilled that God made with Abraham, Moses, and David. There will be a Chosen People and a Promised Land. There will be a *"Seed"* of both Abraham and David, who is none other than the Lord Jesus Christ, to be their King. And finally, God will make a covenant of peace with them. It shall be an everlasting covenant. This is the New Testament of Grace under which we live today. Someday soon the Jewish people will also be brought under this magnificent covenant.

Chapter Nineteen

The Mosaic Tabernacle

On top of a mountain in the middle of a desert long ago and far away, a man stood in the presence of God. His beleaguered followers camped in the desert below awaiting the outcome of his encounter with the Creator.

The man was Moses, and the event occurred 3,500 years ago. Something special happened during those days on Mt. Sinai. God instructed Moses to build a Tabernacle whereby God Himself could dwell among His people. Has not that been the desire of the ages? Oh, that God would dwell among men—that is the blessed hope and, by the way, that is the ultimate message of all prophecy. God will one day dwell among men.

It seems logical then that the Tabernacle should also be a prophetic pattern of God's great plan of the ages pointing toward that golden age when God shall dwell among His people to heal every heartache and wipe away every tear.

The Tabernacle! Everything about it is both symbolic and prophetic. The materials with which it was built bear the message of redemption, and its measurements seem to represent a study in "times." They answer the age-old question, *"When shall these things be? What shall be the sign of thy coming and of the end of the world?"* (Matthew 24:3). The Tabernacle is a symphony of prophecy. More than just a song, it represents a complex harmony of prophetic insight.

Centerpiece of the Camp

The Tabernacle stood in the center of the camp of Israel. The twelve tribes pitched their tents around it, each tribe in its own order.

The tribes of Simeon, Reuben, and Gad lay along its southern side. The tribes of Benjamin, Ephraim, and Manasseh lay along its western side. The tribes of Asher, Dan, and Naphtali lay along its northern side. And the tribes of Issachar, Judah, and Zebulun lay along the eastern side of the Tabernacle.

The tribe of Levi pitched their tents around the perimeter of the Tabernacle. To them was given the religious responsibility of teaching the Law.

The Tabernacle seemed to represent God's second Bible, for those early civilizations did not have the complete written Word. Along with the Tabernacle came the writing of the Torah—the first five books of the Bible: Genesis, Exodus, Leviticus, Numbers, and Deuteronomy. These books, along with the Tabernacle, revealed in further detail God's great plan of the ages.

The White Linen Fence

The courtyard was surrounded by a white linen fence five cubits high. A biblical cubit is said to measure approximately 18 inches. Five cubits, then, represented a fence seven and a half feet tall. The courtyard was 100 cubits (150 feet) long and 50 cubits (75 feet) wide.

The fence was held in place by 60 poles set in sockets of brass rising out of the sand. They were five cubits high, each crowned with a silver cap (called a chapiter). According to Josephus, a first century Jewish historian, each pole had the appearance of a spear. Josephus said:

> "Their chapiters were of silver, but their bases were of brass: they resembled the sharp ends of spears, and were of brass, fixed into the ground."[1]

When Moses prepared for the construction of the Tabernacle, he received a half-shekel offering from each man. The accumulated silver was used in the construction of the Tabernacle.

A half-shekel of silver was used to make each chapiter mounted atop the sixty poles—a total of 30 shekels of silver. Perhaps they correspond to the 30 shekels of silver paid to Judas Iscariot for the betrayal of Jesus Christ.

There were 60 posts made of brass, topped with silver, around the courtyard of the Tabernacle.

---

[1] Flavius Josephus, *The Works Of Josephus*, Trans. William Whiston, A.M. (Lynn, MA: Hendrickson Publishers, 1980), "Antiquities of the Jews," book III, ch. VI, par. 2, p. 71.

The brass represented the judgment of God, and the silver represented redemption. Sixty poles! If the courtyard were a circle, those poles would stand 6 degrees apart, making a total of 360 degrees circumference.

The poles surrounding the courtyard stood five cubits apart. Each linen panel, therefore, was a square five cubits long and five cubits high. I think these numbers could represent a study in "times." Five represents the biblical number of grace. Adding the length and height together produces ten—the number of ordinal perfection. Ten times five is 50—representing the Jubilee.

The width and height of each panel could represent a period of 100 years in the history of the human race. Sixty panels could represent a total of 60 centuries—6,000 years, at the end of which God's Chosen People, who have been living on the perimeter of His presence, will be allowed to enter through gates of glory to stand before God.

Along the eastern side of the linen fence hung the linen gate. The colors of the linen were separated at the gate into the beauty of the blue, the red, and the purple. It is as though the gate provided access whereby the believer could look beyond the white to inspect the intricacies of its source.

Please note, the gate of the Tabernacle lay to the east—facing the rising sun. It was an "eastern gate." That's why we sing, "I'll meet you in the morning just inside the eastern gate." That's why we sing,

"Some golden daybreak Jesus will come,
Some golden daybreak battles all won,
    Then shall the victory break through the blue,
Some golden daybreak for me, and for you."[2]

The Brazen Altar

Just inside the eastern gate stood the brazen altar. It was a place of sacrifice. A repentant sinner could bring his lamb to the altar and have it slain. He would lay his hands upon the head of the animal and confess his sins.

In a spiritual sense, his sins were transferred to that substitute animal being sacrificed in his place. This was a prophetic picture of that day when God would send the ultimate Substitute to take upon Himself the sins of all the world. That's why John the Baptist introduced Jesus Christ in John 1:29 by saying, *"Behold, the Lamb of God which taketh away the sin of the world."*

The word "altar" means "lifted up." It is descriptive of the crucifixion where our Savior was lifted up. Christ was sacrificed as the Substitute for a sinful human race. That is the prophetic fulfillment of the brazen altar which stood just inside the gate—in the courtyard of the Tabernacle. Courtyard? Yes, for there, beside the brazen altar, court convened, and judgment was rendered.

---

[2] Carl Blackmore, *"Some Golden Daybreak"* (Rodeheaver Co., 1962).

The Brazen Laver

Beyond the brazen altar stood the laver. It was also made out of brass—the metal which prophetically portrays judgment. At the brazen altar, men were judged by the Law of God. But at the laver, they judged themselves. The laver was made out of polished mirrored brass so that the one who washed could see himself. It was a place of introspection as one entered the Tabernacle.

The brazen laver appears to be a prophetic picture of baptism. God identified it as such on the Day of Pentecost when 3,000 people were baptized. The number 3,000 corresponds with the number of units of water it took to fill the brazen laver which stood in the courtyard of Solomon's Temple. A description was given by Flavius Josephus:

"Solomon also cast a brazen sea, whose figure was that of a hemisphere. This brazen vessel was called a sea for its largeness, for the laver was ten cubits in diameter, and cast of the thickness of a palm. Its middle part rested on a short pillar ... round about it twelve oxen, that looked to the four winds of heaven, three to each wind, having their hinder parts depressed, that so the hemispherical vessel might rest upon them, which itself was also depressed round about inwardly. Now this sea contained three thousand baths." [3]

II Chronicles 4:5 also reported its contents:

"And the thickness of it was an handbreadth, and the brim of it like the work of the brim of a cup, with flowers

[3] Josephus, *The Works Of Josephus*, "Antiquities of the Jews," book VIII, ch. III, par. 5, p. 175.

of lilies; and it received and held three thousand baths" (II
Chronicles 4:5).

According to the ancient description, the contents
of Solomon's laver seemed to correspond with the
number of people baptized on the day of Pentecost.
The laver then, must have some prophetic
fulfillment in the ordinance of baptism.

May I hasten to add, it is a believer's baptism, for
first the believer must come by way of the brazen
altar with its blood sacrifice. At the brazen altar
the Jew was judged by the Law of God, but at the
laver he judged himself. In like manner, baptism is
a time of self-judgment, a time of introspection, a
time when we prepare ourselves for service as a
priest in "the priesthood of the believer" under the
leadership of our great High Priest and Lord, Jesus
Christ.

The laver seems to represent a transition from
the Dispensation of Law to the Dispensation of
Grace. Under the law men were condemned. Because of our Substitute Sacrifice, however, we can
enter from the condemnation of the Dispensation of
Law into the forgiveness of the Dispensation of
Grace. Pentecost (with its 3,000 baptized believers)
seemed to mark a fulfillment of the prophecy. The
baptized believer is now prepared as a part of the
priesthood to enter into the service of our Savior—
into the Holy Place.

The Tent of the Tabernacle

The Tabernacle was a tent made out of fine-
twined linen. Along the front and the back of that

tent was a border of blue. Upon entering the Tabernacle, the priest could look up and see the blue along the border. It represented heaven, the dwelling place of God. Those blue borders can be seen today on the Israeli flag.

Also, in a symbolic way, the Jewish prayer shawl, called the tallith, represents a miniature Tabernacle. The tallith is worn by the religious Jew when he prays. In a mystical way, when the tallith was worn by the Old Testament Jew, his body became a temple. The fulfillment of that is found in the New Testament. That is why the apostle Paul wrote that the body of the believer becomes the temple of God, and that the Spirit of God dwells or tabernacles within that body:

"Know ye not that ye are the temple of God, and that the Spirit of God dwelleth in you?

"If any man defile the temple of God, him shall God destroy; for the temple of God is holy, which temple ye are" (I Corinthians 3:16,17).

And again, in I Corinthians 6:19 Paul wrote:

"What? Know ye not that your body is the temple of the Holy Ghost which is in you, which ye have of God, and ye are not you own?" (I Corinthians 6:19).

The tallith is made of fine-twined linen with ribbons of blue along its borders. The fringes appear to represent the cords with which the tent of the Tabernacle was staked to the ground. Instructions for the tallith were given at Sinai:

"Speak unto the children of Israel, and bid them that they make them fringes in the borders of their garments

throughout their generations, and that they put upon the fringe of the borders a ribband of blue:

"And it shall be unto you for a fringe, that ye may look upon it, and remember all the commandments of the Lord, and do them ..." (Numbers 15:38-39).

Elijah's mantle was a tallith. Our Savior's vesture, upon which the soldiers gambled, was believed to be a tallith. The Tabernacle represented a giant tallith patterned after the heavenly Tent seen by Moses during his 40 days atop of Mt. Sinai.

The Building

Under the tent of the Tabernacle stood a building 30 cubits long, 10 cubits wide, and 10 cubits high—made of acacia wood, overlaid with gold about the thickness of a postcard. It had two rooms—a Holy Place, and a Holy of Holies.

The Holy Place, with its table of shewbread, altar of incense, and lampstand, corresponds to the Dispensation of Grace. And the Holy of Holies, with its Ark of the Covenant, corresponds to the millennial reign of Christ.

The Tabernacle Disappeared

The Tabernacle disappeared from the pages of history 2,500 years ago, just before the Babylonian army besieged Jerusalem and destroyed Solo-mon's Temple. According to an apocryphal book (II Maccabees 2:4-5) Jeremiah hid the Tabernacle in a cave on Mount Nebo:

"...the prophet, being warned of God, commanded the Tabernacle and the ark to go with him, as he went forth into the mountain, where Moses climbed up, and saw the heritage of God.

"And when Jeremiah came thither, he found an hollow cave, wherein he laid the Tabernacle, and the ark, and the altar of incense, and so stopped the door." [4]

It is also predicted, however, that one day the Tabernacle will be discovered and returned to Jerusalem. Ezekiel 37:26-27 says:

"Moreover I will make a covenant of peace with them; it shall be an everlasting covenant with them: and I will place them, and multiply them, and will set my sanctuary in the midst of them for evermore.

"My tabernacle also shall be with them, yea, I will be their God, and they shall be my people" (Ezekiel 37:26-27).

The prophecy indicates that the Tabernacle will be returned during the days when Magog makes its invasion of Israel. In addition to the Mosaic Tabernacle, it is also predicted that David's Tabernacle will be erected on the Temple Mount:

"In that day will I raise up the tabernacle of David that is fallen, and close up the breaches thereof; and I will raise up his ruins, and I will build it as in the days of old:" (Amos 9:11).

It seems that God led David to copy after Moses in many respects—as we have pointed out in our chapter on the Song of Moses. David produced a Song of Deliverance just before his death—whose

---

[4] *The Apocrypha* (London: Oxford University Press), II Maccabees 2:4-5.

theme was identical to that of the Song of Moses. Also, David used the last words of Moses to introduce the Psalms. David built a tent to house the Ark of the Covenant on Mount Moriah while the Mosaic Tabernacle remained at the high place of Gibeon—just 6 miles northwest of the Temple Mount. These predictions may have a reference to our own generation. If so, both Tabernacles could be discovered and returned to Jerusalem. I believe the Jewish people will reinstitute Temple liturgy after the battle of Gog and Magog—and it appears that we are living in that special generation.

Wouldn't it be exciting to hear on tomorrow's news that the ancient Tabernacle had been found? If and when it is, it will fulfill Bible prophecy.

A Prophetic Pattern

It seems logical that the Tabernacle should be a prophetic pattern of God's great plan of the ages— pointing toward that golden age when God will dwell among us.

Moses was instructed to cover the Tabernacle with additional coverings:

> *"And thou shalt make a covering for the tent of rams' skins dyed red, and a covering above of badgers' skins"* (Exodus 26:14).

There were three other coverings on the tent of the Tabernacle. Though they represented a protection from the elements of wind and weather, they were also symbolic. There was a covering made of goat's hair, a covering made of ram skins dyed red, and an outer covering of leather which was described by Flavius Josephus as silver-grey, or a greyish blue—the color of the desert sky:

> "There were also other curtains made of skins above these, which afforded covering and protection to those that were woven, both in hot weather and when it rained. And great was the surprise of those who viewed these curtains at a distance, for they seemed not at all to differ from the colour of the sky." [5]

The term *"badger skins"* seems unfortunate, for the original Hebrew word appears to be a reference to the color of the leather rather than to the type of leather used.

Jewish scholars have taken exception to the King James translation on the word *"badger."* They have suggested that the badger, being an unclean animal, could never have been used in the construction of the Tabernacle.

I believe the King James Version of the Bible is correct, however, when calling it *"badger"* skins. I consider it to be a reference, not to the type of leather used, but to its color. The World Book Encyclopedia gives the following description:

> "Badgers are silver-grey and about two feet long. Badger fur is a mixture of white, black, and brown. A single hair may have all three colors along the shaft." [6]

---

[5] Josephus, *The Works Of Josephus*, op.cit.., "Antiquities of the Jews," book III, ch. VI, par. 4, pp. 72,73.

[6] "Badger," *The World Book Encyclopedia*, Volume 2, 1973, p. 20.

The term *"badger"* is, therefore, not necessarily a contradiction, but rather simply a description of the silver-grey color of the outer covering of the Tabernacle. The leather covering was probably made from the skins of bullocks.

The sky-blue appearance of the cover represented heaven. Underneath were the ram skins dyed red which may have represented the blood of the sacrifice and/or the evening sky at sunset. All were covered by the skins and hair of the sacrifice animals.

The word atonement means "covering," and that's exactly what these three layers provided for the Tabernacle. They provided a covering which represented the atonement of the sacrifice. There were three basic animals sacrificed in the Jewish religion—the goat, the ram (a male lamb), and the bullock. Therefore, I suggest these were the three kinds of skins used for the covering of the Tabernacle.

The Tabernacle Measurements

The tent covered a building 30 cubits long, 10 cubits wide, and 10 cubits high. It was made of acacia wood planks, each overlaid with a sheet of pure gold, set in sockets of silver. Each plank was about 22 inches wide and 15 feet tall. Five golden bars ran along each side of the building, to hold the planks together. The building consisted of two chambers—the Holy Place and the Holy of Holies. According to Flavius Josephus, the Holy Place was 20 cubits in length, and the Holy of Holies was

10—making a total of 30 cubits.

It is my opinion that these measurements could represent a prophecy in "times." I believe the 10 cubit length of the Holy of Holies could represent 10 centuries, wherein the throne of God will be established upon the earth, and the 20 cubit length of the Holy Place could foreshadow 20 centuries designated for the Dispensation of Grace.

We are approaching the end of the 20th century. Within the foreseeable future, it is possible that mankind could see the establishment of the throne of God upon the earth.

Though the Jewish historian, Flavius Josephus, recorded the measurements of the two chambers to be 20 cubits and 10 cubits, the Bible does not. Perhaps they were not given for a special reason—for *"of that day and hour knoweth no man, no, not the angels of heaven, but my Father only"* (Matthew 24:36). If the Holy Place represents the Dispensation of Grace, then the furniture which occupied the room represents three characteristics of the Christian life in this dispensation.

The Table of Shewbread

Against the northern wall stood the table of shewbread, symbolic of the Word. As believers in Jesus Christ we should read the Word. We should eat and drink the Word. We should consume the Word every day for spiritual nourishment. In so doing, we will become spiritually strong. We will grow in grace and in the knowledge of our Lord and Savior, Jesus Christ.

The Altar of Incense

On the western side of the room near the veil which covered the Holy of Holies stood the golden altar of incense. There was a fire which burned continually upon the altar with the smoke of the incense ascending before the presence of God. According to Revelation 8:3, this represented the prayers of the saints:

> *"And another angel came and stood at the altar, having a golden censer; and there was given unto him much incense, that he should offer it with the prayers of all saints upon the golden altar which was before the throne"* (Revelation 8:3).

As Christians, in the Dispensation of Grace, we should not only learn to read the Word of God as typified by the table of shewbread, but we should also develop a prayer life as expressed by the golden altar of incense.

The Lampstand

Along the southern wall stood the golden menorah—a lampstand holding seven lamps. It reminds us of our testimony before men. In Matthew 5:14, our Savior said, *"Ye are the light of the world."* Those seven lamps represent our witness for Christ.

> *"Let your light so shine before men, that they may see your good works, and glorify your Father which is in heaven"* (Matthew 5:16).

Our Savior challenged us to take the Gospel to every creature. He said:

"Ye shall be witnesses unto me both in Jerusalem, and in all Judea, and in Samaria, and unto the uttermost part of the earth" (Acts 1:8).

In Revelation 1-3, the seven lamps represent the ministries of seven churches which prophetically portray seven characteristics of the church age during the Dispensation of Grace. Down through the centuries, the Christian has borne the responsibility of winning others to Christ.

Please note: the table of shewbread, the golden altar of incense, and the seven golden lampstand represent the whole duty of the believer during the Dispensation of Grace. At the table of shewbread God can speak to us. At the golden altar of incense we can speak to God. And at the seven golden lampstand we can speak to others about God.

The Columns

We know the Holy Place represents the Dispensation of Grace, because of those five golden columns which stood at the entrance to the Holy Place. The number five in the Bible stands for grace. Let us also be reminded that the Church was empowered on Pentecost at the beginning of the fifth millennium of human history.

Five columns stood at the entrance to the Holy Place, but four columns stood at the entrance to the Holy of Holies. Why only four columns? Why not five? Because the numbers have a special prophetic significance. While five is the number of grace, four is the number of the world. E. W. Bullinger published a book on the subject back in 1893. He wrote:

> "Now the number four is made up of three and one (3+1=4), and it denotes, therefore, and marks that which follows the revelation of God in the Trinity, namely, His creative works. He is known by the things that are seen. Hence the written revelation commences with the words, 'In the beginning God created.' Creation is therefore the next thing—the fourth thing, and the number four always has reference to all that is created... Hence it is the WORLD number...
>
> "Four is the number of the great elements—earth, air, fire, and water. Four are the regions of the earth—north, south, east, and west. Four are the divisions of the day—morning, noon, evening, and midnight... Four are the seasons of the year—spring, summer, autumn, and winter.[7]

Four is the number for the world. In reference to this, those four columns which stood before the Holy of Holies seem to be described in Revelation 7:1 as the four corners of the earth:

> *"And after these things I saw four angels standing on the four corners of the earth, holding the four winds of the earth, that the wind should not blow on the earth, nor on the sea, nor on any tree"* (Revelation 7:1).

---

[7] E. W. Bullinger, *Number in Scripture*, (Grand Rapids, Michigan: Kregel Publications, 1981), p. 123.

The four columns which separate the Holy Place from the Holy of Holies represent the four corners of the earth which, in turn, hold up the four winds of the earth. The winds? Yes, a blue oxygen atmosphere covers the sky like a veil and is represented by the blue veil which separated the Holy Place from the Holy of Holies.

On the veil covering the Holy of Holies were four cherubim woven into the fabric. These angelic creatures are also described in Revelation 7:1 as standing on the four corners of the earth holding back the four winds of the earth. These cherubim stand around the throne of God in heaven.

> *"And before the throne there was a sea of glass like unto crystal: and in the midst of the throne, and round about the throne, were four beasts full of eyes before and behind.*
>
> *"And the first beast was like a lion, and the second beast like a calf, and the third beast had a face as a man, and the fourth beast was like a flying eagle.*
>
> *"And the four beasts had each of them six wings about him; and they were full of eyes within; and they rest not day and night, saying, Holy, holy, holy, Lord God Almighty, which was, and is, and is to come"* (Revelation 4:6-8).

We are told that four angelic creatures stand around the throne. One had the face of a man, another had the face of a calf, another had the face of an eagle, and another had the face of a lion. These living creatures also seem to represent the four divisions of the constellations. The man compares with Aquarius; the calf corresponds with Taurus; the Eagle replaces Scorpio; and the Lion represents Leo.

The prophet Isaiah saw, not four, but six of these creatures which he called seraphim. Why six? Perhaps because, though four can be seen upon the veil, there are two others mounted upon the Ark of the Covenant just beyond the veil. They hover over the mercy seat—the throne of God.

> *"In the year that king Uzziah died I saw also the Lord sitting upon a throne, high and lifted up, and his train filled the temple.*
>
> *"Above it stood the Seraphim: each one had six wings; with twain he covered his face, and with twain he covered his feet, and with twain he did fly.*
>
> *"And one cried unto another, and said, Holy, holy, holy, LORD of hosts: the whole earth is full of his glory"* (Isaiah 6:1-3).

What did these angelic creatures look like? No one knows. Josephus referred to their appearance when making his description of the Tabernacle:

> "...they are flying creatures, but their form is not like to that of any of the creatures which men have seen, though Moses said he had seen such beings near the throne of God." [8]

The veil was woven with blue and red threads and gave the appearance of purple. Blue represents the color of the sky. The red and purple can be seen at sunset. Yes, the veil represents the oxygen atmosphere which surrounds our planet. Throughout the day the blue sky veils our view of outer space—that Holy of Holies where God lives

---

[8] Josephus, *The Works Of Josephus*, "Antiquities of the Jews," book III, ch. VI, par. 5, p. 73.

and performs His miracles.

The only thing we can see through the blue veil or sky is a ball of fire we call the sun. In like manner, the only thing the priests could see from beyond the veil covering the Holy of Holies was the radiance of a ball of fire hovering between the cherubim on the mercy seat of the Ark of the Covenant. It was called the Shekinah Glory and represented the presence of God. Again, Josephus described it:

> "...this portion of the measures of the tabernacle proved to be an imitation of the system of the world; for that third part thereof which was within the four pillars, to which the priests were not admitted, is, as it were, a heaven peculiar to God. But the space of the twenty cubits, is, as it were, sea and land, on which men live."[9]

At night, however, that veil we call a blue oxygen atmosphere is removed, and we can see out into the universe where God lives. One day you and I, who are in the royal priesthood of the believer, will enter beyond the veil into the Holy of Holies of heaven to stand before the throne of God. Our High Priest, Jesus Christ, is there today and will come to the veil one day to call us up into his presence.

After seven years of tribulation the sun will turn as black as sackcloth of ashes and the moon will turn as blood. The heavens will be rolled back like a scroll and the Shekinah Glory will return to the earth in the person of Jesus Christ.

---

[9] Josephus, *The Works Of Josephus*, "Antiquities of the Jews," book III, ch. VI, par. 4, p. 72.

Chapter Twenty

The Passover

"The catechism of the Jew consists of his calendar." With this seemingly casual statement, the late Rabbi Samson Rafael Hersch began his monumental series of lectures, "Judaism Eternal."

The Jewish calendar is one factor that has united the scattered nation. A Jew may be rich or poor, educated or ignorant, orthodox or atheist—still, every week Sabbath calls him, "Come." Every year Passover, Pentecost, the Day of Atonement, the Feast of Tabernacles bring to him forgotten truths from the Word of God. Rabbi Hersch went on to say,

"On the pinions of time which bear us through life, God has inscribed the eternal words of His soul-inspiring doctrine making days and weeks, months and years the heralds to proclaim His truths. Nothing would seem more fleeting than these elements of time, but to them God has entrusted the care of His holy things thereby rendering them more imperishable and more accessible than any mouth of any priest or any monument, any temple or altar could have done.

"Priests die, monuments decay, temples and altars fall to pieces, but time remains forever, and every newborn day emerges fresh and vigorous from its bosom. The priest can only visit a few. Priests and monuments, temples and altars must wait till you come to them, and you are most in need of them precisely when you do not come to them, when you do not feel yourself drawn to the sanctuary or when misery dooms you to isolation.

"Not so the children of time. They do not wait for you to come to them; they come to you unannounced, and you cannot refuse them. They are able to find you when you are immersed in the busy mart of life or in the full career of enjoyment, in the stillness of the prison or on the painful bed of sickness." [1]

The calendar of the Jew yields spiritual insight. It relates a prophetic plan for the ages. God gave the Passover (Pesach), the Feast of Unleavened Bread, First Fruits (Omer), Pentecost (Shavuot), the Feast of Trumpets (Rosh Hashanah), the Day of Atonement (Yom Kippur), and the Feast of Tabernacles (Sukkot) as prophecies of Israel's future confrontations with their Messiah. These Jewish feasts were instituted about 1,490 years before the birth of Christ, and reveal God's purpose in the redemption of mankind.

The events prophesied by the first three feasts were fulfilled at the First Advent of Christ. The prophecy behind Pentecost has, in my opinion, a double fulfillment. It represents the pouring out of His Spirit, which first occurred 10 days after the Ascension. A future final fulfillment should occur at the close of this dispensation—the pouring out of the Holy Spirit upon the house of Israel. The last three feasts yield prophetic insight about the Return of Christ.

[1] Rabbi Samson Rafael Hersch, *"Judaism Eternal."*

The Passover Feast

"In the fourteenth day of the first month at even is the Lord's passover" (Leviticus 23:5).

Historically speaking, Passover reminds Israel of their years in Egyptian bondage. On that first Passover, Moses told the people to slay a lamb and roast it for a quick meal. They were instructed to display its blood on the doorposts and lintels (symbolic of the cross) as an act of faith in God. If there was a poor family nearby who could not afford a lamb, they were to invite that family to join their Passover meal. All were to eat the meal standing, ready to leave Egypt on a moment's notice. God said,

> *"For I will pass through the land of Egypt this night, and will smite all the firstborn in the land of Egypt, both man and beast; and against all the gods of Egypt I will execute judgment: I am the LORD.*
>
> *"And the blood shall be to you for a token upon the houses where ye are: and when I see the blood, I will pass over you, and the plague shall not be upon you to destroy you, when I smite the land of Egypt"* (Exodus 12:12-13).

The Passover represented more than just an historical event in Egypt, it was a prophecy as well. The Passover lamb offered an allegory of a future sacrifice which would be made for the purpose of providing salvation, not only to Israel, but for the whole world. That simple ceremony prophesied the grand plan of God to save all of humanity—all, that is, who would apply the blood.

According to I Corinthians 5:7, Jesus Christ fulfilled the prophecy hidden in the observance of Passover:

"For even Christ our passover is sacrificed for us" (I Corinthians 5:7).

Jesus Christ, the Lamb of God, Who gave His life on Passover Day 2,000 years ago, was our greater Passover Lamb. It matters not whether we are educated or uneducated; whether we are moral or immoral; we are all sinners; *"there is none righteous, no, not one."* The only way we will ever get to heaven is through the blood of Christ. Therefore, we understand that Israel's first great feast day represents the Lord Jesus Christ, Who was our Passover.

Passover is celebrated on the first full moon following the blooming of the almond trees. This occurs around April each year. The Hebrew month is called Nisan, meaning "start." Nisan opens the religious year (a picture of the Age of Grace) and six months later, on the first of Tishri (September), Israel celebrates Rosh Hashanah, New Year's Day for their civil New Year. It is a prophetic picture of that day when Jesus Christ will return to establish the promised kingdom.

The Feast of Unleavened Bread

The second feast is that of the Unleavened Bread. In Leviticus 23:6, God said,

"On the fifteenth day of the same month is the feast of unleavened bread unto the Lord: seven days ye must eat unleavened bread" (Leviticus 23:6).

It was important that the bread not be leavened. Leaven is a type of sin. The bread contained only flour and water and was to be cooked immediately—not allowed to rise. It contained no salt or yeast—nothing in it but the fruit of the field. The grain was ground up and made into a simple bread.

During the course of the Passover meal, one of the three cakes of unleavened bread was broken and hidden. The meal could not be concluded, however, until the missing piece was found. This offers a prophetic picture of Christ as that part of the Trinity whose body was broken and buried. The unleavened bread represents the perfect and sinless body of Jesus Christ. Finding the broken piece pictures the Resurrection of Christ.

On the night before His crucifixion, as He broke the bread, Jesus said, *"Take ye. This is My body which is broken for you."* After feeding the 5,000, Jesus told His disciples, *"I am that bread of life: he that cometh to me shall never hunger"* (John 6:35). The Passover pictures His crucifixion and the unleavened bread pictures His sinless perfection and burial.

The Feast of Firstfruits

There is a third feast—the Feast of First Fruits. God instructed the Israelites in Leviticus 23:

> *"Speak unto the children of Israel, and say unto them, When ye be come into the land which I give unto you, and shall reap the harvest thereof, then ye shall bring a sheaf of the firstfruits of your harvest unto the priest:*
>
> *"And he shall wave the sheaf before the LORD, to be accepted for you: on the morrow after the sabbath the priest shall wave it"* (Leviticus 23:10-11).

Here is a picture of the Resurrection of the Lord Jesus Christ. The Apostle Paul wrote about it in his epistle to the Corinthians:

> *"But now is Christ risen from the dead, and become the **firstfruits** of them that slept.*
>
> *"For since by man came death, by man came also the resurrection of the dead.*
>
> *"For as in Adam all die, even so in Christ shall all be made alive.*
>
> *"But every man in his own order: Christ the **firstfruits**; afterward they that are Christ's at his coming.*
>
> *"Then cometh the end, when he shall have delivered up the kingdom to God, even the Father; when he shall have put down all rule and all authority and power.*
>
> *"For he must reign, till he hath put all enemies under his feet.*
>
> *"The last enemy that shall be destroyed is death"* (I Corinthians 15:20-26).

Jesus fulfilled the Feast of Firstfruits in His Resurrection. The first three Jewish feast days, Passover, Unleavened Bread, and Firstfruits, occurred in conjunction with each other and represented our Lord Jesus Christ in His death, burial, and Resurrection.

On the first Sunday after the Passover meal, the Jewish people would bring a sheaf of grain to the priest. He would take the stalks and wave them before the Lord. Thus would begin the 50 days wait until Pentecost. Israel's grain harvest began on the Day of Firstfruits and concluded at Pentecost. The harvest season offers a prophetic picture of this Dispensation of Grace. Since the Resurrection of our Savior, Christians have been reaping a harvest by preaching the gospel and winning people to Christ. We will continue to do so until the end of the harvest. We are gathering in a harvest of souls.

Will a future Pentecost see the conclusion of that harvest? Read on.

Chapter Twenty One

The Day
of Pentecost

Many theologians regard the Feast of Trumpets
(Rosh Hashanah) as a prophetic picture of the
Resurrection and Rapture. Some have even speculated that the Resurrection could occur on that
very day. The trumpet blasts on Rosh Hashanah
appear to correspond with the "trump of God,"
which, according to the apostle Paul, will attend
the Resurrection:

*"For the Lord himself shall descend from heaven with
a shout, with the voice of the archangel, and with the
trump of God: and the dead in Christ shall rise first:*

*"Then we which are alive and remain shall be caught
up together with them in the clouds, to meet the Lord in
the air: and so shall we ever be with the Lord"*
(I Thessalonians 4:16-17).

Resurrection Day offers a glorious prospect. It is
our "Blessed Hope!" We shall be reunited with our
friends and relatives, be rewarded for our faithfulness and live forever!

The Question Is, "When?"

The age-old question has been, "When?" We are anxious for that day to come! Will the Resurrection occur on a future Rosh Hashanah as some believe?

I think we should not "put all of our eggs into one basket." Let us not forget that *"of that day and hour knoweth no man"* (Matthew 24:36). Rosh Hashanah is not the only Jewish feast day which forms a prophetic picture of the Resurrection.

The Harvest Festivals

There are at least three other Jewish festivals that offer prophetic views of the Resurrection. At these three harvest festivals, all Jewish men were required to travel to Jerusalem and *"appear before the Lord:"*

> *"Three times in a year shall all thy males appear before the LORD thy God in the place which he shall choose; in the feast of unleavened bread, and in the feast of weeks, and in the feast of tabernacles: and they shall not appear before the LORD empty"* (Deuteronomy 16:16).

Any one of them could represent Resurrection Day, when we shall stand before the Judgment Seat of Christ.

The Feast of Weeks

Pentecost, the second of these festivals, was called the *"feast of weeks"* because it involved the counting of seven weeks from the time of offering the Firstfruits (Omer). Pentecost concludes the grain harvest. The Hebrew name for Pentecost is "Shavuot," meaning "weeks." It was instituted by God in Exodus 23:15-17:

> *"And ye shall count unto you from the morrow after the sabbath, from the day that ye brought the sheaf of the wave offering; seven sabbaths shall be complete:*
>
> *"Even unto the morrow after the seventh sabbath shall ye number fifty days; and ye shall offer a new meat offering unto the Lord.*
>
> *"Ye shall bring out of your habitations* **two wave loaves** *of two tenth deals: they shall be of fine flour; they shall be baken with leaven; they are the* **firstfruits** *unto the Lord"* (Exodus 23:15-17).

At the beginning of the harvest, some stalks of the first-ripe grain were to be waved before the Lord. Fifty days later, this grain was baked into two loaves of bread and waved again before the Lord. Further instructions for the festival are repeated in Deuteronomy 16:9-10:

> *"Seven weeks shalt thou number unto thee: begin to number the seven weeks from such time as thou beginnest to put the sickle to the corn.*
>
> *"And thou shalt keep the feast of weeks unto the Lord thy God with a tribute of a freewill offering of thine hand, which thou shalt give unto the Lord thy God, according as the Lord thy God hath blessed thee"* (Deuteronomy 16:9-10).

In the New Testament, the Festival of Weeks was called Pentecost—from the Greek word for "fiftieth." It was celebrated fifty days after Firstfruits (Omer), in the Jewish festival cycle. The observance of the Omer (waving stalks of grain) prophetically pictured Christ, who is our Firstfruits of the Resurrection. The two loaves of bread made from the grain and waved before the Lord on the day of Pentecost may prophetically represent New Testament Christianity, which we shall consider later.

The Order of Resurrections

The apostle Paul wrote about the Resurrection of Christ and its relationship with the future Resurrection. In I Corinthians 15:23, he talked about a specific order of resurrections to be observed:

> *"But every man in his own order: Christ the firstfruits; afterward they that are Christ's at his coming"* (I Corinthians 15:23).

Let's consider this word, *"order."* There is a special order in the Jewish feast cycle and there is a special order of resurrections. Paul, an Israelite of the tribe of Benjamin, had been schooled in the Scriptures at the feet of Gamaliel. Without a doubt, he was intimately aware of the tiniest details of the feast cycle. Therefore, when he speaks of Christ the *"firstfruits"* in the context of an order of events, he knows that the next event in that order is Pentecost.

But this was not the Pentecost at which the Holy Spirit was given to the infant church. It had already taken place. Perhaps Paul was referring to a future Pentecost which would conclude the harvest—Christ's resurrection being the *"firstfruits,"* and our resurrection coming at the end of harvest. Could this possibly occur on a future Pentecost? Could that be the time when Christ will come to take those who are His? Pentecost, remember, concludes the grain harvest.

It seems that when Paul used the word, *"order,"* he intended the reader to see the order of the Jewish festival cycle. It is at least possible he was suggesting that the Resurrection could take place on a future Pentecost.

Apparently the early Church thought so. The ZONDERVAN PICTORIAL ENCYCLOPEDIA OF THE BIBLE offers the following comment:

> "The Church Fathers highly regarded Pentecost. Easter was always on Sunday, so Pentecost was also. Between Easter and Pentecost, there was to be no fasting. Praying was done standing, rather than kneeling. During this time, catechumens [new converts] were baptized. Many expected, because the Ascension had taken place near Pentecost, that **Christ would return in the same season.**" [1]

Pentecost was a time of expectation for the early Church. They felt that Christ might come for His own during this period. Why did they believe this? Was it because of its closeness to the time of the Ascension, or was it because of something else they had been taught? Remember, Christ's actual

---

[1] Merrill C. Tenney, *Zondervan Pictorial Encyclopedia of the Bible,* (Grand Rapids, MI: Zondervan Publishing House, 1976) p. 694.

Ascension took place forty days after His Resurrection. Ten days later, the Holy Spirit empowered the Church for its future role in the harvest of souls.

Pentecost is called the "Feast of the Harvest." And in Matthew 13:39, Jesus said, *"the harvest is the end of the world."* He, Himself, was the Firstfruits of the *"harvest"* which will be manifested at the Resurrection and Rapture.

The Harvest

Think for a moment about the traditions that originated in the first years of the Church. Its central doctrines were handed down through men brought up in the traditions of Jewish history and prophecy. Their lives had literally revolved around the keeping of the festival calendar.

They had heard the teachings of Christ—some no doubt, in person. They had heard His parable of the harvest, when the good wheat and the tares which had grown up together would be separated. They knew about the Festival of Harvest (Pentecost).

When Peter preached that historic sermon on the Day of Pentecost, he quoted the prophet Joel, whose entire book was centered around the harvest cycle. Please remember that before Joel wrote the prophecy, *"I will pour out my Spirit upon all flesh,"* he set the theme of the harvest. Joel said, *"The field is wasted, the land mourneth..."* (Joel 1:10). He said, *"That which the palmerworm hath left hath the locust eaten"* (Joel 1:4). That was a prediction of Israel's exile. The Jews must be scattered from their land, to suffer among the nations.

But that's not all. Joel also spoke of Israel's restoration and linked it to the time of the spring harvest. Joel 2:23-25:

"Be glad then, ye children of Zion, and rejoice in the Lord your God: for he hath given you the former rain moderately, and he will cause to come down for you the rain, the former rain and the latter rain in the first month.

"And the floors shall be full of wheat, and the fats shall overflow with wine and oil.

"And I will restore to you the years that the locust hath eaten" (Joel 2:23-25).

This is a prophecy fulfilled in 1948. Furthermore, Israel was restored on May 15th, during the season of the harvest cycle.

The Early Rain and Latter Rain

When the Holy Spirit was poured out in Jerusalem on the day of Pentecost, the prophecy of the *"early rain"* was fulfilled. Some day, the Holy Spirit will be poured out again in Jerusalem. It should be a fulfillment of the promise of a *"latter rain."* Will it also occur on Pentecost? In Peter's second sermon, he spoke of the ultimate fulfillment of the festival cycle. In Acts 3:19-21, he said:

"Repent ye therefore, and be converted, that your sins may be blotted out, when the times of refreshing shall come from the presence of the Lord;

"And he shall send Jesus Christ, which before was preached unto you:

"Whom the heaven must receive until the times of restitution of all things, which God hath spoken by the

mouth of all his holy prophets since the world began" (Acts 3:19-21).

The prophetic implications of the festival cycle lie in God's promise to restore the earth to the state of glory that He originally intended. So that His people would always remember what He has in mind, He planted this prophetic scenario in their culture. At some future time known only to Him, the story will become a reality. This story is arranged around events in their calendar that foreshadow their future counterparts.

The Harvest Is the End of the World

In the parables recorded in Matthew 13, Jesus likened the cultivation of the harvest fields to the progression of events leading to the kingdom of heaven. *"The harvest,"* He said, *"is the end of the world"* (Matthew 13:39).

Just prior to giving these parables, Jesus had been criticized by the Pharisees for breaking their Sabbath-day restrictions against any sort of labor. Jesus had healed a man who was blind and dumb— a sign to the nation that He was indeed the Messiah. The Pharisees responded by accusing Him of casting out demons by the power of Beelzebub, prince of the devils. They ignored one of their own traditional signs by which they had always said the Messiah might be recognized. From that time, Jesus taught in parables difficult for them to understand. He said:

"Therefore, I speak to them in parables: because they seeing see not; and hearing they hear not, neither do they understand" (Matthew 13:13).

He began with the parable of the soils, which speaks of the hearing and acceptance of the word of God. He spoke about the wheat and the tares; of the harvest that would finally separate the good grain from the weeds. He taught about the grain of mustard seed and about the leavening of the meal. He couched His descriptions about the kingdom of heaven within the framework of planting, harvest, and nourishment.

After Jesus had taught the people, He entered a house to rest. His disciples asked Him to explain the parable of the wheat and the tares. In Matthew 13:37-43, this is what He told them:

"He that soweth the good seed is the Son of Man;

"The field is the world; the good seeds are the children of the kingdom; but the tares are the children of the wicked one;

"The enemy that soweth them is the devil; **the harvest is the end of the world;** *and the reapers are the angels.*

"As therefore the tares are gathered and burned in the fire; so shall it be in the end of this world.

"The son of man shall send forth his angels, and they shall gather out of his kingdom all things that offend, and them which do iniquity;

"And shall cast them into a furnace of fire: there shall be wailing and gnashing of teeth.

"Then shall the righteous shine forth as the sun in the kingdom of their Father. Who hath ears to hear, let him hear" (Matthew 13:37-43).

Here, we see the harvest of souls at the END of the age! Pentecost (the Festival of Harvest) seems to be at least as much of a prophetic scenario for end-time events as it was for the days following the crucifixion.

Judgment of the Fruit

Jewish families observe Pentecost by wearing bright and festive clothing. Homes are decorated with green plants and festive foods are prepared. Michael Strassfeld tells us that on this day, "there are various religious and secular celebrations of the firstfruits of the season, which hark back to bringing the firstfruits to the Temple on Shavuot."[2] According to Hayyim Schauss, writing in THE JEWISH FESTIVALS:

> "The custom of decorating the homes and synagogues with green plants is variously explained. One theory is that the day is marked in heaven as the day of judgment for the fruit of the trees." [3]

Here is the theme of fruit bearing, which points to the Judgment Seat of Christ following the Rapture and Resurrection. In Matthew 7:15-20, Jesus likened true versus false teaching to the fruit of trees:

> *"Beware of false prophets, which come to you in sheep's clothing, but inwardly they are ravening wolves.*

---

[2] Ibid, p. 76.

[3] Hayyim Schauss, *The Jewish Festivals*, (New York, NY: Schocken Books, 1962), p. 94.

"Ye shall know them by their fruits. Do men gather grapes of thorns, or figs of thistles?

"Even so every good tree bringeth forth good fruit; but a corrupt tree bringeth forth evil fruit.

"A good tree cannot bring forth evil fruit, neither can a corrupt tree bring forth good fruit.

"Every tree that bringeth not forth good fruit is hewn down, and cast into the fire.

"Wherefore by their fruits ye shall know them" (Matthew 7:15-20).

Jesus teaches that false prophets can be known by their *"fruits."* The righteous will bring forth *"good fruit."* This *"good fruit"* is the *"fruit of the Spirit,"* spoken of in Galatians 5:22-23:

*"But the **fruit** of the Spirit is love, joy, peace, longsuffering, gentleness, goodness, faith, meekness, temperance: against such there is no law"* (Galatians 5:22-23).

Pentecost, associated with the giving of the Law, is a time for reviewing one's *"fruit."* The Law is seen as the way toward such *"good fruit."* But the apostle Paul wrote that only through the Resurrection of Christ can we bring forth *"fruit"* unto God.

*"Wherefore, my brethren, ye also are become dead to the law by the body of Christ; that ye should be married to another, even to him who is raised from the dead, that we should bring forth **fruit** unto God"* (Romans 7:4).

By His Resurrection, Christ became our *"First-fruits."* He laid the *"foundation"* that made it possible for the Church to bring forth *"fruit."* This principle is clearly stated in I Corinthians 3:11-13:

"*For other* **foundation** *can no man lay than that is laid, which is Jesus Christ.*

"*Now if any man build upon this foundation gold, silver, precious stones, wood, hay stubble;*

"*Every man's work shall be made manifest: for the day shall declare it, because it shall be revealed by fire; and the fire shall try every man's work of what sort it is*" (I Corinthians 3:11-13).

The judgment of the fruit of trees corresponds to the reward of the believer in heaven. This is exactly the theme seen in the Jewish festival of Pentecost.

The Date Cannot Be Fixed

According to Rabbi Hayyim Schauss, in his book, THE JEWISH FESTIVALS, the date for Pentecost cannot be fixed. It is the "only Jewish festival for which there is no fixed date."[4] The Penteteuch does not state on what day of the month Pentecost is to be observed. It says only that it is to be celebrated fifty days after the offering of the Omer, the first sheaf of the grain harvest, which was to be offered on "*the morrow after the Sabbath,*" as we have already seen in Leviticus 23:15-17.

The Sadducees interpreted this as meaning that the Omer was to be offered on the first Sunday after Passover, and that Pentecost would always fall on the seventh Sunday thereafter ... exactly fifty days later.

Even though the actual counting of forty-nine

---

[4] Hayyim Schauss, p. 87.

weekdays would always remain the same, Shavuot itself would continually drift back and forth on the calendar. Could this be the reason why Jesus said, *"But of that day and hour knoweth no man?"* (Matthew 24:36).

The Pharisees, who sought to interpret the Law in accordance with the conditions of their day, came to interpret the word "sabbath," as merely meaning the first day of the festival of Passover. According to the Pharisees, it was necessary to offer the Omer on the sixteenth day of Nisan; Pentecost, therefore, would always come on the sixth day of Sivan (late May or early June). Sometimes it would come on a Tuesday, or Friday or some other day. Christians, however, held to the biblical view, as did the Saducees, that the Day of Pentecost should be observed on a Sunday.

Two Wave Loaves of Bread

Shavuot was considered to be a minor festival. It was thought to be no more than a mere continuation of the Festival of Unleavened Bread. As we have already noted, its location in the feast cycle depended on the date of Passover, plus a count of seven weeks from the offering of the Omer. This counting of days linked it with the major festival of Unleavened Bread.

To conclude the seven weeks, another wave offering was given. It was made up of two loaves of bread, but this time the bread was made with leaven. It appears to be a prophetic picture of New Testament Christianity. The two loaves may indicate a divided Christianity, and the leaven in the loaves seem to represent the presence of sin. We must admit that New Testament Christianity is a divided and imperfect group of people, saved, not by their own goodness, but only by the grace of God. That which was begun on the Feast of Firstfruits with the resurrection of Christ will someday be presented to God at the conclusion of the great spiritual harvest of souls, just as the two loaves were presented at Pentecost. This is yet another reason why some future Pentecost could be a good day for the Rapture and Resurrection.

The Omer was a specific offering of new wheat, harvested on the second evening of Passover and brought to the Temple. It represented the firstfruits of the harvest. As we have already pointed out, the Omer or Firstfruits is a picture of the Resurrection of Christ.

Our Savior's Resurrection is the greatest single event in human history. It, and it alone, points the way that mankind may move back toward God. Christ is the Lamb of God—literally the Passover Lamb. The events of His death, burial and Resurrection coincided with the actual dates of Passover in the year of His sacrifice. He was crucified on Passover, buried on the Feast of Unleavened Bread and resurrected on the day of the Firstfruits offering.

So we see that while the Jewish festivals are notes of remembrance and prophetic guideposts—at least the first three—they also mark those actual historical events that fulfilled the prophecies typified by each observance.

The Earnest of Our Inheritance

Pentecost is regarded as the day when life and power was given to the Church. Some theologians consider it to be the birthday of the New Testament church. But could it be more than just the day when the Holy Spirit came? Could it also be a prophecy of that future day when the Holy Spirit, who is the "*the earnest* [downpayment] *of our inheritance*" (Ephesians 1:14) will fulfill His ministry with Resurrection and Rapture?

The Pentecost Trumpet

We have noted before, the blowing of the ram's horn on Rosh Hashanah has been suggested as representing the final trumpet of resurrection. But does it really? Is it possible that the trumpet blast on Rosh Hashanah represents instead, a "*memorial*" of the heavenly Pentecost trumpet?

> "*In the seventh month, in the first day of the month, shall ye have a sabbath, a **memorial** of blowing of trumpets, an holy convocation*" (Leviticus 23:24).

Let us review the part Pentecost has played at the beginning of two dispensations—Law and Grace. The rabbis say that the Dispensation of Law began on Pentecost. On that day, a heavenly trumpet was heard at Mount Sinai. The Jews remember this as a time when their national identity took a new direction.

> *"And when the voice of the trumpet sounded long, and waxed louder and louder, Moses spoke, and God answered him by a voice"* (Exodus 19:19).

Some Jewish scholars say that this first mention of a trumpet blast in Exodus was regarded by the spiritual leaders of Israel as having occurred on Shavuot or Pentecost. Exodus 19:1 tells us that this event came about in the third month—Sivan.

Furthermore, that trumpet was blown, not by man, but by a heavenly being. Moses and the Chosen People had gathered at Mt. Sinai, on the third day of preparation, wherein they washed themselves, cleaned their clothes, and were forbidden to touch the mountain.

Writing in his book, THE JEWISH HOLIDAYS, A GUIDE & COMMENTARY, Michael Strassfeld wrote:

> "At some point in the rabbinic period, connections began to be made with the Revelation at Sinai, which, as the biblical text tells us, took place in the third month—that is, during Sivan (see Exodus 19:1). The exact date of Sinai is not given, and in fact there is a disagreement in the Talmud over whether the Revelation took place on the sixth or seventh of Sivan!" [5]

When God came down, a trumpet sounded long and loud, frightening the people. On that occasion, the fire of God's glory descended, and God gave the Ten Commandments. It is the only heavenly trumpet recorded in the Old Testament. The next

---

[5] Michael Strassfeld, *The Jewish Holidays: A Guide and Commentary*, (New York, NY: Harper & Row, 1985), p. 71.

heavenly trumpet should occur on the day of Rapture and Resurrection, making the day of Pentecost an interesting possibility for that event.

According to Jewish tradition, God took the two horns from the ram, given to Abraham as a substitute sacrifice in the place of Isaac, and made two ram's horns. The left horn was called the "first trumpet" and was blown at Sinai. The right horn is called the "last trumpet" and will be blown on the day of Resurrection. The question is, will the last trumpet be blown on Pentecost or on Rosh Hashanah? By the way, this early Jewish tradition may be the origin of Paul's use of the term "last trumpet" in I Corinthians 15:51-53.

"Behold, I shew you a mystery; We shall not all sleep, but we shall all be changed,

"In a moment, in the twinkling of an eye, at the last trump: for the trumpet shall sound, and the dead shall be raised incorruptible, and we shall be changed.

"For this corruptible must put on incorruption, and this mortal must put on immortality" (I Corinthians 15:51-53).

Ruth Was a Gentile Bride

Of all the festivals, Shavuot (Pentecost), is the most mysterious. As a harvest festival, it is perhaps best remembered in the Story of Ruth—read in all synagogues on Pentecost.

The grain harvest comes in the springtime. Trees are laden with fresh foliage. Flowers are in bloom. The heart of humanity is light and optimistic. Jewish homes are decorated with fresh greenery and floral decoration. Hayyim Schauss, writing in THE JEWISH FESTIVALS, says:

> "Even in school the instruction is festive and breathes the spirit of the holiday. **The children are taught the Book of Ruth.** So clear is the imagery thereof that they are carried back to the days of old, when Jews reaped the harvest of the fields of their own land.
>
> "The older children sit around a long table with the teacher and study the Book of Ruth. But their thoughts are not on their studies; they are thinking of Bethlehem, the town where David was born and spent his childhood. They imagine they are standing at harvest time in the fields that surround the town. Gentle breezes blow from the hills of Judah. The fields are filled with the freshly cut sheaves. They hear the whir of the reaping scythe, and the song of the workers in the fields. And everywhere is the pleasing aroma of the newly-fallen gleanings which Ruth is gathering in the field.
>
> "Their thoughts are carried still farther afield when the teacher recites, or rather sings, as he interprets 'Akdomus.' [This is an eleventh-century Aramaic poem.] King David is descended from Ruth and Boaz, and from David's seed, it is believed, will come the Messiah. In 'Akdomus' is presented vividly a picture of the day when the Messiah will have arrived, the time of eternal bliss on earth." [6]

Many have said that the book of Ruth is the most beautiful narrative in the entire Bible. Ruth was a Gentile woman of Moab, who married into a Hebrew family. Not only that, there was a famine in Israel, which the family hoped to escape by emigrating from Bethlehem to Moab. These events took place during the period of time in which the

---

[6] Hayyim Schauss, p. 91.

judges ruled the land after the death of Joshua. It was a time of deep moral and spiritual decline.

The husband and both sons died in Moab, widowing Ruth, her mother-in-law, Naomi, and her sister-in-law, Orpah, who soon left. Naomi elected to return to her home in Bethlelem, urging Ruth to stay with her own people, as Orpah had done. But Ruth faithfully determined to go with her and to remain by her side until death separated them.

They arrived in Bethlehem at harvest time. As was the right of the poor, Ruth gleaned in the fields for their food. As a poor foreigner, she had nothing to expect by a future of perpetual widowhood. Yet she found favor in the sight of Boaz, a wealthy landowner. He allowed her to glean even among the sheaves of the field. At Naomi's instruction, Ruth went to the threshing floor and laid down at the feet of Boaz on the night of Pentecost, the festival of harvest. That night, he claimed her and redeemed her as a near kinsman had the right to do. After securing the legal right to marry her, they were united and she bore him a son. That son was Obed, the grandfather of David the king.

This is the story of a Gentile bride in a strange land, who started out with only her faith. She provides a prophetic picture of the Gentile bride of Christ—the Church. On the very night of Pentecost, Ruth came to lie at the feet of Boaz. What a beautiful picture of that day when we will go to our Bridegroom! Ruth 3:7-11 tells of the exciting culmination of her story:

"And when Boaz had eaten and drunk, and his heart was merry, he went to lie down at the end of the heap of corn: and she came softly, and uncovered his feet, and laid her down.

"And it came to pass at midnight, that the man was afraid, and turned himself: and behold, a woman lay at his feet.

"And he said, Who art thou? And she answered, I am Ruth thine handmaid: spread therefore thy skirt over thine handmaid; for thou art a near kinsman.

"And he said, Blessed be thou of the Lord, my daughter: for thou hast shewed more kindness in the latter end than at the beginning, inasmuch as thou followedst not young men, whether poor or rich.

"And now, my daughter, fear not; I will do to thee all that thou requirest: for all the city of my people doth know that thou art a virtuous woman" (Ruth 3:7-11).

Boaz had finished the Feast of Harvest. He laid down by the mound of grain that was rightfully his, and fell asleep. Quietly, Ruth came and uncovered his feet before lying down there. According to the custom of the day, this constituted a petition for his acceptance.

At midnight, startled, he awoke to discover the woman of whom he had taken earlier note as she gleaned in his fields. His acceptance of her set in motion a series of legal steps, which he undertook promptly, in order that he might marry her. Ruth had remained completely faithful to Naomi. Boaz knew of her reputation as a virtuous woman. He completed her righteousness in their marriage, making her an heir to the Messianic promises. A poor woman of Moab had been brought into the lineage of the throne of David, from which the

Messiah would one day rule over the nations.

Moab was a name held in disrepute by the Jews, since Moab was the son of Lot, born as a result of an incestuous union with his eldest daughter. His name had been given to the land lying to the east and south of the Dead Sea.

The book of Judges records that Eglon, king of Moab, subjugated the Israelites for eighteen years. Scripture depicts the Moabites as a warlike people, who were always in conflict with their neighbors. Yet, in the book of Ruth, God graciously places one Moabite family into a renewed relationship with Himself. This perfectly depicts the individual salvation of those whom God calls to righteousness. According to Michael Strassfeld, rabbinical authority calls for the book of Ruth to be read at Pentecost, because:

1. The story is set at the time of harvest.

2. Ruth's conversion to Judaism is thought to bear a close resemblance to one's voluntary acceptance of the Torah and God's covenant at Sinai.

3. King David, according to tradition, was born and died on Shavuot. (The book of Ruth, of course, ends with a genealogy from Ruth down to King David.) And,

4. Reading Ruth means that the totality of the Torah is celebrated on Shavuot, for Ruth is part of the ... writings that together with the Torah and the prophets compose the whole Bible. [7]

Strassfeld adds a curious note at this point. He says,

---

[7] Michael Strassfeld, p. 73.

"Most commonly the book of Ruth is read without a blessing during the morning services of Shavuot (on the second day for those observing two days of Shavuot.)" [8]

Why, "without a blessing?" Could it be because the Jews are jealous of Gentile Christianity?

Jews Stay Up All Night

At this point, it is of great interest to note another element of the Jewish festival: The Jews stay up all night in their synagogue's house of study, poring over "tikkun." This consists of little sections from each book of the Torah and the Talmud, representing all of the most important texts of Judaism. But even this act of staying up all night sets forth the theme of resurrection. Michael Strassfeld writes of this custom:

"A kabbalistic custom emanating from the mystics in Safed (sixteenth century) is to stay up the whole (first) night of Shavuot studying Torah. The tikkun—a set order of study—was composed of selections from the Bible, rabbinic literature, and even mystical literature such as the ZOHAR. In this fashion the kabbalists prepared for the momentous revelation of the following morning.

"This practice of staying up all night is in stark contrast to that of the Israelites at Sinai, who according to tradition slept late that morning and had to be awakened by Moses. In atonement for this, Jews nowadays stay awake all night. The sense of preparation for Sinai is heightened by a mystical tradition holding that the skies open up during this night for a brief instant. At that very moment, we are told, God will favorably answer any prayer. The kabbalists also regard Pentecost as the wed-

[8] Ibid.

ding of God and Israel. Therefore, we stay up all night to 'decorate the bride.' " [9]

What an incredible picture of the Rapture! The opening of the heavens *"for a brief instant"* corresponds with the message in I Corinthians 15:51:

"Behold, I show you a mystery: We shall not all sleep, but we shall all be changed, in a moment, in the twinkling of an eye..." (I Corinthians 15:51).

Here is a perfect picture of Christ coming to catch away His Bride! And where does He take them?—to the Marriage Supper of the Lamb! This corresponds with Pentecost when the Jews "stay up all night to decorate the bride."

Israel Was the Bride of Jehovah

Writing on the theme of Shavuot as marriage, Strassfeld says:

"One of the most beautiful images of Shavuot is that of the marriage between God (the groom) and Israel (the bride). Developing this image, [Passover] is the period of God's courtship of Israel, and Shavuot celebrates the actual marriage...

"Even the midrash's problematic imagery of God holding the mountain of Sinai over the Israelites' heads while saying 'accept my Torah or else!' is transformed in this romantic symbolism as the mountain becomes a huppah— a wedding canopy for the marriage. According to this view, Moses smashes the tablets because they are God's ketubah or marriage contract to Israel, and Moses, as messenger, chooses to smash them rather than de-

---

[9] Michael Strassfeld, pp. 73-74.

liver them to Israel and thereby complete the marriage of Israel and God. To complete the marriage would have meant that the Israelites, who were worshiping the golden calf, were in fact being unfaithful in their marriage." [10]

Because of their unfaithfulness to Jehovah, Israel could not become a June bride. Moses ground the golden calf to powder. He mixed it with water and made the people drink it. In our chapter on Moses and the Messiah, we observed the various events that transpired.

On the first day of Elul (late August) Moses went back up the mountain for another 40 days. When he returned on the tenth of Tishri, he presented the second set of tablets to Israel. Those tablets (containing the Ten Commandments) represented a marriage contract (Ketubah). Israel became a September bride.

Each year, from the first day of Elul until the tenth of Tishri, a series of trumpet blowings commemorate the Pentecost trumpet. That heavenly trumpet at the first Pentecost should have marked Israel's happy marriage to Jehovah. For thousands of years now, on every Rosh Hashanah, Israel blows a series of sad and sorrowful notes on their shofar trumpets. Instead of becoming a June bride, Israel became a September bride.

Someday, at the sound of another heavenly trumpet, the Church (the Bride of Christ) will be taken out of this world. No man knows the *"day nor hour"* of this great event. Will it occur on a fu-

---

[10] Michael Strassfeld, p. 75.

ture Pentecost—or on a Rosh Hashanah? Will we be a June bride, like Ruth, or a September bride, like Israel?

The Battle of Leviathan and Behemoth

According to Jewish legend, Pentecost also represents the day when the Messiah will have arrived. There will be eternal bliss on earth.

Hayyin Schauss, writing in THE JEWISH FESTIVALS, tells of the glorious picture that the Jews associate with Pentecost:

> "They see golden thrones, approached by seven stairs; **seated** on the thrones are the saints, gleaming and shining like the stars of heaven. Above them are spread canopies of light, and below ripple streams of fragrant balsam. There is no end to the joy and happiness of the saints. They dance in Paradise, arm-in-arm with God himself; He entertains them with a mammoth spectacle, arranged especially for them, the combat between the **Leviathan and the Behemoth**."

> "The teacher tells of the feast which God will prepare after the coming of the Messiah, and his imagination makes it more vivid and colorful even than its description in AKDOMUS. He pictures the saints **seated** around a table made of precious stones, eating the flesh of the **Leviathan and the Behemoth**." [11]

Once again, we find within the complex observance of Pentecost a reference to prophetic fulfillment. Here, Leviathan and Behemoth are seen in

---

[11] Hayyim Schauss, pp. 91-92.

a final battle. Note that the struggle is being witnessed by the saints who are safely seated in heaven around a table made of precious stones. What a picture of the Marriage Supper of the Lamb!

The saints here are "seated." While on earth, the Christian way of life is characterized as a *"walk."* We are to be positive and active, led by the Holy Spirit. In Ephesians 5:15, we are told, *"See then that ye walk circumspectly, not as fools, but as wise."* This posture is reflected in virtually all of Scripture, even setting the tone for the Book of Psalms: *"Blessed is the man that walketh not in the counsel of the ungodly..."* (Psalm 1:1) This is the way that Jesus walked, when He was on earth.

Now, in heaven, He is seated. His position is on the throne of heaven, with the Father. In the concluding words of the letters to the seven churches in Revelation, Jesus says, *"To him that overcometh will I grant to sit with me in my throne, even as I also overcame, and am set down with my Father in his throne."* Amazingly, the Jewish observance of Pentecost includes this very picture of the saints seated with the Messiah. But it also includes a view of the climactic battle, of which we read in Revelation 17:17-20:

"And I saw an angel standing in the sun; and he cried with a loud voice, saying to all the fowls that fly in the midst of heaven, Come and gather yourselves together unto the supper of the great God;

"That ye may eat the flesh of kings, and the flesh of captains, and the flesh of mighty men, and the flesh of horses, and of them that sit on them, and the flesh of all

men, both free and bond, both small and great.

"And I saw the beast and the kings of the earth, and their armies, gathered together to make war against him that sat on the horse, and against his army.

"And the beast was taken, and with him the false prophet that wrought miracles before him, with which he deceived them that had received the mark of the beast, and them that worshiped his image. These both were cast alive into a lake of fire burning with brimstone" (Revelation 17:17-20).

This description, depicting the events that will occur when Christ returns in glory with His saints, immediately follows the account of the Marriage Supper of the Lamb! This is the battle of Leviathan and Behemoth witnessed by the saints. God seems to have placed this future prophetic fulfillment in the context of the Jewish Pentecost.

Year after year, as the rabbis recount the story of the saints in heaven watching the battle of the beasts, they are planting the seeds of recognition in the minds of their people. When the time comes, the Jews will recognize the event.

Leviathan and Behemoth seem to be the subjects of Revelation 13:1 and 13:11. Verse 1 says,

"And I stood upon the sand of the sea, and saw a **beast** rise out of the sea, having seven heads and ten horns, and upon his horns ten crowns, and upon his heads the name of blasphemy" (Revelation 13:1).

"And I beheld **another beast** coming up out of the earth; and he had two horns like a lamb, and he spake as a dragon" (Revelation 13:11).

These beasts are empowered by satan, the dragon. And though for a time, they enrapture and captivate the whole world, their doom is certain as they finally clash with the armies of heaven.

The beast rising from the sea is that evil force which supports the final form of world government. In the Old Testament, this monster is given the name, *"Rahab."* Psalm 87:4 says,

> *"I will make mention of Rahab and Babylon to them that know me..."* (Psalm 87:4).

According to UNGER'S BIBLE DICTIONARY, the term Rahab as used in this passage refers also to a "sea monster." NELSON'S ILLUSTRATED BIBLE ENCYCLOPEDIA calls it "Rahab the Dragon"—an allegorical sea monster or dragon representing the evil forces of chaos.

The Old Testament usage compares perfectly with the revived Roman empire and MYSTERY BABYLON THE GREAT who is seen by John as the harlot riding upon a seven-headed dragon (Revelation 17:3-5). Isaiah also described it:

> *"Awake, awake, put on strength, O arm of the LORD; awake, as in the ancient days, in the generations of old. Art thou not it that hath cut Rahab, and wounded the dragon?"* (Isaiah 51:9).

The terms *"Rahab and Babylon"* in Psalm 87 correspond to the Revived Roman Empire predicted to dominate the world under the leadership of the antichrist during the Tribulation Period.

The mystery city will be destroyed—as related in Psalm 89! Ethan completes the picture of God's judgment upon the harlot city as he wrote:

*"Thou hast broken Rahab in pieces, as one that is slain;
thou hast scattered thine enemies with thy strong arm.*

"The heavens are thine, the earth also is thine: ..."
(Psalm 89:10,11).

This Jewish story about the battle of the beasts is
a part of the observance of Pentecost. Yes, the
prophecies behind Pentecost were not completed
when the Holy Spirit descended two thousand years
ago. There are still some prophecies about the
festival yet to be fulfilled.

A strange story is related by the first century historian, Flavius Josephus, which occurred a few
years before the destruction of Herod's Temple in
A.D. 70. It could have happened as much as seven
years before the Temple was burned.

> "... at that feast which we call Pentecost, as the priests
> were going by night into the inner court of the temple, as
> their custom was, to perform their sacred ministrations,
> they said that, in the first place, they felt a quaking, and
> heard a great noise, and after that they heard a sound as
> of a great multitude, saying, 'Let us remove hence.' "[12]

The sound could be viewed as a prophetic reference to the Rapture. Some day, at the Rapture, we
will indeed "remove hence!" Could that future
event occur on a Pentecost? Was the quaking, the
noise, and the shout indicative of the Rapture?
Also, Josephus recounts another event which may
help to date this one. He said that a man named

---

[12] Flavius Josephus, "Wars of the Jews," book 6, chapter 5, section 3,
Translated by William Whiston, *The Works of Josephus*, (Lynn, MA:
Hendrickson Publishers, 1980), p. 582.

Jesus came to Jerusalem at the Feast of Tabernacles some seven years and five months before the siege and began crying aloud,

> "A voice from the east, a voice from the west, a voice from the four winds, a voice against Jerusalem and the holy house, a voice against the bridegrooms and the brides, and a voice against this whole people!" [13]

He continued this cry day and night for seven years and five months, at which time the city was besieged and "a stone came out of one of the [Roman] engines and smote him and killed him immediately."[14]

Some day, in the not-too-distant future, the world will advance to the next stage in the festival cycle. The next prophetic event may be the pouring out of the Holy Spirit upon Jerusalem. Some time between now and then, Christians will be taken out of the world. No man knows the *"day nor hour"* of this great event. Will it occur on a future Pentecost—or on a Rosh Hashanah? Will we be a June bride, like Ruth, or a September bride, like Israel? Nobody knows.

---

[13] Ibid.

[14] Ibid.

Chapter Twenty Two

The Feast of Trumpets

The Resurrection of the saints is connected with the blowing of a trumpet. In the book of I Thessalonians the apostle Paul wrote:

> *"For the Lord himself shall descend from heaven with a shout, with the voice of the archangel, and with the trump of God"* (I Thessalonians 4:16).

In I Corinthians 15:51-52, he wrote:

> *"Behold, I shew you a mystery; We shall not all sleep, but we shall all be changed,*
>
> *"In a moment, in the twinkling of an eye, at the last trump..."* (I Corinthians 15:51-52).

In each of these verses the apostle Paul refers to a trumpet. The use of the trumpet has an important spiritual and prophetic significance. Every born-again Christian who looks forward to the Second Coming of Christ *"as a thief in the night"* to snatch away His bride is listening for that spine-tingling, exhilarating sound of God's divine trumpet.

The ram's horn trumpet is blown each year on

Rosh Hashanah, the Jewish New Year. In the Bible it is called the Feast of Trumpets. This Jewish Holy Day, along with Yom Kippur (the Day of Atonement) and the Feast of Tabernacles, makes a very interesting prophetic scenario. According to Jewish theologians, they look forward to that day when Messiah will judge the world, and establish His kingdom.

There are seven Holy Days given in Leviticus 23. They tell the story of God's plan of the ages. The first three feast days have already been fulfilled. They are the feasts of Passover, Unleavened Bread, and Firstfruits. They pictured the suffering of Christ—His death, burial, and resurrection.

Christ fulfilled the prophecy of the Passover Lamb through His death on Passover day. He fulfilled the Feast of Unleavened Bread through His burial. And He fulfilled the Feast of Firstfruits through His Resurrection on the first day of the week—the very day the wave offering of firstfruits was made. He fulfilled the prophecy of each of these three Jewish Holy Days on the very day of each feast.

The prophecy of Pentecost was at least partially fulfilled on the exact day of that feast. In fulfillment of Joel's promise of the *"early rain,"* the Holy Spirit came to Jerusalem and empowered the church for its great worldwide mission. Some day, the promise of the *"latter rain"* will come. It will be another pouring out of the Holy Spirit. Perhaps it will also occur on a Pentecost.

In our study on the prophecies behind Pentecost, we considered the possibility that the snatching away of the Bride of Christ might occur on a future Pentecost. In this study, we shall consider the alternative. Some theologians believe that the Resurrection could occur on Rosh Hashanah, the Jewish Feast of Trumpets.

A controversy has continued down through the centuries among rabbis as to whether the Messiah will come during the autumn festivals around Rosh Hashanah or during the spring season between Passover and Pentecost. That is why, at the conclusion of both the spring festival of Passover and the autumn festival of the High Holy Days, the Jews repeated the hope of future redemption by saying, "Next year in Jerusalem."

It is easy to see how the controversy developed when you take note that Rosh Hashanah, or New Year's day, is observed on the first day of the seventh month rather than on the first day of the first month. Passover is celebrated in the first month and Rosh Hashanah is observed in the seventh month. Passover is a happy festival and Rosh Hashanah is a solemn time for self analysis.

Hayyim Schauss writes:

> "Both Rosh Hashanah and Yom Kippur are different, in atmosphere, from other Jewish festivals and are therefore known as the Days of Awe. In all other festivals the spirit is one of exalted joyfulness. The exaltation of Rosh Hashanah and Yom Kippur, however, has no traces of joy, for these are profoundly serious days, with a feeling of the heavy moral responsibility which life puts on all." [1]

---

[1] Hayyim Schauss, *The Jewish Festivals*, (New York: Schocken Books, 1938), p. 112.

He further wrote,

"Rosh Hashanah is the Jewish New Year but, in contrast with the New Year of other peoples, it is greeted not with noise and joy, but with a serious and contrite heart." [2]

Rosh Hashanah, the Feast of Trumpets, occurs on the first day of the month called Tishri in late September or early October each year. It represents that great day in the future when God's judgment will be set.

Following Rosh Hashanah are seven days called the Days of Affliction—a time of introspection. They are also called the Days of Awe and, prophetically, represent the Tribulation Period.

The tenth day of Tishri is called Yom Kippur, the Day of Atonement. Prophetically, it represents the salvation of the nation of Israel in the height of the Battle of Armageddon. It pictures the time when the Messiah will come to save His people. It is a day of repentance for the Jew as he seeks the forgiveness of God for his unbelief.

Five days later the Jewish people move into tents to celebrate the Feast of Tabernacles. Prophetically, this is believed to represent the Millennial reign of Christ—when for a thousand years we will rule and reign with Christ on earth.

The High Holy Days—those of Rosh Hashanah, Yom Kippur, and the Feast of Tabernacles—all refer to future events.

---

[2] Ibid.

Preparation for the High Holy Days

Unlike the other festivals of the Jewish calendar, both Rosh Hashanah and Yom Kippur do not commemorate any historical event in the life of the Jewish nation.

The two festivals are such High Holy Days that preparation for them actually begins a month earlier on the first of the Jewish month called Elul (corresponding to late August). Each day throughout the month, the ram's-horn trumpet is blown. On the day before Rosh Hashanah (the last day of the month of Elul), no trumpet is blown. The final trumpet is sounded on Rosh Hashanah, the first of Tishri. It is the final trumpet in the series of 30 days of trumpet blowing.

The Blowing of Trumpets

The possibility of the Resurrection occurring on Rosh Hashanah centers around the blowing of the trumpet. However, there is another possible interpretation. When the ram's-horn trumpet is blown on Rosh Hashanah, it is blown in a series of trumpet blasts—some short, some long. Some of the sounds are very short staccato notes. There is a wailing note that is always preceded and followed by a long clear blast.

The wailing or sobbing note can be one of three alternatives—three short blasts of the horn, a series of extremely short blasts, or a combination of the two—three short blasts followed by a series of staccato notes. Each is repeated three times making a total of 30 blasts. They are blown at the beginning of a special Jewish service, called the Musaf. Another 60 blasts are blown during the service. The last Teki'ah blast is drawn out, and is called "Teki'ah Gedolah." It is the great Teki'ah.

On the first day of every month, the short blasts of the trumpet are sounded in Jewish ritual, but on the first day of the seventh month, the long alarm blast is added. It is said to remind the people of the long sounding of the horn attending God's appearance on Mt. Sinai. Evidently, the heavenly trumpet which was sounded on Pentecost at the giving of the Ten Commandments is commemorated on Rosh Hashanah, some four months later. And there is a reason why. You may recall, at Pentecost, Moses ascended Mount Sinai and stayed 40 days. When he returned, the people were worshiping a golden calf. Moses promptly broke the tablets of stone representing God's marriage contract with Israel.

After several days of judgment, Moses ascended the mountain again—to spend another 40 days. He returned on the tenth day of the seventh month with another set of tablets. The marriage contract with Israel was finally accepted, but it was a somber occasion. The joy of Pentecost was turned into the sorrow of Yom Kippur, the Day of Atonement. The Jews would rather remember the Pentecost trumpet of the first marriage contract during the time when Moses was receiving the second marriage tablets.

The shofar used in Jewish worship does not have to be a ram's horn. It can be the horn of any clean animal, with the exception of the ox or calf.

God refused to allow the people to use the horn of a calf or ox because of their worship of the golden calf while Moses was on top of the mountain. Generally, however, a ram's horn is used.

My Light and My Salvation

During the month of Elul, Psalm 27 is recited together with the blowing of the shofar. The psalm opens with a reference to Rosh Hashanah, Yom Kippur, and the Feast of Tabernacles:

"The Lord is my light and my salvation; whom shall I fear?..." (Psalm 27:1).

The words *"my light"* are taken to refer to Rosh Hashanah, and the words *"my salvation"* are believed to refer to the Day of Atonement. Remember, it was during those 40 days, beginning with the first of Elul, that Moses and the people of Israel finally received the Torah from God. After those 40 days, when he descended from the mountain on Yom Kippur, the face of Moses glistened with the strange light of God's glory:

"For in the time of trouble he shall hide me in his pavilion: in the secret of his tabernacle shall he hide me" (Psalm 27:5).

This is a reference to the Feast of Tabernacles, at which time, the psalm is recited daily. The *"light"* of Psalm 27 could represent a light of understanding which will illuminate the darkened minds of the Jewish people and will climax seven years later with their salvation.

Rosh Hashanah Represents . . .

According to Jewish theologians, the festival of Rosh Hashanah represents three things: the anniversary of Adam's creation, the future day of judgment, and the future day of renewing the bond between God and Israel.

Not only do the Jews regard Rosh Hashanah as the day of Adam's creation and the future day of judgment, but they also believe that on some future Rosh Hashanah, God will renew His bond with Israel. Perhaps this is a reference to the 70th week of Daniel. God's dealing with the Jewish people will be renewed during the Tribulation Period. Israel will come to repentance and receive Christ as their Messiah. The Second Coming of Christ at the height of Armageddon is believed to be the fulfillment of the prophetic Yom Kippur and will usher in the glorious Feast of Tabernacles—representing the Millennial reign of Christ.

Observed for Two Days

There's another interesting bit of information about Rosh Hashanah, the Jewish New Year—it is observed for two days, not one. These two days, however, are considered one long day. There's a reason for this. Tradition required that the new month be determined not by mathematical calculation, but by the evidence of eyewitnesses who had seen the new moon. Accordingly, the people would look out for the new moon on the nights of the 29th and 30th of Elul. When spotted, the Sanhedrin court would receive the witnesses, and declare that day to be Rosh Chodesh, the first of the new month. But the Jews were eventually scattered throughout the world, having no contact with Jerusalem. Therefore, two days were eventually observed as Rosh Hashanah to insure that all Jews throughout the world were observing the same day.

That makes the timing of the day somewhat obscure. Some have considered that to be the reason why the Savior said that men cannot determine the day of His coming by calculation.

The Shofar

In the Bible, Rosh Hashanah is described as a day for sounding the horn. According to Jewish theology, the ram's horn is reminiscent of the ram caught in the thicket which was used by Abraham as a substitute sacrifice for his son, Isaac. Much of the ceremony of the day hinges around that historic event. The central ceremony of the festival is the sounding of the shofar, the ram's horn.

The shofar should be curved, a symbol that man must bend his will before God. It is usually softened and shaped in hot water. There must be no impairment in the sound of a shofar. A split or hole in the shofar is liable to render it unfit.

Before blowing the shofar, the Jewish congregation recites Psalm 47 seven times. This psalm exalts God as King of all the earth, a befitting theme for the blowing of the shofar. It also includes the verse, *"God is gone up with a shout, the Lord with the sound of a trumpet"* (Psalm 47:5).

This verse is given as the reason for holding the shofar with the wide end pointing upward. Another six verses are then recited. The first letters of each verse form an acrostic, reading "Kera Satan," which means "tear up Satan." This, of course, is exactly what will happen when God's great future Rosh Hashanah comes.

Ten Reasons for Blowing the Trumpet

According to Rabbi Saadiah Gaon, who lived in the ninth century, there are ten reasons for sounding the shofar on Rosh Hashanah:

1. Rosh Hashanah, as the day of creation, is the anniversary of God's rule. It is a coronation day, and Israel proclaims His kingship.

2. Rosh Hashanah introduces the Days of Penitence. The shofar calls for repentance.

3. The shofar evokes the revelation at Sinai when the Torah was given to Israel amidst the blowing of the horn.

4. The sound of the shofar is compared to the inspiring message of Ezekiel 33:7 which says,

> *"I have set thee a watchman unto the house of Israel; therefore thou shall hear the word at my mouth, and warn them from me"* (Ezekiel 33:7).

5. The shofar is the sound of battle and the clash of arms. The memory of the capture of Jerusalem and the destruction of the Temple evokes prayers for the speedy return of Israel's national glory.

6. The shofar is symbolic of the ram Abraham

sacrificed instead of Isaac.

7. The horn arouses fear. Amos 3:6 says,

"Shall a trumpet be blown in the city, and the people not be afraid?"(Amos 3:6).

8. The shofar evokes the ultimate Day of Judgment, as in Zephaniah 2:14 and 16:

"The great day of the Lord is near, it is near, and hasteth greatly..."

"A day of the trumpet and alarm..." (Zephaniah 2:14,16).

9. The final ingathering of the exiles is also associated with the blowing of the horn. Isaiah 27:13:

"And it shall come to pass in that day, that the great trumpet shall be blown, and they shall come which were ready to perish in the land of Assyria, and the outcasts in the land of Egypt, and shall worship the Lord in the holy mount at Jerusalem" (Isaiah 27:13).

10. The shofar is connected with the Resurrection. It is in this sense (according to Saadiah Gaon) the ancient Jewish rabbi, that Isaiah wrote in Isaiah 18:3:

"All ye inhabitants of the world, and dwellers on the earth, see ye, when he lifteth up an ensign on the mountains; and when he bloweth a trumpet, hear ye" (Isaiah 18:3).

Three Books Will Be Opened

According to the Talmud, Rabbi Johanan, who lived in the third century, wrote that on that day (some future Rosh Hashanah) three books will be opened before God. One is the Book of Life, in which the names of the just are entered and confirmed. One is the Book of Death in which the wicked are entered. The third is the book for those who are neither wholly just nor wholly wicked, in whose case the verdict is delayed until the Day of Atonement.

This picturesque description seems to concur with the New Testament concept of the Tribulation Period. Those whose names are written in the Lamb's Book of Life, having been saved by the blood of the Lamb, will be raised and raptured into heaven. Those who have refused Christ as Savior will be doomed to judgment.

However, there is a third group of people who could be given an opportunity to be saved during the days from Rosh Hashanah to Yom Kippur. These seven Days of Awe seem to graphically represent the Tribulation Period. In the book of Revelation we are told that 144,000 Jews will be saved—plus a great multitude of people from every nation.

That's quite a concept wrapped around the Jewish festivals of the Feast of Trumpets, the Day of Atonement, and the Feast of Tabernacles. Rosh Hashanah is certainly a prophetic picture of the beginning of the Tribulation. It also rivals the Day of Pentecost as a prophetic scenario of the Resurrection. But of course, we must remember that our Savior said, *"Of that day and hour, knoweth no man."*

Chapter Twenty Three

The Days of Awe

The "Days of Awe" are observed for ten days commencing with Rosh Hashanah on the first of Tishri (September) and concluding with Yom Kippur ten days later. Rosh Hashanah is also called the "Feast of Trumpets" (opening the Jewish New Year) and Yom Kippur is a term used for the "Day of Atonement." The prophetic implications of these ten days are quite significant.

Following the celebration of Rosh Hashanah on the first and second days of the month of Tishri, there are seven Days of Penitence—from the third day of Tishri until the ninth. These seven days of affliction for the Jewish people seem to be a prophetic reference to the future seven years of the Tribulation.

This is not unusual, for there are other prophecies in the Old Testament where a day is made to equal a year. Briefly, by way of example, consider Kadesh-Barnea, where God pronounced a judgment upon Israel. Because of their unbelief, God proclaimed that the people would have to wander in the wilderness for forty years—a year for each day of the forty days the spies had spent in the Promised Land.

Again, in Ezekiel 4:4-6, God commanded the prophet to lie on his left side for 390 days and then to lie on his right side for 40 days as a picture God's judgment upon Israel and Judah. Ezekiel was told that this judgment would be upon the people for a total of 430 years, a year for each day Ezekiel had lain on his side. So it is not unusual for a single day to prophetically represent an entire year in God's prophetic plan. These seven Days of Penitence appear to be a prophetic scenario of the seven years of the Tribulation.

During the seven Days of Penitence, observed each year by the Jewish people, three days are prominent. They are called the Fast of Gedaliah, observed on the first day; Shabbat Shuvah, observed on a Sabbath in the midst of the week; and Erev Yom Kippur, observed on the last day of the seven.

The Fast of Gedaliah

The Fast of Gedaliah is observed in remembrance of the murder of Gedaliah, son of Ahikam, during the days of the Babylonian occupation of Jerusalem. After the destruction of Solomon's Temple in 586 B.C., the king of Babylon appointed Gedaliah governor of the country. Ishmael, of the Judean royal family, came to Gedaliah at Mizpah and murdered him. The murder was said to have taken place on Rosh Hashanah and is observed by the Jewish people each year on the day following Rosh Hashanah.

In Zechariah 7:3-5, the prophet commented on two fast days—the fast of the fifth month and the fast of the seventh month. The fast of Gedaliah was the *"fast of the seventh month."* In that chapter, a delegation of men had come from Babylon to inquire of the priests which were in the House of the Lord, saying:

> *"... Should I weep in the fifth month, separating myself, as I have done these so many years?"* (Zechariah 7:3).

The fast of the fifth month was observed on the ninth of Av—the date on which the Temple of Solomon was destroyed. The prophet's reply is given in Zechariah 7:4-5:

> *"Then came the word of the Lord of hosts unto me, saying, Speak unto all the people of the land, and to the priests, saying, When ye fasted and mourned in the fifth and seventh month, even those seventy years, did ye at all fast unto me, even to me?"* (Zechariah 7:4-5).

The fast of the seventh month is still observed on the first day of the seven Days of Penitence, between Rosh Hashanah and Yom Kippur. It appears to be a prophetic picture of events which could occur in the first year in the Tribulation Period. Will the leader of the nation of Israel be murdered at the beginning of the Tribulation? Maybe. Or maybe it pictures a greater devastation to the entire nation at the onset of the Tribulation. Perhaps it is a prophetic picture of the Battle of Gog and Magog. At any rate, the death of Gedaliah seems to be a prophecy which may be fulfilled at the beginning of the seven years of Tribulation.

Shabbat Shuvah

During the seven days between Rosh Hashanah and Yom Kippur a special Sabbath is observed. It is called Shabbat Shuvah and is observed with the reading of the words, *"Return, O Israel, unto the Lord thy God."* Today, in most Jewish congregations, Shabbat Shuvah is observed with a sermon from the rabbi. His message is expected to arouse the congregation to repentance and good deeds. Prophetically, this seems to correlate with the middle of the Tribulation Period when the antichrist commits the abomination of desolation.

It is also about this time that *"Mystery, Babylon the Great, that great city which reigneth over the kings of the earth"* is destroyed by fire. In Revelation 18:4, a great voice from heaven proclaims, *"... Come out of her, my people, that ye be not partakers of her sins, and that ye receive not of her plagues."* How fitting that in the middle of these seven Days of Penitence the Jewish people read the Scripture, *"Return, O Israel, unto the Lord thy God."*

The Fast of Gedaliah, observed on the first of these seven days, in memory of the murder of their beloved governor, could well represent the beginning of the Tribulation Period along with the Battle of Gog and Magog. And Shabbat Shuvah, observed in the midst of these seven days, could well represent a worldwide exodus of Jews from all the countries of the world, particularly *"Mystery Babylon,"* to their home country and their sacred city, Jerusalem.

The Eve of Yom Kippur

The third special day observed during these seven Days of Awe is called Erev Yom Kippur, or the "Eve of Yom Kippur." It is observed on the seventh day and could well have a prophetic significance to the seventh year of the Tribulation Period.

Erev Yom Kippur is regarded as a semi-festival, which is usually spent in making preparations for the Day of Atonement. Early in the morning, often before breakfast, the religious Jew takes a chicken and waves it above his head, while he recites three times, "This is my substitute, this is my exchange, this is my atonement; this fowl will go to its death, and I shall enter a good and long life in peace." The ceremony is symbolic and reminiscent of the Temple sacrifices.

One of the ideas behind the atonement sacrifice in the Temple is that guilt is transferred to the sacrificial animal which pays the penalty for the sinner, while the person is cleansed. Through the offering of the animal, the person should be brought to the realization that it is he who should, in reality, be paying the penalty.

After the brief ceremony, the chicken is redeemed with money which is given to the poor and it is immediately slaughtered to be eaten for the evening meal preceding the Fast of Yom Kippur. The intestines of the chicken are thrown outside in a place where "the birds can eat them."

One day, in the Battle of Armageddon, when it looks as if the Jewish people will have to pay the ultimate price for their unbelief, a spirit of repentance will come over then. They will turn to Jesus Christ as their Messiah and beg for forgiveness. They will have no choice. The genocide of·the Jewish people will be imminent. Half of the city of Jerusalem will have fallen to the enemy, the houses will be rifled and the women ravished. When the Jewish people are finally driven to repentance, a substitute sacrifice will be given. Instead of the Jewish people being destroyed, the armies of the world will be destroyed.

Revelation 14:20 tells us that instead of the blood of Jews running in the streets, the blood of Gentiles will flow up to the horses' bridles (approximately 3 to 4 feet) for the length of the land of Israel (almost 200 miles). Just as birds are invited to eat the entrails of the chicken on the Eve of Yom Kippur, John describes its prophetic counterpart:

> *"And I saw an angel standing in the sun; and he cried with a loud voice, saying to all the fowls that fly in the midst of heaven, Come and gather yourselves together unto the supper of the great God;*
>
> *"That ye may eat the flesh of captains, and the flesh of mighty men, and the flesh of horses, and of them that sit on them, and the flesh of all men, both free and bond, both small and great"* (Revelation 19:17-18).

It is also on Erev Yom Kippur that the people pray a confessional prayer of repentance before eating the sacrificed chicken. Another custom, seldom seen nowadays, is to receive lashes. On Erev Yom Kippur, token blows, usually with a leather strap, are administered lightly. The penitent Jew recites the short confessional while the striker recites, "For He is merciful and forgives iniquity." It is reminiscent of Isaiah 53:4-5:

> *"Surely he hath borne our griefs, and carried our sorrows ...*
>
> *"But he was wounded for our transgressions, he was bruised for our iniquities: the chastisement of our peace was upon him; and with his stripes we are healed"* (Isaiah 53:4-5).

It is significant, also, that these things should be observed on the last day of the seven Days of Penitence. They appear to represent the seventh year of the Tribulation Period.

After the seven Days of Penitence comes Yom Kippur, the Day of Atonement. It is the day on which both the Jew as an individual and the nation as a whole are cleansed of their sins and granted atonement. The concept that a man can achieve atonement for his sins is basic to Judaism. Man is a dynamic organism who has free choice to do good or evil. But even after having committed evil, he can regain his former purity through atonement.

Yom Kippur, as a day of atonement, concerns primarily the Jewish people as a nation rather than the atonement of the individual—the observance of Passover represents the atonement of the individual. In the ancient days of the Temple in Jerusalem, the High Priest acted as the representative of the nation. A great part of the atonement service was for the nation as a whole. Even today, the confessional prayers are conducted in the plural form, thereby including all Israel.

Traditionally, Yom Kippur is the anniversary of the day on which Moses came down from Mount Sinai with the second set of stone tablets after obtaining God's forgiveness for Israel's sin with the golden calf. This day was set aside for generations to come as a day of forgiveness for the nation. The second-century rabbis have written that during the Second Temple period, it was customary to tie some red wool to the Temple gate which would turn white as a sign that the people had found forgiveness. It was also recorded by the rabbis that during the forty years before the destruction of Herod's Temple in A.D. 70, that red wool tied to the Temple gate remained red. The rabbis concluded that God was saying, "I will not forgive, I will not forgive."

Apart from the description of the Yom Kippur ceremony in Leviticus 23:27-32, there is no information in the Bible as to how the day was observed prior to the Babylonian exile. There is a detailed description of the atonement service in the Second Temple period found in the Mishnah. Fragments of a prayer for the Day of Atonement have also been found in one of the caves at Qumran on the northwestern shore of the Dead Sea. It is remarkable how little the content and theme of Yom Kippur has changed during these past 2,000 years.

There is a famous description by Rabbi Simeon Ben Gamaliel of Yom Kippur, in which he writes that the maidens of Jerusalem would go forth, all dressed in white, and would call out to the young men to choose each man a wife for himself. The plain girls would say, "Set not your eyes on beauty," and the beautiful girls would say, "Set not

your eyes on family lineage." Could this be a
prophetic picture of the Bride of Christ, representing the difference between the Gentile Bride of this
dispensation and the Jews of the Old Testament?
One can almost hear the plain Bride, or Jews, saying to Christ, "Set not your eyes on beauty," and the
beautiful Bride, the New Testament church, saying, "Set not your eyes on family lineage." Only in
the book of Jubilees do we find Yom Kippur
connected with mourning. The day on which
Jacob heard of young Joseph's supposed death
was said to be the tenth of Tishri, and because of
Jacob's grief, this day was ordained as a day for
seeking atonement. The goat, offered in the
Temple as an atonement sacrifice, was a reminder of the goat which Joseph's brothers
slaughtered. They dipped his coat in the goat's
blood and sent it to Jacob to deceive him after
selling Joseph. When Christ returns, His vesture
will also be dipped in blood. Joseph, by the way,
was made governor of Egypt (second to Pharaoh)
on a Rosh Hashanah, the first day of Tishri.

Rosh Hashanah also marked the beginning of
the seven-year famine in Egypt. Joseph, as governor of the land, revealed himself to his brothers
two years later. His revelation, as brother to the
sons of Jacob, also occurred in the month of
Tishri. How prophetic! One day the Lord Jesus
Christ, who was rejected by His brethren and of
whom Joseph was a type, will return to be declared King over a Gentile world and be revealed
to the Jewish people as the Messiah whom they rejected.

Chapter Twenty Four

The Day of Atonement

On the Jewish High Holy Day of Yom Kippur (the Day of Atonement) the book of Jonah is read in synagogues around the world. This has been a ritual for hundreds of years. The question is— why? Why would the story of Jonah be read on the Day of Atonement? What connection does it have with Yom Kippur?

Jonah appears to have a tremendous prophetic significance. It seems as if Jonah is a prophetic type of the nation of Israel, who shirked its responsibility to take the message of God's judgment and justice to a Gentile world. Israel has suffered three millennia in the proverbial whale's belly because of it. At the same time, many Gentiles have repented. Let's take a few moments to look at Jonah.

The story divides naturally into three parts. In the first part, Jonah tries to escape from his destiny, but he cannot. The second part demonstrates the efficacy of repentance, both when Jonah repents to do the will of God, and when Nineveh repents and is spared the judgment of God. The third section shows how God explains the workings of His providence to Jonah. God demonstrates to Jonah His love for His creatures, whose lives are dear to Him.

Jonah appears to represent the Jewish people who have tried to escape from their destiny, but cannot. God's judgment has thus been unleashed upon the Chosen People. Finally, instead of utterly destroying the world, God redeems them.

Jonah, of course, also represents the Lord Jesus Christ, who took the punishment of Israel upon Himself as their substitute, and thus was in the heart of the earth for three days and three nights. Jesus referred to this in Matthew 12:40:

> *"For as Jonah was three days and three nights in the whale's belly; so shall the Son of man be three days and three nights in the heart of the earth"* (Matthew 12:40).

Yes, Jesus took Israel's punishment and He took our punishment, as well, on the Cross of Calvary. One day He will return to complete the work of redemption and fulfill the prophecies portrayed in the Day of Atonement.

The ritual of the High Priest on the Day of Atonement during the Temple Period is most interesting. For seven days before Yom Kippur, the High Priest lived in the Temple precincts in order to prepare himself for the ritual sacrifice.

There were two kinds of services on Yom Kippur: the regular everyday service and the specific Yom Kippur service. For the regular Temple service the High Priest wore his normal priestly garments, ornamented with gold. But at the special Yom Kippur service he wore white, for the gold evoked the memory of the golden calf.

Several times during the day the High Priest had to change his clothes from gold to white, and back again. Every time he did this, he sanctified himself by a ritual immersion.

One of the principal parts of the special atonement service in the Temple consisted of three prayers recited by the High Priest over the sacrifice animals. During these prayers, the High Priest spoke the holy name—the ineffable name of God.

The first prayer was recited when the High Priest placed his hands on the head of the bullock and prayed for an atonement for himself and his family. Later, he used the same bullock when praying for the priests—the descendants of Aaron.

His third prayer requested atonement for the whole nation. For this prayer, the scapegoat was used. It was called the Azazel goat. The order of the atonement prayers was not accidental, nor did it denote self-interest. Before the High Priest could become the people's representative in their atonement, he first had to be utterly free from sin himself.

Similarly, the priests who helped with the service had to have their sins atoned for before it was possible to seek an atonement for the nation as a whole.

The scapegoat, or Azazel goat, was one of a pair. Two goats were used for this part of the service. One of the goats was to be used for a sacrifice and his blood would be sprinkled upon the Mercy Seat of the Ark of the Covenant. The other goat would be taken out to the wilderness of Judea, near the area of Qumran, and driven over a cliff.

When the High Priest first received the two animals, he drew lots to decide which goat should be sacrificed. On one lot were written the words, "A sin offering for the Lord," and on the other lot, the words, "For Azazel." As the High Priest drew the lots, he would raise the hand in which he held the lot for the sin offering and cry aloud, "A sin offering for the Lord," again using the ineffable name of God.

It was considered a good omen if the lot for the sin offering came up in the High Priest's right hand, for right is symbolic of good and left is symbolic of evil.

In the second century, the rabbis wrote that during the 40 years prior to the destruction of the Temple in A.D. 70, this lot always came up in the left hand of the High Priest. It was believed to be one of the signs of the impending doom placed by God upon the Temple of Herod.

The sacrificial goat was then slaughtered and its blood sprinkled on the Ark of the Covenant in the Holy of Holies. Afterward, the second goat (the scapegoat) was taken by the High Priest, who laid his hands upon its head and recited the atonement prayer on behalf of the nation of Israel. This goat was then taken out to the Judean desert and pushed backward over a high cliff to its destruction.

Neither the Bible nor the Mishnah explains the inner meaning of this ceremony. However, I think we can determine the prophetic significance of the two goats. They both appear to represent the Messiah—in His two natures.

The sacrificial goat appears to represent the humanity of Jesus Christ who was sacrificed for the sins of all men. Remember, it was John the Baptist who proclaimed, "... *Behold the Lamb of God, which taketh away the sin of the world"* (John 1:29). According to calculations, John made this proclamation during the season of the High Holy Days—when the High Priest sacrificed the atonement animal at the Jerusalem Temple.

The scapegoat appears to represent the deity of the Savior, who carried our sins into the wilderness of God's forgetfulness. God placed our sins behind His back to *"remember them no more"* (Isaiah 38:17). This was seen also in the Toshlek ceremony where the prophet Micah was quoted as saying, "... *thou wilt cast all their sins into the depths of the sea"* (Micah 7:19).

Every time the High Priest uttered the ineffable name of God, the people who were gathered in the court of the Temple would fall on their faces and say, "Blessed be his glorious sovereign name forever and ever." That part of Yom Kippur is still practiced in synagogues today.

On the ancient Day of Atonement the High Priest would enter the Holy of Holies three times—once with a special incense offering and twice to sprinkle the blood of the sacrifices.

The people waiting in the courtyard of the Temple were unable to see the High Priest until he emerged from the outer sanctuary. It was believed that if the High Priest was unworthy to enter the Holy of Holies, he would not survive. For this reason a rope was tied to the leg of the High Priest so that if he collapsed while in the presence of God, his body could be pulled from the inner sanctuary. As far as we know, history never recorded the death of a High Priest while in the Holy of Holies.

When the High Priest entered the inner sanctuary with the blood of the sacrificed animal, he sprinkled it upon the Mercy seat of the Ark of the Covenant.

After three hours in the darkness of the Holy of Holies, the High Priest would emerge with the empty basin, hold it high and proclaim, "It is finished." The people were then confident that the sacrifice had been accepted and their sins had been forgiven.

Prophetically, the blood atonement found its fulfillment on Calvary. Our High Priest, the Lord Jesus Christ, has taken His own blood into the presence of God the Father. Another future fulfillment will come to pass when our High Priest returns from the Holy of Holies of God's presence in Heaven to proclaim, "It is finished."

At the close of the day following the afternoon service, as the sun reaches treetop height, the Ne'ilah service is recited. This is the concluding service of the Day of Atonement. Ne'ilah means "closing."

The full name for the Ne'ilah service is "Ne'ilat Ha Shearim" (the closing of the gates). It refers to the daily closing of the Temple gates at sunset, but prophetically may represent the closing of the heavenly gates—when all who are going to be saved will be saved, and the gate of Heaven will be shut.

At the close of the Ne'ilah service, the shofar is blown on Yom Kippur, even if it is a sabbath, because it is already night. Various reasons are given for the blowing of the shofar. It is a reminder of the Jubilee year when all property is returned to its original owners, all debts are forgiven, and all slaves are set free. This was announced by the blowing of the shofar on Yom Kippur. Again, there appears to be a prophetic reference to the Second Coming of Jesus Christ. When the Savior returns to win the Battle of Armageddon, He will establish His Jubilee. All property throughout planet Earth will be returned to its original owner and every spiritual slave will be set free.

The blowing of the shofar trumpet at the end of Yom Kippur is also an allusion to Psalm 47:5:

"God is gone up with a shout, the Lord with the sound of a trumpet" (Psalm 47:5).

When God concluded the Sinai visitation and went up from the mount, the blast of the trumpet was heard. It signified the termination of God's presence on the mountain.

In Jerusalem, it is customary to blow the shofar at the Western Wall. Following the Arab riots of

1929, British authorities set up a committee of inquiry, followed by an international committee, which decided that, although the Jews had a right to worship at the wall, they were not to blow the shofar there.

The Jews regarded this ruling as a searing humiliation, and every year the young Jewish men would make it a point of honor to blow the shofar at the wall at the termination of Yom Kippur—despite the danger from the Arabs and the intervention of the British police. Many of those young men were arrested and imprisoned.

Immediately following the capture of the old city of Jerusalem in 1967, Rabbi Shlomo Goren, who (at that time) was the chief chaplain of the Israel Defense Forces, blew the shofar at the Western Wall as a symbol of its redemption.

After the concluding service at the end of Yom Kippur, the Jewish people say to each other, "Next year, in Jerusalem." Only twice a year is this wish expressed—one at the termination of the Haggadah on Passover night and the other at the conclusion of Yom Kippur. This is in accordance with a difference of opinion found in the ancient writings of two rabbis, Rabbi Elliazer and Rabbi Joshua, as to whether the Messiah will come to redeem Israel in the first month of Nisan or in the seventh month of Tishri—around Passover and Pentecost, or around Rosh Hashanah and the Day of Atonement.

In the Bible, Yom Kippur is described as Shabbat Shabbaton, "a sabbath of sabbaths." All of the commandments concerning the sabbath also applies to Yom Kippur. But it transcends the sabbath in sanctity because of the sacrificial service, and by virtue of its ultimate purpose. It also differs from the sabbath in the practice of the five forms of self-denial, observed on Yom Kippur as a part of the repentance ritual.

These forms of self-denial, or afflictions, affecting the basic functions of the human body, make Yom Kippur even more a day of rest than the regular sabbath.

Yom Kippur is referred to four times in the Pentateuch—three times in Leviticus and once in Numbers. Leviticus 16 describes the sacrificial service on the Day of Atonement. Yom Kippur is mentioned again in the list of festivals and a third time in connection with the Year of Jubilee.

In the book of Numbers, the sacrifices of the day are listed. In each instance, except in the reference to the Jubilee year, the Bible stresses the commandment that a person must afflict himself. This commandment is directly related to the atonement which is granted on Yom Kippur. How prophetic that during the seven year Tribulation Period the Jewish people will be afflicted! The holocaust of Germany during the 1940's will pale in comparison with the attempted genocide of the Jewish people during the war of Armageddon.

The affliction of Yom Kippur is observed by the Jewish people today through the method of fasting. Fasting appears frequently in the Bible as a sign of repentance. The people of Nineveh fasted after hearing Jonah's message. So did Esther and the Jews for three days before she risked her life by going uninvited to see King Ahasuerus.

Fasting also serves the purpose of enhancing the spiritual inner man. By restraining the material requirements of the body, the mind can focus more clearly on the spiritual.

A fast also reduces the fat content of the body, which is reckoned as if the worshiper had brought a sacrifice, the fat of which was offered on the brazen altar. On Yom Kippur, washing and bathing is prohibited only when it causes gratification or comfort. For this reason, a Jewish person does not wash his hands or face on Yom Kippur. As the evening sun sets, marking the end of Yom Kippur, the fast is broken and it is considered commendable to eat and drink.

The High Holy Days of Rosh Hashanah and Yom Kippur are remarkable for the impact they make on the Jewish people. The Days of Awe (those seven days between Rosh Hashanah and Yom Kippur) seem to embody the whole spirit of Judaism. Thus, for the religious Jew, they become the climax of the year. Prophetically, they seem to represent the climax of the centuries.

It is surprising how little the High Holy Days have changed in the course of 2,000 years. They have remained essentially the same since the days of the Second Temple, with the exception of the sacrifice made on Yom Kippur and the entrance of the High Priest into the Holy of Holies.

Originally, the Holy of Holies contained the Ark of the Covenant with the tablets of stone and the Torah. In the Second Temple, the Holy of Holies was empty, much to the astonishment of Pompey, the Roman general, who, in 63 B.C. forced his way into the inner sanctuary.

When the High Priest entered the Holy of Holies on the Day of Atonement, he was completely alone. As the representative of the Jewish people, this was understood as a direct confrontation with God. According to the ancient writings of the rabbis, even the angels were denied access to this encounter.

Someday, in fulfillment of the Day of Atonement, the Messiah will make his exit from the heavenly Holy of Holies. In Revelation 11:15,19, the apostle John described it this way:

> *"And the seventh angel sounded; and there were great voices in heaven, saying, The kingdoms of this world are become the kingdoms of our Lord, and of his Christ; and he shall reign forever and ever."*

> *"And the temple of God was opened in heaven, and there was seen in his temple the ark of his testament: and there were lightnings, and voices, and thunderings, and an earthquake, and great hail"* (Revelation 11:15,19).

Perhaps it will be on a future Day of Atonement when the Temple of God will be opened in heaven and our High Priest will come forth to judge the wicked and establish His Kingdom.

Chapter Twenty Five

The Feast of Tabernacles

The Feast of Tabernacles is a holiday for rejoicing and celebration immediately following the somber and judgmental High Holy Days of Rosh Hashanah and Yom Kippur. It is the third "pilgrimage festival," in which the ancient Jew was expected to make a trip to Jerusalem and, once there, to participate in the pageantry of the season.

This festival continues the story of the early Israelites. At these three "harvest festivals" Passover, Pentecost, and Tabernacles, all Jewish men must go to Jerusalem. The Jew celebrated the Exodus at Passover. He observed the giving of the Law at Pentecost. And finally, he remembered the forty year's wilderness journey by dwelling in a tent during the Feast of Tabernacles.

Another name for the Feast of Tabernacles is the Festival of Ingathering, which concludes the three harvest festivals—Passover, Pentecost and Tabernacles. It marks the final ingathering of produce before the approaching winter. At the giving of the Law, the Lord commanded that this feast be kept as one of three major festivals:

> *"Three times thou shalt keep a feast unto me in the year.*
>
> *"Thou shalt keep the feast of unleavened bread (thou shalt eat unleavened bread seven days, as I commanded thee, in the time appointed of the month Abib; for in it thou camest out from Egypt: and none shall appear before me empty);*
>
> *"And the feast of harvest, the first fruits of thy labors, which thou hast sown in the field; and the feast of ingathering, which is in the end of the year, when thou hast gathered in thy labors out of the field.*
>
> *"Three times in the year all thy males shall appear before the Lord God"* (Exodus 23:14-17).

The Israelites were commanded to construct booths with open roofs decked with fruit and foliage where they were to live for a week, while meditating on God's providence and celebrating His blessing. Present-day Jews are divided about whether the practice of living in booths came from an agricultural tradition or from the dwelling in tents during the desert wandering. But the fact is, both the agricultural and historical elements of the early Israelites have been woven into the modern celebration of this Jewish festival.

A Time of Rejoicing

The basic element in the Feast of Tabernacles is the act of rejoicing. This holiday directly follows Rosh Hashanah and Yom Kippur. Rosh Hashanah (the Feast of Trumpets) is observed on the first two days of Tishri (a Jewish month corresponding to September). Yom Kippur (the Day of

Atonement) is observed on the tenth. Five days later, on the fifteenth of Tishri, The Feast of Tabernacles launches a week of observances. There is the symbolic sense of having completed the process of repentance. The harvest has passed and God's providence is joyfully celebrated.

The prospects for a millennial reign of the Messiah was most important to the Jews, even from their earliest days. During the days of the Kings of Israel, the Feast of Tabernacles was considered the most important festival of all. For example, The Feast of Tabernacles was the time chosen by Solomon to consecrate the First Temple. It was also the occasion every seven years for the public reading of the Torah before the people. But in time, this important festival was eclipsed by the spring festivals associated with Passover and the fall festivals following Rosh Hashanah. It was almost as though the people wanted to forget the tents of their desert wandering during the Exodus.

A Type of the Coming Kingdom

But the festival of Tabernacles is more than a remembrance of times past. It also looks forward to the earthly reign of the Messiah. It will be the ultimate fulfillment of the Lord's prayer, as written in Matthew 6:10: *"Thy kingdom come. Thy will be done, in earth as it is in heaven."* Zechariah pointed up the prophetic importance of the Feast of Tabernacles:

> *"And it shall come to pass, that every one that is left of all the nations which came against Jerusalem shall even go up from year to year to worship the King, the Lord of hosts, and to keep the feast of tabernacles.*
>
> *"And it shall be, that whoso will not come up of all the families of the earth unto Jerusalem to worship the King, the Lord of hosts, even upon them shall be no rain"* (Zechariah 14:16-17).

Zechariah looks forward to the time when the Lord, as King, requires even the Gentile nations to go up to Jerusalem and keep the festival of ingathering. The bounty of the harvest is associated with the Lord's blessing, even to the control of the weather! As the Lord sits upon the throne of the Millennial Temple, the prophetic picture is that of an earth at peace and in the process of restoration. This is the picture implied in the celebration of the Feast of Tabernacles.

The harvest, of course, is also a picture of God's harvest of souls. From the time of Adam's fall, God's redemptive plan has been in action. His plan of the ages revolves around this principle. The Feast of Tabernacles, as a feast of harvest, is a prophetic picture of the harvest of the souls of men. Among the current hymns of the church is "Bringing in the Sheaves," a song of salvation and redemption. We live in an age of technology, but until very recently, the world lived in an agricultural environment. How significant that God would phrase His plan in terms easily understood by men.

The Great Sabbath

The Feast of Tabernacles pictures the great sabbath rest—the seventh millennium in world history. For six thousand years, the nations have warred against each other. Finally, at the last, they will even try to fight against God. Revelation 19:19 tells of the "... *armies, gathered together to make war against* [Christ] *him that sat on the horse, and against his army."*

In Revelation 20, we are told that satan will be bound for a thousand years. In the first seven verses of this chapter, the thousand-year period is mentioned six times, comparable to the number of millennia that will precede the final millennium. This seventh millennium corresponds with the seventh day, the day of God's rest after the creation of the heavens and the earth.

Nehemiah Restored the Feast

In the Old Testament book of Nehemiah, there is a similar story of restoration and renewal. Nehemiah, who lived in the fifth century, B.C., was cupbearer to the king of Persia. He was granted permission by the king to return to Jerusalem. During his return, he led the third and final group of exiles back to the land. Upon his arrival, he challenged his countrymen to rebuild the dilapidated wall around the holy city. He had prayed earnestly that the Lord would bless his efforts. In spite of much resistance from those already living in and around the city, he completed his task in only 52 days.

Then came the even more arduous task of spiritually reviving the people. After organizing leaders from among the elders and registering the priests who could display valid genealogical records, the remnant brought gifts to the Temple. And then they gathered to hear the reading of the Law:

> *"And Ezra the priest brought the law before the congregation both of men and women, and all that could hear with understanding, upon the first day of the seventh month.*
>
> *"And he read therein before the street that was before the water gate from the morning until midday, before the men and the women, and those that could understand; and the ears of all the people were attentive unto the book of the law"* (Nehemiah 8:2,3).

The eighth verse of this chapter is a simple and beautiful example of the spirit of revival:

> *"So they read in the book in the law of God distinctly, and gave the sense, and caused them to understand the reading"* (v. 8).

Verses 14-17 remind us of Zechariah's prophecy concerning the Messianic Kingdom. Just as the rule of Christ upon the throne is associated with the Feast of Tabernacles among the nations, so the rebuilding of the Holy City under Nehemiah is memorialized in the first fully-realized Feast of Tabernacles since the days of Joshua:

> *"And they found written in the law which the Lord had commanded by Moses, that the children of Israel should dwell in booths in the feast of the seventh month:*

"And that they should publish and proclaim in all their cities, and in Jerusalem, saying, Go forth unto the mount, and fetch olive branches, and pine branches, and myrtle branches, and palm branches, and branches of thick trees, to make booths, as it is written.

"So the people went forth, and brought them, and made themselves booths, every one upon the roof of his house, and in their courts, and in the courts of the house of God, and in the street of the water gate, and in the street of the gate of Ephraim.

"And all the congregation of them that were come again out of the captivity made booths, and sat under the booths: for since the days of Joshua the son of Nun unto that day had not the children of Israel done so. And there was very great gladness" (vv. 14-17).

This particular Feast of Tabernacles points up the importance of the prophetic nature of the festival. These people had returned from the Babylonian captivity in hopes of setting up the Kingdom and restoring the throne of David. To them, history had reached a climax. They were ready for the Messiah to come. But alas, their hopes were not fully realized. The Kingdom of Heaven must await another day. Nevertheless, the fact that the verse says, *"there was very great gladness,"* indicates that the people had an expectation of an imminent fulfillment of the Blessed Hope, which implies a resurrection of the dead, along with the coming of Messiah.

Just a few years before, Daniel had published his prophecy. It predicted, *"And at that time shall Michael stand up ... and many of them that sleep in the dust of the earth shall awake"* (Daniel 12:1-2). With this ancient observance of the Feast of Tabernacles under Nehemiah, the people were anticipating the Kingdom, perhaps even the Messiah.

A thousand years had elapsed since Joshua had conquered the land. The Feast of Tabernacles, once the most important in Israel's calendar, had fallen into neglect for exactly one millennium. This fact implies the prophetic nature of the Feast of Tabernacles. Its ultimate fulfillment will see a millennial kingdom established by the Messiah. The throne of David will be restored.

Three Commandments Observed

The spirit of the Feast of Tabernacles (or Booths) can be found in the rejoicing over the culmination of God's plan. For today's Jews, this festival is still the most joyful of all the holidays. There are three commandments that they observe during its celebration.

1. They Must Live in the Booth

First, they are to live in the booth, itself. This command can be found in Leviticus 23:42-43:

> *"Ye shall dwell in booths seven days; all that are Israelites born shall dwell in booths:*
>
> *"That your generations may know that I made the children of Israel to dwell in booths, when I brought them out of the land of Egypt: I am the Lord your God"* (Leviticus 23:42-43).

Some modern Jews deny that the Feast of Tabernacles commemorates their wilderness sojourn. But the last verse of this passage flatly states that the booths were to remind them of those forty detestable years in the desert. At this point, we can well understand why the Jews neglected the Feast of Tabernacles from the days of Joshua to the days of Nehemiah. They simply didn't want to be reminded of their past failures. After all, when they finally entered into the Promised Land—a land of milk and honey—why would they want to remember their desert testing?

As earlier stated, the division among Jewish scholars about the true nature of the booth's origin has brought a variety of traditions into this celebration. Hayyim Schauss writes:

"The Pentateuch tells us that the sukkoh [booth] is a reminder of ancient days, when the Jews wandered in the desert and lived in tents. This is, however a forced interpretation and was evolved in later times. If the sukkoh was really connected with the Exodus, then Pesach [Passover] would be the time for dwelling in booths. Besides, the Jews resided in tents during their wanderings in the desert, and there is quite a difference between a tent and a booth. The tent of the desert Bedouin consists of a sheet of goatskin, hung over poles driven into the earth. The main feature of a sukkoh is the open roof, which is covered with branches and leaves.

"In addition to the reason for dwelling in booths as given in the Pentateuch, the Jewish philosopher of Alexandria, Philo, evolved a new meaning for the sukkoh. He said that it was erected to bring evidence of misfortune at a time of good fortune, and a reminder of poverty to those who were wealthy. Maimonides gave the same interpretation for the sukkoh." [1]

---

[1] Hayyim Schauss, *The Jewish Festivals*, (New York: Schocken Books, 1962), p. 200.

From this comment, which represents a common philosophy among rabbis, we can see that there is still a reluctance among Jews to associate booths with their 40-year wilderness sojourn. This remains true even though God's Word states,

> *"... all that are Israelites born shall dwell in booths: That your generations may know that I made the children of Israel to dwell in booths, when I brought them out of the land of Egypt"* (Leviticus 23:42-43).

Schauss tells us that the booth is to be thought of as an agricultural shelter, once built as a temporary shelter for the fruit of the orchard and the produce of the field. But in spite of this interpretation, the Bible clearly states that the booth must typify the tents used by the Israelites during the Exodus.

Michael Strassfeld comments that the Jews believe the booth "must be a temporary structure, not a permanent one. This, he says, is to remind us of the portability of the huts in the desert as the Israelites wandered from place to place for forty years. It also stresses one of the themes of the holiday—the impermanence of our lives."[2]

Strassfeld's comments show us that modern Jewish interpretations of this holiday are somewhat blurred. He tells us that the Jews believe the booth should be regarded as a permanent home for seven days. One should eat and drink and study there. The roof of the booth must be

---

[2] Michael Strassfeld, *The Jewish Holidays, A Guide and Commentary*, (New York: Harper and Row, 1985), p. 127.

temporary and created from some organic material. It should be something that has grown and then is detached from the ground, such as branches and boughs. Finally, it should reflect beauty and fertility, including handmade objects of art, nuts, almonds, peaches, pomegranates, grape vines, decanters of oil, fine meal, and wreaths made with ears of corn—even pictures of Jerusalem.

Usually, however, the booth is used for eating, particularly on the first night of the festival. The primary mandate for the booth is that it be a place of happiness and conversation, of candlelight and relaxation.

2. Gather Four Species of Produce

The second commandment concerning this festival is that four symbolic species of produce be gathered: The lulav (palm branch), the etrog (citron), the hadasim (myrtle branch) and the aravot (willow branch). These four species emphasize the agricultural nature of the festival.

They are also said to characterize four Jewish spiritual types:

1. The etrog has taste and fragrance and symbolized those Jews who have demonstrated both learning and good deeds.

2. The palm branch has taste but not fragrance, picturing those Jews who possess learning but not good deeds.

3. The myrtle has fragrance but not taste, and is a symbol of those who have shown good deeds but

not learning.

4. Finally, the willow branch has neither fragrance nor taste, telling of those Jews who are neither good nor learned.

During the Festival of Tabernacles, a "hallel" (praise ceremony) is held every day, during which the four species are held out and shaken in the four directions of the compass, then upward and downward. These six directions acknowledge the necessity of God's blessing to obtain the good fruit of His earth. They are accompanied by the recitation of Scripture, from Psalms 118:1,25,29:

> *"O give thanks unto the Lord; for he is good: because his mercy endureth for ever."*

> *"Save now, I beseech thee, O Lord: O Lord, I beseech thee, send now prosperity."*

> *"O give thanks unto the Lord; for he is good: for his mercy endureth for ever"* (Psalms 118:1, 25,29).

3. Rejoice and Be Glad

The final commandment concerns rejoicing during the holiday ... the passionate remembrance of food, prosperity, and friends. Happiness is commanded, telling of that time when the Messiah shall have brought the earth into a condition of peace and prosperity. One of the chief observances of the Feast of Tabernacles is the recitation of the hoshanot. On this subject, Rabbi Strassfeld writes,

> "Each day of Sukkot [booths], the hoshanot are recited during the morning service. These are hymns that begin with the words hosha na ('save us'), hence the name. One is recited each day as a circuit is made of the syna-

gogue. Hoshanot recall the procession in the temple, which was done around the altar. Today the Torah replaces the altar." [3]

The seventh day of Tabernacles is given a special name: "Hoshanna Rabbah," or the Great Hoshanna. Its customs and rituals involve two observances:

1. The synagogue is circled seven times while carrying the four species and reciting the hoshanna prayers.

2. The aravot, or willow branches, are beaten on the ground.

This additional step, involving the willow branches, is said to symbolize a casting away of sins and is the reason the Hoshanna Rabbah is still known by the rabbis as the final day of judgment. Today, this ritual comes at the end of hoshanot and involves beating a bunch of willows against a chair or the ground. Rabbi Strassfeld comments that this ritual is very important to the rabbis, so much so that it was held to supersede the Shabbat laws. He writes,

"According to some authorities, Hoshanna Rabbah marked the conclusion of the High Holiday period. There is a tradition that harsh judgments can still be changed before Hoshanna Rabbah—that the final seal is not put on the Books of Life and Death until then. Therefore, the morning service ... is a solemn one." [4]

---

[3] Ibid. p. 133.

[4] Ibid. p. 136.

After the Millennium,
the Judgment

What an amazing picture of the millennium! Just as in the Jewish holiday, the millennial reign of Christ will end with a final judgment at the end of this future thousand-year period. Satan is to be released for a short time to *"deceive the nations"* (Revelation 20:8). His goal will be to destroy the saints and the Holy City, Jerusalem. But he is destroyed by fire that comes down from God out of heaven. He will be thrown into the lake of fire and brimstone with the beast and the false prophet to be tormented forever. After that, the Bible tells of a time when the Books of Life and Death will be opened, exactly as pictured in the Jewish observance of the Feast of Tabernacles:

"And I saw a great white throne, and him that sat on it, from whose face the earth and the heaven fled away; and there was found no place for them.

"And I saw the dead, small and great, stand before God; and the books were opened: and another book was opened, which is the book of life: and the dead were judged out of those things which were written in the books, according to their works.

"And the sea gave up the dead which were in it; and death and hell delivered up the dead which were in them: and they were judged every man according to their works.

"And death and hell were cast into the lake of fire. This is the second death.

"And whosoever was not found written in the book of life was cast into the lake of fire" (Revelation 20:11-15).

Here again, the Feast of Tabernacles offers the very image of scriptural prophecy. During the celebration of Hoshanna Rabbah, people wish each other "pikta tava," which literally means, "a good writ of judgment." On the afternoon of this final day, some visit the booth one last time and recite the following prayer: "May it be that we merit to dwell in the sukkot [booth] made of Leviathan." According to Jewish legend, God will make a booth out of the body of the leviathan at the end of days and will place the righteous there. Of course, leviathan is the great world political, economic, and religious system which has thrived under satan. And at the end of the millennium, the entire evil world system will be finally destroyed.

Once again, we observe a Jewish festival and discover that, by the grace of God, it gives an exact picture of His redemptive plan. His work is right on schedule. And His Chosen People are being prepared, so that when His Kingdom comes and His will is done, evil will at last be destroyed.

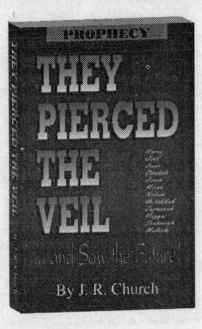